UNIX™ SYSTEM PROGRAMMING

INTERNATIONAL COMPUTER SCIENCE SERIES

Consulting editors **A D McGettrick** University of Strathclyde
J van Leeuwen University of Utrecht

OTHER TITLES IN THE SERIES:

Programming in Ada (2nd Edn.) *J G P Barnes*

Computer Science Applied to Business Systems *M J R Shave and K N Bhaskar*

Software Engineering (2nd Edn.) *I Sommerville*

A Structured Approach to FORTRAN 77 Programming *T M R Ellis*

The Cambridge Distributed Computing System *R M Needham and A J Herbert*

An Introduction to Numerical Methods with Pascal *L V Atkinson and P J Harley*

The UNIX System *S R Bourne*

Handbook of Algorithms and Data Structures *G H Gonnet*

Office Automation: Concepts, Technologies and Issues *R A Hirschheim*

Microcomputers in Engineering and Science *J F Craine and G R Martin*

UNIX for Super-Users *E Foxley*

Software Specification Techniques *N Gehani and A D McGettrick* (eds.)

The UNIX System V Environment *S R Bourne*

Data Communications for Programmers *M Purser*

Prolog Programming for Artificial Intelligence *I Bratko*

Modula-2: Discipline & Design *A H J Sale*

Introduction to Expert Systems *P Jackson*

Local Area Network Design *A Hopper, S Temple and R C Williamson*

Programming Language Translation: A Practical Approach *P D Terry*

Data Abstraction in Programming Languages *J M Bishop*

System Simulation: Programming Styles and Languages *W Kreutzer*

The Craft of Software Engineering *A Macro and J Buxton*

An Introduction to Programming with Modula-2 *P D Terry*

Pop-11 Programming for Artificial Intelligence *A M Burton and N R Shadbolt*

PROLOG *F Giannesini, H Kanoui, R Pasero and M van Caneghem*

UNIX™ SYSTEM PROGRAMMING

Keith Haviland
The Instruction Set Ltd
(formerly of Sphinx Ltd)

Ben Salama
Data Logic Ltd
(formerly of Sphinx Ltd)

ADDISON-WESLEY PUBLISHING COMPANY

Wokingham, England · Reading, Massachusetts · Menlo Park, California
New York · Don Mills, Ontario · Amsterdam · Bonn
Sydney · Singapore · Tokyo · Madrid · San Juan

The programs in this book have been included for their instructional value. They have been tested with care but are not guaranteed for any particular purpose. The publisher does not offer any warranties or representations, nor does it accept any liabilities with respect to the programs.

Cover illustration courtesy of Julius Vitali.
Typeset by Quorum Technical Services Ltd.
Printed and bound in Great Britain by T. J. Press, Padstow, Cornwall.

First printed 1987. Reprinted 1988 and 1989 (twice).

British Library Cataloguing in Publication Data

Haviland, Keith Frank
UNIX system programming—(International computer science series).
1. UNIX (Computer operating system)
I. Title II. Salama, Ben III. Series
005.4′3 QA76.76.063

ISBN 0–201–12919–1

Library of Congress Cataloguing in Publication Data

Haviland, Keith, 1958–
UNIX system programming.
(International computer science series)
Bibliography: p.
Includes index.
1. UNIX (Computer operating system) I. Salama, Ben, 1954– . II. Title. III. Series.
QA76.76.063H38 1987 005.4′2 87–11560

ISBN 0–201–12919–1 (pbk.)

To our wives and families
Angela and Alice
Tacchi, Rebecca and Claire

Preface

The purpose of this book

Since its humble beginnings at Bell Laboratories in 1969, the UNIX Operating System has become increasingly popular, finding favour first in the academic world and then as a *de facto* standard operating system for a new generation of multi-user micro- and minicomputers in the 1980s. At the time of writing this growth seems set to continue.

Of course, as the installed base of UNIX systems has increased from tens to tens of thousands, its user base has also grown proportionately. Once, relatively few people had direct experience of software development under UNIX. Now many professional programmers will spend much of their working lives in the environment provided by the system.

The popularity of this operating system has been matched by the increasing availability of UNIX textbooks. The majority of these books have concentrated on how to use standard UNIX programs and UNIX tools, covering the utilities provided by the system for file management, program development, text processing and communications.

Our aim with this book is substantially different. We will concentrate on the programming interface that exists between the UNIX kernel (that part of UNIX which qualifies as an operating system proper) and applications software that runs in the UNIX environment. This interface is called the UNIX system call interface. As we shall see, system calls are the primitives upon which all UNIX programs – whether supplied along with the operating system or independently developed – are ultimately built. Our target audience consists of programmers with some UNIX experience who will be developing UNIX software in the C language. The text will be relevant to developers of systems level software, and applications and business programs – anyone in fact with a serious interest in developing UNIX programs.

Aside from system calls, we shall also consider some of the more important subroutine libraries provided with a UNIX system. These library routines are, obviously, written using system calls and in many cases perform the same action as a system call, but at a higher level or perhaps in a more programmer friendly manner. By exploring both system calls and subroutine libraries we hope that you will get an appreciation of when not to re-invent the wheel as well as a better understanding of the internal workings of this elegant operating system.

The AT&T System V Interface Definition: a reference standard

For over ten years hardware manufacturers and software houses throughout the world have been implementing, under licence from AT&T, their own versions of the UNIX Operating System. Prior to 1983, however, AT&T took little interest in these implementations or the development of UNIX as a commercial operating environment.

This lack of control had both positive and negative effects. On the positive side, AT&T's hands-off attitude allowed UNIX to establish itself, and be accepted, as a non-proprietary operating system standard, a position that could never be achieved if UNIX was launched today as the child of the new look AT&T – AT&T the computer company.

On the negative side, the lack of control from AT&T has meant a proliferation of many different versions of UNIX. To take just one example, all but the most recent of the AT&T releases of UNIX lacked file and record locking facilities, essential for the commercial acceptance of the system. These features were added in a variety of incompatible forms by the hardware manufacturers and software companies who implemented their own versions of the system. As a result, a program that uses record locking and is intended to run on any UNIX system will need a different interface for each locking mechanism.

The large number of differing UNIX implementations has made the portability of applications from one UNIX system to another considerably harder than it should ever have been. Thankfully, great emphasis is now placed on standardization by the international UNIX community and by AT&T in particular. One concrete manifestation of this new attitude is a document called the AT&T *System V Interface Definition (SVID)* which was first published in 1985 and describes UNIX System V in terms of its system calls, subroutine libraries and utility programs. It provides a baseline definition of UNIX System V to which all suppliers of the system must comply. For the software author it means that programs written using only the primitives described in the *SVID* will be portable in source form to all other System V environments whether they be microcomputers, minicomputers or mainframes.

Because of its importance, we have firmly based this book on *Issue 2* of the AT&T *System V Interface Definition*. Almost all of the system calls and subroutines described in the text are defined in the *SVID*. With few exceptions (and they are noted in the text) the program examples should run on any computer system conforming to the *SVID*. When we need to describe details of a particular implementation of UNIX, we will usually focus on *UNIX System V Release 2.0* as supplied on the AT&T 3B2 computer. This implementation of the system was developed at AT&T and conforms fully to the *SVID*.

The contents of this book are almost equally relevant to two other important standards documents: the *X/OPEN Portability Guide* and the IEEE P1003 Committee's trial-use *POSIX* standard. Both documents define operating system interfaces derived from UNIX System V and follow the *SVID* closely. Of the two, the *POSIX* standard in particular seems set to become important.

Other versions of UNIX

Despite the moves to standardize around UNIX System V, there remain a large number of different versions of UNIX and UNIX-like operating systems still in use. The following list puts the most important of these into context:

- *UNIX System III* This is the version of UNIX that immediately preceded System V (no System IV was ever publicly released). It is becoming increasingly rare as manufacturers upgrade their versions of UNIX to System V. It is essentially a subset of System V.
- *UNIX Version 7* (sometimes called *UNIX 7th Edition)* Surprisingly enough, given the '7', this predates even System III. Again, Version 7 can be regarded for most purposes as a subset of System V. There are, however, areas where things differ substantially, for example, in terminal handling.
- *Berkeley UNIX,* versions *4.1bsd, 4.2bsd,* and *4.3bsd* Berkeley UNIX is a much expanded derivative of Version 7 that was developed at the University of California, Berkeley. It was designed initially to run on VAX computers and has proved very popular in the academic world. Although recognizably a UNIX derivative, it is in a few areas, such as the file store structure and communications, very different from System V. Some of the enhancements developed at Berkeley, such as the `curses` screen handling package and the `vi` editor, have found their way back into System V.
- *Xenix* The Microsoft version of UNIX, Xenix has become particularly popular on microcomputers based on Intel processors. The latest versions conform to the *SVID* standard, although extra features are provided.

Much of this book will apply to all the versions of UNIX described above. The most serious divergences will be with Berkeley UNIX, which really deserves a text of its own.

Organization of the text

This book is organized as follows:

- Chapter 1 is a review of some fundamental concepts and basic terminology. The two most important terms discussed are **file** and **process**. We hope that most readers of the book will be familiar with at least some of the material presented here (see the following section on prerequisites).
- Chapter 2 describes the system call primitives for handling files. It covers opening and creating files, reading and writing data to and from files, and random access. We also introduce ways of handling the errors that can be generated by system calls.
- Chapter 3 is a study of the file in context. Here we look at the issues of file ownership, how file system privileges are managed under UNIX, and how these attributes can be manipulated with system calls.
- Chapter 4 looks primarily at the UNIX **directory** concept from a programming viewpoint. We also include a short discussion on the underlying structure of the UNIX file store, covering **file systems** and the **special files** used to represent devices.
- Chapter 5 deals with the fundamental nature and control of UNIX **processes**. The important system calls `fork` and `exec` are introduced, and explained at length. Among the examples is a small **shell** or command processor.
- Chapter 6 is the first of two on interprocess communication and looks at the most basic ways separate processes can cooperate. The important concepts introduced here are **signals** and **pipes.**
- Chapter 7 deals with interprocess communication techniques that have been introduced into UNIX with System V. **Record locking**, **message passing**, **semaphores** and **shared memory** are described here.
- Chapter 8 deals with the terminal at system call level. As a major example, the code for a file transfer program is given.
- Chapter 9 is where we turn away from system calls and start an examination of major library packages. This chapter contains a systematic study of the important **Standard I/O Library**, which offers many more file handling facilities than the system call primitives introduced in Chapter 2.
- Chapter 10 is a brief introduction to the `curses` screen handling library. We include it because many developers will want to add a screen-based interface to their programs.
- Finally, Chapter 11 is a review of miscellaneous system calls and library routines. String handling, time functions and memory management are among the topics discussed.

What you need to know

This book is not intended as a general introduction to UNIX or the C language, but as a detailed study of the UNIX system call interface. To make best use of it you should be familiar with the following topics:

- logging into your UNIX system;
- creating files using one of the standard editors provided on your system;
- the tree-like directory structure presented by UNIX;
- basic commands for manipulating files and directories;
- creating and compiling simple C programs (including programs with code held in several source files);
- making simple use of the I/O routines `printf` and `getchar` from within a C program;
- using command line arguments, i.e. `argc` and `argv`, within a C program;
- using your system's manual. (Unhappily, it is no longer possible to give absolutely specific advice in this area since the once-standard format of the manual has been rearranged by several manufacturers. The traditional arrangement divides the manual into eight sections, where each section is arranged alphabetically. The first three are of most relevance to us: *Section 1* describes commands; *Section 2* describes system calls; and *Section 3* covers subroutines.)

Those of you who are unhappy with any of these points should limber up with the exercises listed below. If you need more help, the Bibliography at the end of this book should direct you to a suitable text.

One final point: computing is *not* a spectator sport and throughout this book there is a strong emphasis on exercises and examples. Before starting, you should ensure you have access to a suitable UNIX machine.

Exercise P.1 Explain the purpose of the following UNIX commands:
`ls cat rm cp mv mkdir cc`

Exercise P.2 Using your favourite editor, create a small text file. Use `cat` to create another file consisting of five repetitions of this.

Using `wc` count the number of characters and words in both. Explain the result.

Create a subdirectory and move the two files into this.

Exercise P.3 Create a file containing a directory listing of both your home directory and the directory `/bin`.

Exercise P.4 Devise a single command line which displays the number of users currently logged onto your system.

Exercise P.5 Write, compile and execute a C program that prints a welcoming message of your choice.

Exercise P.6 Write, compile and run a C program that prints its arguments.

Exercise P.7 Using `getchar()` and `printf()`, write a program that counts the number of words, lines and characters in its input.

Exercise P.8 Create a file containing a C subroutine which prints the message `"hello, world"`. Create a separate file containing the main program which calls this routine. Compile and execute the resulting program, calling it `hw`.

Exercise P.9 Look up the entries for the following topics in your system's manual: the `cat` command, the `printf` subroutine and the `write` system call.

Acknowledgements

We would like to acknowledge the help of a number of people: Steve Ratcliffe, for reading the many versions of each chapter and checking all the program examples, making sure they worked under UNIX System V.2; and Jonathan Leffler, Greg Brougham, Dominic Dunlop, Nigel Martin, Bill Fraser-Campbell, Dave Lukes and Floyd Williams for their comments, suggestions and assistance during the preparation of the text.

All example programs in this book were run on an AT&T 3B2 computer under UNIX System V.2. The original manuscript was also prepared on this system using the UNIX troff software. We are grateful to Sphinx Ltd. for the provision of these computing facilities.

And finally, special thanks go to Angela and Tacchi for their encouragement and patience over the last two years.

Keith Haviland
Ben Salama
June, 1987

Contents

Chapter 1 Basic Concepts and Terminology

In this chapter we will briefly review some basic ideas and terminology that we shall make use of throughout this book. We will start by examining the notion of the UNIX **file.**

1.1 The file

Information on a UNIX system is stored in files. Typical UNIX commands that manipulate files include

```
$ vi test.c
```

which will invoke the `vi` editor in order to create or edit the file *test.c*,

```
$ cat test.c
```

which will display the contents of *test.c* on the terminal, and

```
$ cc -o test test.c
```

which will invoke the C compiler to generate the program file *test* from the source file *test.c*, assuming, of course, that *test.c* contains no syntactical errors.

Most files will be given some sort of logical structure by the user who created them. A document, for example, will consist of words, lines, paragraphs and pages. To the system, however, all UNIX files actually appear as simple, unstructured sequences of bytes or characters. The file access primitives provided by the system allow individual bytes to be accessed either sequentially or randomly. There are no record or file terminator characters embedded into files and no multiple record types to negotiate.

This simplicity is entirely deliberate and typical of the UNIX philosophy. The UNIX file is a clean, general concept from which more complex and specific structures (such as an indexed file organization) can be developed. Premature detail and special cases have been ruthlessly eliminated. For example, within ordinary text files the newline character (actually ASCII line-feed) that indicates the end of a line of text is, as far as UNIX is concerned, just another character, to be read or written by system utilities and user programs. Only programs that expect their input to be made up of lines need concern themselves with the semantics of the newline character.

Nor does UNIX distinguish between different types of file. A file can contain readable text (such as a shopping list or the paragraph you are reading now) or it can contain 'binary' data (such as the compiled form of a program). In either case the same primitive operations or utilities can be used to manipulate the file. As a corollary of this, you will find none of the formal naming schemes encountered under other operating systems; UNIX file names are entirely arbitrary as long as they don't exceed the maximum length of 14 characters. (However, some programs, such as `cc`, follow certain simple naming conventions.)

1.1.1 Directories and Pathnames

An important concept allied to the file is the **directory**. Directories are collections of files, allowing some logical organization of the file system. For example, each user has his or her own 'home' directory to work in, while commands, system libraries and administrative programs are generally located in their own specific directories. As well as containing files, directories can also contain any number of sub-directories. These in turn can contain their own sub-directories and so on. In fact, directories can be nested to any depth. The UNIX file store can therefore be thought of as a hierarchical, tree-like structure where each non-terminal node corresponds to a directory. The top of this tree is a single directory, conventionally called the **root directory.**

We will study the UNIX directory structure in detail in Chapter 4. However, because we will use them throughout the text, it is worth noting that the full names of UNIX files – called **pathnames** – reflect this tree structure. Each pathname gives the sequence of directories that lead to the file. For example, the pathname

```
/usr/keith/chap1.doc
```

can be dissected as follows: the first '/' character means the pathname starts at the root directory, i.e. this pathname gives the *absolute* location of the file within the file store. Next comes `usr`, which is a sub-directory within the root directory. The directory `keith` is another step down and is therefore a sub-directory of `/usr`. The final component, `chap1.doc`, is the name of the file within the directory `/usr/keith`. In fact, `chap1.doc` could equally well be a directory instead of an ordinary file since directories are identified by the same naming scheme as files.

A pathname that doesn't begin with a '/' character is called a **relative pathname** and gives the route to the file relative to a user's **current working directory.** For example, the pathname

```
chap1/intro.txt
```

describes a file `intro.txt` which is contained in the sub-directory `chap1` of the current directory. In the limiting case, a name such as

```
intro.txt
```

simply identifies the file `intro.txt` within the current working directory. Note that each individual component of a pathname is limited to 14 characters in length.

1.1.2 Ownerships and permissions

A file is not characterized just by the data it contains, and there are a number of other primitive attributes associated with any UNIX file. For example, each file is **owned** by a particular user. Ownership bestows certain rights, one of which is the ability to change another file attribute, namely **permissions**. As we shall see in Chapter 3, permissions determine which users can read or write a file, or execute it if it contains a program.

1.1.3 Generalization of the file concept

UNIX extends the file concept to cover not only disk files but also peripheral devices and interprocess communication channels. This means that the same primitive operations can be used to read and write text files, binary files, terminals, magnetic tape units and even main memory. This scheme allows programs to be thought of as general tools, capable of using any type of output device. For example,

```
$ cat file > /dev/rmt0
```

is a crude way of writing a file to a tape (the pathname `/dev/rmt0` being a common mnemonic for a magnetic tape drive).

1.2 The process

A **process** in UNIX terminology is simply an instance of an executing program. The easiest way to create a process is to give a command to the UNIX command processor or **shell**; for example if a user types

```
$ ls
```

the shell process that accepts the command will create another process specifically to run the directory listing program `ls`. Since UNIX is a multitasking system, more than one process can run concurrently. In fact there will be at least one, usually more, for each current user of a UNIX system.

1.2.1 Interprocess communication

UNIX allows concurrent processes to cooperate by using a variety of interprocess communication methods.

One such method is the **pipe**. Pipes are normally used to couple the output of one program to the input of another without having to store data in an intermediate file. Again users can take advantage of this general facility within the shell. The command line:

```
$ ls|wc
```

causes the shell to create two processes to run `ls` and the word-count program `wc` concurrently. It also links the output of `ls` to the input of `wc`. The result is to produce a count of the number of files in the current directory.

Other UNIX interprocess communication facilities include **signals**, which offer an interrupt-based communications model, and, in the more recent implementations of UNIX, **shared memory** and **semaphores**.

1.3 System calls and library subroutines

In the Preface we said that the primary focus of this book is on the **system call interface**. For some readers of this book, the term **system call** is one that will need further definition.

System calls are in fact the software developer's passport into the UNIX **kernel**. The kernel, which we first met in the Preface, is a single piece of software which is permanently memory-resident and deals with a UNIX system's process scheduling and I/O control. In essence, the kernel is that part of UNIX which qualifies as an operating system proper. All user processes, and all file system accesses, will be resourced, monitored and controlled by the kernel.

System calls are invoked in the same way a programmer would call an ordinary C subroutine or function. For example, data could be read from a file by using the `read` system call as follows:

```
nread = read(filedes, inputbuf, BUFSIZ);
```

The essential difference between a subroutine and a system call is that when a program calls a subroutine the code executed is always part of the final object program, even if it was linked in from a library; with a system call the major part of the code executed is actually part of the kernel itself and not the calling program. In other words the calling program is making direct use of the facilities provided by the kernel. The switch between user process and kernel is usually achieved via a software interrupt mechanism.

You shouldn't be surprised to learn that the majority of system calls perform operations on either files or processes. In fact system calls constitute the fundamental primitive operations associated with both types of object.

In the case of a file these operations may include transferring data to and from the file, randomly seeking through the file or changing the access permissions associated with the file.

In the case of processes, the system call operations may create a new process, terminate an existing one, obtain information about the state of a process or establish a communications channel between two processes.

A small number of system calls have nothing to do with either files or processes. Typically, system calls in this category are concerned with system-wide information or control. For example, one system call allows a program to interrogate the kernel to find out its idea of the current date and time; another allows a program to reset these.

As well as the system call interface, UNIX systems also provide libraries of standard subroutines. One very important example is the **Standard I/O Library**. This provides facilities not directly offered by the system calls which make up the file access primitives, including formatted conversions and automatic buffering. It also provides them with guaranteed efficiency. However, the Standard I/O routines ultimately use the system call interface themselves. They should be seen as presenting an extra layer of file access facilities based on system call primitives, not a separate subsystem. The real point here is that any process that interacts with its environment, in however small a way, must make use of system calls at some point.

Exercise 1.1 Explain the meaning of the following terms:
kernel system call C function process directory pathname

Chapter 2 The File

2.1 UNIX file access primitives

2.1.1 Introduction

In this chapter we will look at the fundamental primitives UNIX provides for handling files from within programs. These primitives consist of a small set of system calls that give direct access to the I/O facilities provided by the UNIX kernel. They form the building blocks for all UNIX I/O and any other file access mechanism will ultimately be based around them. Their names are listed in Table 2.1.

Table 2.1 UNIX file access primitives.

Name	*Meaning*
`open`	opens a file for reading or writing
`creat`	creates an empty file
`close`	closes a previously opened file
`read`	extracts information from a file
`write`	places information into a file
`lseek`	moves to a specified byte in a file
`unlink`	removes a file

A typical UNIX program will call `open` (or `creat`) to initialize a file, then use `read`, `write` and `lseek` to manipulate data within that file. It will indicate it has finished by a call to `close`.

The following trivial program, which simply reads the first part of a file, shows this general structure more clearly. Since it is only an introductory example, we have omitted some normally essential refinements such as error handling. Be warned, for in production programs this kind of omission is bad practice.

```
/*a rudimentary example program*/

#include <fcntl.h>
```

```
main()
{
        int fd, nread;
        char buf[1024];

        /*open file "data" for reading*/
        fd = open("data", O_RDONLY);

        /*read in the data*/
        nread = read(fd, buf, 1024);

        /*close the file*/
        close(fd);
}
```

The first statement in the example to involve one of the system call primitives is:

```
fd = open("data", O_RDONLY);
```

This causes the file `data` to be opened for use by the program. The second argument in the call `O_RDONLY` is an integer constant defined in the header file `fcntl.h`, that tells the system to open the file **read only.** In other words, the program will only be able to read the contents of the file. It will not be able to alter the file by writing to it.

The return value from the `open` call, which is placed into the integer variable `fd`, is extremely important. If `open` is successful, `fd` will contain something called a **file descriptor**. A file descriptor is a small, non-negative integer (whose exact value is determined by the system). It identifies the open file and is passed as a parameter to the other file access primitives, such as `read`, `write`, `lseek` and `close`. It can be usefully compared to the unit numbers found in FORTRAN. If the `open` call fails, it would instead return −1, which is the number returned by almost all system calls to indicate an error. In a real program we would test specially for this value, and take appropriate action if it arose.

Once the file is opened, our example program uses the `read` system call:

```
nread = read(fd, buf, 1024);
```

This means: take 1024 characters, if possible, from the file identified by `fd` and place them into the character array `buf`. The return value `nread` gives the number of characters actually read, which will normally be 1024, but would be less if the file is smaller than 1024 bytes in length. Like `open`, if something goes wrong, `read` can also return −1.

This statement demonstrates another important point: the file access primitives deal in simple, linear sequences of characters or bytes. The `read` call will not, for example, perform any useful conversions such as translating the character representation of an integer into the form used internally by a computer. Both `read` (and `write` for that matter) should not be confused with higher-level namesakes in FORTRAN or Pascal. `read` is typical of the philosophy that underlies the system call interface; it performs a single, simple function and provides a building block on which other facilities can be built.

At the end of the example the file is closed with:

```
close(fd);
```

This tells the system that the program has finished with the file associated with `fd`. It is easy to see that the `close` call is the inverse of `open`. Actually, since the program is just about to terminate anyway, the call to `close` isn't really necessary, all open files being automatically closed when a process stops.

This brief example should give you a flavour of the UNIX file access primitives. We will now discuss each of the file access primitives in greater detail.

2.1.2 The `open` system call

Before an existing file can be read or written it must be opened with the `open` system call. This can be used in two ways. For the time being we will just consider the simplest.

Usage

```
#include <fcntl.h>

int filedes, flags;
char *pathname;
  .
  .
  .
filedes = open(pathname, flags);
```

The first argument, `pathname`, is a pointer to a string that contains the pathname of the file to be opened. The file must already exist before an `open` call of this type is made, otherwise an error will result. To create a new file the programmer can use the `creat` primitive, which is described in the next section (however, see also Section 2.1.12 on the extended uses of `open`).

`pathname` can be an absolute pathname, such as:

```
/usr/keith/junk
```

which gives the location of the file in relation to the root directory. It can also be a relative pathname giving the file's location in relation to the current directory; for example:

```
keith/junk
```

or simply:

```
junk
```

In the last case, of course, the program would open a file `junk` in the current directory. In general, whenever a system call or library subroutine takes a file name argument, it will accept any valid UNIX pathname.

The second argument of `open`, called `flags` in our usage description, is of integer type and specifies the access method. The value of `flags` is taken from constants defined in the system include file `fcntl.h` by means of the preprocessor directive `#define` (the term `fcntl` by the way stands for **file control**). Like most standard include files, `fcntl.h` lives in the directory `/usr/include` and can be incorporated into a program with the directive:

```
#include <fcntl.h>
```

There are three constants defined in `fcntl.h` that are of immediate interest to us:

`O_RDONLY`	open file for reading only
`O_WRONLY`	open file for writing only
`O_RDWR`	open file for both reading and writing

If the `open` call succeeds and the file is successfully opened, the return value `filedes` will contain a non-negative integer – the file descriptor. The value of the file descriptor will actually be the smallest non-negative integer that isn't already being used as a file descriptor by the process making the call; a fact you won't often need to know. As we saw in the introduction, if an error occurs, `open` will instead return −1. This can happen, for example, if the file does not exist.

The following skeleton program opens a file `junk` for reading and writing, and also checks to see if an error has occurred during opening. This last point is an important one; it makes good sense to build error checking into all programs that use system calls, since things will sometimes go wrong, however straightforward the application. The example makes use of the library routine `printf` for displaying a message, and the system call `exit` which terminates the calling program. Both of these are provided as standard with any UNIX system.

```
#include <fcntl.h>      /*include fcntl.h file*/

char workfile[]="junk";/*define workfile name*/

main()
{
        int filedes;

        /*Open using O_RDWR from include file*/
        /*file to be opened for read/write   */
```

```
            if((filedes = open(workfile, O_RDWR)) == -1){
                printf("Couldn't open %s\n", workfile);
                exit(1); /*error, so exit*/
            }

            /*rest of program follows*/

            exit(0);     /*normal exit*/
    }
```

Notice how we use `exit` with an argument of 1 when an error occurs, and 0 on successful completion. This conforms to UNIX conventions and is good programming practice. As we shall see in later chapters, the argument passed to `exit` (the program's **exit status**) can be accessed after execution has finished.

Caveats

There are a number of caveats we can add to this discussion. First, note that there is a limit on the number of files that may be left open simultaneously by an executing program – typically 20. To get around this the `close` system call can be used to tell the system you have finished with a file. We will look at `close` in Section 2.1.4. There is also a system-wide limit on the number of files that can be opened by all processes taken together, determined by the size of a table inside the kernel.

Second, a word of warning: in early versions of UNIX the include file `fcntl.h` did not exist and actual numeric values were used to form the `flags` parameter. It is still a common, though not wholly satisfactory, practice to use these numeric values rather than the constant names defined in `fcntl.h`. So in many programs you will often see a statement like

```
filedes = open(filename, 0);
```

which under normal circumstances opens a file for read-only access and is equivalent to

```
filedes = open(filename, O_RDONLY);
```

Exercise 2.1 Create the small skeleton program described above. Test it when the file `junk` does not exist. Then create `junk` with your favourite editor and rerun the program. The contents of `junk` are entirely arbitrary.

2.1.3 The `creat` system call

The `creat` system call is used to either create a new file from scratch or truncate an existing one, i.e. reset its length to zero characters. Like `open`, it returns either a non-negative file descriptor or the error code −1. If the return value is a valid file descriptor, then the file will be open for writing. `creat` is called as follows.

Usage

```
int filedes, mode;
char *pathname;
 .
 .
 .
filedes = creat(pathname, mode);
```

The first parameter, `pathname`, points to a UNIX pathname. This gives the name and location of a new file, or the name of an existing file which is to be truncated.

The second, `mode`, is an `int` and gives the **access permissions** of the file. Without going into too much detail here, file access permissions determine which users of the system can read, write or execute the file. For example, if `mode` is set to 0644 (octal), this will allow the user who created the file to read and write to it. Other users will only be allowed read access. We will explain just how this value is constructed in the next chapter. For simplicity we shall use it in examples throughout the rest of the current chapter. In any case the value of `mode` only has meaning when a file is being created. It does not affect a truncated file, which retains its original permissions.

The following skeleton program attempts to create a file `newfile` (we are assuming the file doesn't already exist):

```
#define PERM 0644          /*Permissions for creat*/

char filename[]="newfile";

main()                     /*start of main program*/
{
        int filedes;


        if((filedes = creat(filename, PERM)) == -1){
             printf("Couldn't create %s\n", filename);
             exit(1); /*error, so exit*/
        }

        /*rest of program follows*/

        exit(0);
}
```

It should be stressed that `creat` opens a file for writing only. A program cannot, for example, create a file, write data to it, then move backwards and attempt to read from it, unless it closes the file and reopens it with `open`.

Exercise 2.2 Write a short program that first creates a file using `creat`, then without calling `close`, immediately opens it with the `open` system call for reading and writing. In both cases make the program indicate success or failure by using `printf` to display a message.

2.1.4 The `close` system call

The system call `close` is the inverse of `open`. It tells the system that the calling process has finished with a file. It is useful because there is a limit, usually 20, to the number of files a running program may keep open at the same time.

Usage

```
int retval, filedes;
 .
 .
 .
retval = close(filedes);
```

`close` takes just one argument – the file descriptor to be closed. This file descriptor will normally come from a previous call to either `open` or `creat`. The following program fragment illustrates the simple relationship between `open` and `close`:

```
filedes = open ("file", O_RDONLY);
 .
 .
 .
close(filedes);
```

`close` returns 0 if successful, −1 on error (which can happen if the integer argument is not a valid file descriptor).

Note that, to prevent total chaos, all open files are automatically closed when a program completes execution.

2.1.5 The `read` system call

`read` is used to copy an arbitrary number of characters or bytes from a file into a buffer under the control of the calling program, the buffer being declared as an array of `char`.

(Note that C programmers use the terms 'characters' and 'bytes' interchangeably. A byte is the unit of storage required to hold a character, and is eight bits in length on most machines. The term 'character' usually describes a member of the ASCII character set, which consists of a pattern of just seven bits. A byte therefore can typically hold more values than there are ASCII characters. The C `char` type represents the more general notion of byte, and its name is a bit of a misnomer.)

Usage

```
int nread, filedes, n;
char *bufptr;
  .
  .
  .
nread = read(filedes, bufptr, n);
```

`read's` first parameter `filedes` is an integer file descriptor which has been obtained from a previous call to either `open` or `creat`. The second, `bufptr`, is a pointer to the character array into which data will be copied. In many cases, this will simply be the name of the array itself. For example:

```
int fd, nread;
char buffer[SOMEVALUE];
  .
  .
  .
nread = read(fd, buffer, SOMEVALUE);
```

As you might guess from this example, `read`'s third parameter is a positive integer which gives the number of bytes to be read from the file.

The integer returned by `read` (called `nread` above) records the number of bytes actually read. Usually, this will be the number of characters requested by the program, but as we shall see, this isn't always the case, and `nread` can take smaller values. In addition, when an error occurs `read` will return −1. This happens, for example, when `read` is passed an invalid file descriptor.

The read-write pointer

Naturally enough, a program can call `read` successively in order to scan sequentially through a file. For example, if we assume the file '`foo`' contains at least 1024 characters, the fragment:

```
int fd;
char buf1[512], buf2[512];
  .
  .
  .
if((fd = open("foo", O_RDONLY)) < 0)
      return(-1);

read(fd, buf1, 512);
read(fd, buf2, 512);
```

should place the first 512 characters from 'foo' into buf1, and the second 512 characters into buf2.

The system keeps track of a process's position in a file with an entity called the **read-write pointer.** Essentially, this records the position of the next byte in the file to be read (or written) by a process, and can be thought of as a kind of bookmark. Its value is maintained internally by the system and the programmer does not have to explicitly allocate a variable to contain it. Random access, where the position of the read-write pointer is explicitly changed, can be performed with the lseek system call, described in Section 2.1.9. In the case of read, the system simply advances the read-write pointer by the number of bytes read after each call.

Since read can be used to scan through a file from beginning to end, a program must be able to detect the end of a file. This is where the return value from read becomes important. When the number of characters requested in a read call is greater than the number of characters left in the file, the system will transfer only the characters remaining, setting the return value appropriately. Any further calls to read will return a value of 0. There is, after all, no data remaining to be read. Checking for a return value of 0 from read is, in fact, the normal way of testing for end of file within a program, or at least a program which uses the file access primitives.

The next example program count puts some of these points together:

```
/*count  -- counts the characters in a file*/

#include <fcntl.h>
#define BUFSIZE 512

main()
{
        /*buffer holds data from read*/
        char buffer[BUFSIZE];

        /*file descriptor and count*/
        int filedes, j;

        /*variable to record total chars*/
        long total = 0;

        /*open "anotherfile" read only*/
        if((filedes = open("anotherfile", O_RDONLY)) < 0){
                printf("error in opening anotherfile\n");
                exit(1);
        }

        /*loop until EOF, shown by return value 0*/
```

```
        while( (j = read(filedes, buffer, BUFSIZE)) >  0)
             total += j; /*increment total*/

        printf("total chars in anotherfile: %ld\n", total);
        exit(0);

}
```

This program will read through the file `anotherfile` in chunks of 512 characters. After each call to `read`, it increments the `total` variable by the number of characters actually copied into the array `buffer`. (Why do you think `total` is declared as a long integer?)

We used the value 512 for the number of characters to be read. This is because a UNIX system is configured to work most efficiently when moving data in blocks that are multiples of a standard size (in fact the blocking factor of the disk). This standard size is often 512, sometimes 1024. However, we could have given `read` any number we might have thought of, including 1. There is no functional benefit in using the particular figure appropriate to your system, just a useful efficiency gain, but as we shall see in Section 2.1.8 this gain can be very considerable.

To make use of the true disk blocking factor for your system, you can utilize the definition of BUFSIZ in the file `/usr/include/stdio.h` (which is actually part of the well-known Standard I/O Library). For example:

```
#include <stdio.h>
  .
  .
  .
nread = read(filedes, buffer, BUFSIZ);
```

Exercise 2.3 If you know how, make `count` accept a command line argument instead of using a fixed file name. Test it on a small file, with several lines.

Exercise 2.4 Make `count` also display the number of words and lines in the file. Define a word as being either a punctuation mark or any alphanumeric string not containing 'white space' characters such as space, tab or newline. A line, of course, is any sequence of characters terminated by newline. Can you think of any ways to simplify the structure of the resulting program?

2.1.6 The `write` system call

The `write` system call is the natural inverse of `read`. It copies data from a program buffer, again declared as an array of characters, to an external file.

Usage

```
int nwrite, filedes, n;
char *bufptr;
  .
  .
  .
nwrite = write(filedes, bufptr, n);
```

Like `read`, `write` takes three arguments: `filedes` which is an integer file descriptor, `bufptr` which is a pointer to the character buffer and `n`, a positive integer giving the number of characters to be written. The value returned into `nwrite` is either the number of characters `write` managed to output, or the error code −1. Actually, if it is not −1, then `nwrite` will almost always be equal to `n`. If it is any less, something has gone badly wrong. This can occur, for example, when the `write` call fills up the output medium before it has completed. (If the medium is already full before the `write` call is made, then −1 will be returned.)

The `write` call is often used with a file descriptor that has been obtained from `creat`. In this case it is easy to see what happens. The file is initially zero bytes long (it has either been freshly created or truncated). Each call to `write` simply adds data to the end of the file, with the read-write pointer being advanced to the position immediately after the last byte written. For example, the fragment

```
int fd;
char header1[512], header2[1024];
  .
  .
  .
if((fd = creat("newfile", 0644)) < 0)
     return(-1);

write(fd, header1, 512);
write(fd, header2, 1024);
  .
  .
  .
```

results in a file of 1536 bytes containing the contents of `header1` and `header2` in succession.

What happens if a program opens an *existing* file for writing with `open` instead of `creat`, then immediately writes to that file? The answer is equally simple: the old data in the file will be overwritten by the new, character by character. For example, suppose the file `oldhat` is 500 characters in length. If a program opens `oldhat` in the usual manner for writing, then outputs 10 characters, the first 10 characters of `oldhat` will be replaced by the contents of the program's write buffer. The next such write will replace the next 10 characters and so on. Once the end of the original file is reached the file, now containing all new data, will be extended with each successive call to `write`.

2.1.7 The `copyfile` example

We are now in the position to tackle our first practical example. The task is to write a subroutine `copyfile` which will copy the contents of one file to another. The return value should either be zero indicating success, or a negative number to indicate an error.

The basic logic is clear: open the first file, then create the second; read from the first and write to the second until the end of the first is reached. Finally close both.

The finished solution might look something like:

```
/*copyfile  -- copy name1 to name2*/

#include <fcntl.h>

#define BUFSIZE   512   /*size of chunk to be read*/
#define PERM      0644  /*file permission for creat*/

int copyfile(name1, name2)     /*copy name1 to name2*/
char *name1, *name2;
{
     int infile, outfile, nread;
     char buffer[BUFSIZE];

     if( (infile = open(name1, O_RDONLY)) < 0)
          return(-1);

     if( (outfile = creat(name2, PERM)) < 0){
          close(infile);
          return(-2);
     }

     /*now read from name1 BUFSIZE chars at a time*/
     while( (nread = read(infile, buffer, BUFSIZE)) > 0){

          /*write buffer to output file*/
          if(write(outfile, buffer, nread) < nread){
               close(infile);
               close(outfile);
               return(-3);     /*write error*/
          }

     }
```

```
        close(infile);
        close(outfile);
        return(0);
}
```

`copyfile` can now be used with a call like:

```
retcode = copyfile("squarepeg", "roundhole");
```

Exercise 2.5 Adapt `copyfile` so that it accepts two file descriptors rather than two file names as parameters. Test this new version.

Exercise 2.6 If you are familiar with command line arguments, use one of the `copyfile` routines to create a program `mycp` that copies one file name argument to another.

2.1.8 `read`, `write` and efficiency

The `copyfile` routine provides a way of gauging the efficiency of the file access primitives in relation to buffer size. One technique is to simply compile `copyfile` with different values for `BUFSIZE`, then time the resulting program with the UNIX **time** command. We did this using the following main function.

```
/*main function to test "copyfile"*/

main()
{

        copyfile("test.in", "test.out");
}
```

and obtained the results shown in Table 2.2 by copying the same large file (74 315 bytes) on a computer running System III UNIX with a natural disk blocking factor of 512. Here the format of the table reflects the output from the **time** command. The first column gives the value of `BUFSIZE`. The second column gives the real, or actual, elapsed time the process took to run in minutes, seconds and tenths of a second. The third column gives the 'user' time, which is the amount of time taken up by those parts of a program which aren't system calls. Because of the granularity of the clock used by **time,** some entries in this column are misleadingly reported as being zero. The fourth and final column is the amount of time the kernel spent servicing system calls. As you can see, columns three and four don't add up to give the real elapsed time. This is because a UNIX system runs several, maybe many, processes simultaneously. It will not spend all its time running your programs!

Table 2.2 Results of `copyfile` test.

BUFSIZE	*Real time*	*User time*	*System time*
1	3:42.8	4.1	3:24.8
64	0:27.3	0.0	0:05.1
511	0:24.0	0.0	0:01.9
512	0:22.3	0.0	0:01.0
513	0:25.1	0.0	0:02.4
4096	0:13.3	0.0	0:00.9
8192	0:12.9	0.0	0:01.1

Our results are pretty conclusive; reading and writing one byte at a time gives appalling performance, while increasing the buffer size improves performance greatly. The best performance of all is achieved when `BUFSIZE` is a multiple of the system's natural disk blocking factor, as shown by the results for `BUFSIZE` values of 512, 4096 and 8192 bytes. Notice how `BUFSIZE` values of 511 and 513 bytes markedly worsen the system time over a value of 512 bytes.

We should stress that a large part (but not all) of any efficiency gain comes simply from reducing the number of system calls. Switching mode between program and kernel when a system call is made is expensive. In general, you should minimize the number of system calls made by a program.

2.1.9 `lseek` and random access

The `lseek` system call enables the user to change the position of the read-write pointer, i.e. change the number of the byte that will be read or written next. `lseek` therefore enables random access into a file.

Usage

```
long newpos, offset, lseek();
int filedes, direction;
  .
  .
  .
newpos = lseek(filedes, offset, direction);
```

`filedes` is an open file descriptor. The second parameter, the long integer `offset`, actually determines the new position of the read-write pointer. It gives the number of bytes to add to a starting position. What this position will be is determined by the third argument, the integer `direction`. If the value of `direction` is 0 then `offset` is simply taken as the number of a byte, counting from the start of the file. `offset` in this case is being treated like an index into an array. If on the other hand `direction` is 1, then `offset` is added to the current position of the file pointer. Finally, if `offset` is 2, it will be added to the number of the last byte in the file.

In all three cases the return value contained in `newpos` will give the new position in the file. If an error occurs then `newpos` will contain the usual error code of −1.

There are a number of points worth noting here. Firstly, both `newpos` and `offset` are long integers because the file size (in bytes) might well exceed the maximum value of a normal integer, which corresponds to `short` on many machines. Secondly, `offset` can be negative. In other words it is possible to move backwards from the starting point indicated by `direction`. An error will only result if you try to move to a position before the start of the file. Thirdly, it is possible to specify a position beyond the end of a file. If this is done there is obviously no data waiting to be read – UNIX doesn't yet support time travel – but a subsequent write is perfectly meaningful and will cause the file to be extended. Any empty space between the old end of file and the starting position of the new data may not actually be physically allocated but it will appear to future `read` calls to be filled with the ASCII null character.

As a simple example we can construct a program fragment that will append to the end of an existing file by opening the file, moving to the file end with `lseek`, and starting to write:

```
filedes = open(filename, O_RDWR);
lseek(filedes, 0L, 2);
write(filedes, outbuf, OBSIZE);
```

Here the direction parameter for `lseek` is set to 2 to move the read-write pointer to the end of the file. Since we want to move no further, the offset given is zero, represented as '`0L`'. This, of course, is because the offset is defined as a long quantity.

`lseek` can also be called in the same way to give the size of the file, since it returns the new position in the file.

```
long filesize;
int filedes;
  .
  .
  .
filesize = lseek(filedes, 0L, 2);
```

Exercise 2.7 Write a function that uses `lseek` to get the size of an open file, but appears not to have changed the value of the read-write pointer.

2.1.10 The hotel example

As a highly contrived, but possibly illuminating example, suppose we have a file `residents` for recording the names of the residents of a hotel. Line 1 contains the name of the occupant of room 1, line 2 the name of the occupant of room 2 and so on (as you can see this is a hotel with a peculiarly well behaved room-numbering system). Each line is exactly 41 characters in length, the first 40 characters containing the occupant's name while the forty-first is a newline which makes the file readable with the UNIX `cat` command.

The following `getoccupier` subroutine will, given an integer room number, calculate the location of the first byte of the occupier's name, then move to that position and read the data contained there. It returns either a pointer to a string containing the occupier's name, or a null pointer on error (we will use the name `NULLPTR` for this). Note how we give the file descriptor variable `infile` an initial value of −1. By testing for this we can ensure the file is opened just once.

```
/*getoccupier -- get occupier's name from residents file*/

#include <fcntl.h>

#define NULLPTR    (char *)0
#define NAMELENGTH 41

char namebuf[NAMELENGTH];       /*buffer to hold name*/
int  infile = -1;               /*will hold file descriptor*/

char *getoccupier(roomno)
int roomno;
{
        long offset, lseek();
        int nread;

        /*open the file first time around*/
        if( infile == -1){
             if((infile = open("residents", O_RDONLY)) < 0)
                  return(NULLPTR); /*couldn't open file*/
        }

        offset = (roomno-1) * NAMELENGTH;


        /*find room slot and read occupier's name*/
        if(lseek(infile, offset, 0) < 0)
              return(NULLPTR);

        nread = read(infile, namebuf, NAMELENGTH);
```

```
          if(nread <= 0)
               return(NULLPTR); /*read unsuccessful*/
          else{
               namebuf[nread -1] = '\0';
               return(namebuf);
          }
}
```

Assuming that the hotel contains 10 rooms, the following program will successively call `getoccupier` to scan through the file, using the `printf` routine from the Standard I/O Library to display each name it finds.

```
/*listoc - list all occupants' names*/

#define NROOMS     10
#define NULLPTR    (char *)0

main()
{
          int j;
          char *getoccupier(), *p;

          for(j = 1;j <= NROOMS;j++){
               if((p = getoccupier(j)) != NULLPTR)
                    printf("Room %2d, %s\n", j, p);
               else
                    printf("Error on room %d\n", j);
          }
}
```

Exercise 2.8 Invent a mechanism for deciding whether a room is empty. Modify `getoccupier`, and the data file if necessary, to reflect this. Now write a routine called `findfree` to locate the lowest numbered free room.

Exercise 2.9 Write a routine `freeroom` to remove a guest from his or her room. Then write `addguest` to place a new guest into a room, checking whether it is empty.

Exercise 2.10 Incorporate `getoccupier`, `freeroom`, `addguest` and `findfree` into a simple utility program `frontdesk` which maintains the data file. Use either command line arguments or write an interactive program that calls `printf` and `getchar`. In either case you will need a way of converting strings to integers in order to calculate room numbers. You can use the library routine `atoi` as follows:

```
i = atoi(string);
```

where `string` is a character pointer and `i` an integer.

Exercise 2.11 As a more general exercise write a program around `lseek` that copies the bytes of one file to another in reverse order. Is your solution efficient?

Exercise 2.12 Using `lseek`, write routines to copy the last 10 characters, the last 10 words and the last 10 lines of one file to another.

2.1.11 The `unlink` system call

The `unlink` system call can be used to remove a file from the system. This is useful for dealing with temporary workfiles, and the like.

Usage

```
int retval;
char *filename;
  .
  .
  .
retval = unlink(filename);
```

It takes one argument: a string containing the name of the file to be removed. For example:

```
unlink("/tmp/tmpfile");
```

`unlink` returns either 0, indicating success, or -1 to indicate failure.

2.1.12 Extended features of the `open` call

The form of `open` we met in Section 2.1.2 is rather limited. In recent versions of UNIX, from System III onwards, `open` provides additional features. It is these we shall now turn to.

We have already discussed three possible values for `open`'s second flag parameter, which determine the access mode of an opened file. They were `O_RDONLY` (meaning open for reading only), `O_WRONLY` (meaning open for writing only) and `O_RDWR` (which allows both). In each case the read-write pointer is placed at the beginning of the file. Clearly the use of these three flags is mutually exclusive. However, the exact effect of each one can be modified by additional flags, again taken from the include file `fcntl.h`. The additional constants are combined with the basic flag values by using the C bitwise OR operator. This is meaningful because each of the constants taken from `fcntl.h` actually specifies a bit to set in the flag argument passed to `open`. Combining several of the constants with the bitwise OR operator simply means setting more than one bit in the flag argument.

This isn't as intimidating as it might at first seem. The best way to demonstrate it is by introducing the first of the additional flags: `O_APPEND`. If set, `O_APPEND` causes the file pointer to be positioned at the end of a file whenever a write takes place. This is useful if the programmer wants just to add data to the end of a file and protect the original contents against accidental corruption.

O_APPEND can be used as follows. The important thing to note is the way O_WRONLY is combined with O_APPEND by the use of the '|' symbol (the C bitwise OR operator):

```
filedes = open("yetanother", O_WRONLY|O_APPEND);
```

Each subsequent use of write, such as

```
write(filedes, appbuf, BUFSIZE);
```

is functionally equivalent to

```
/*seek to file end*/
lseek(filedes, 0L, 2);
write(filedes, appbuf, BUFSIZE);
```

Creating files with open

open can be used to create or truncate a file in a manner similar to creat, but with greater flexibility. As before, this requires one of the three basic flags to be modified by ORing it with additional flags from fcntl.h, taken in this case from the set: O_CREAT, O_TRUNC, or O_EXCL.

O_CREAT allows open to create a file if it does not exist. If O_CREAT is set then open must be given a third, file mode argument which gives the permissions of the file, exactly like the second argument of creat. If the file already exists then, providing neither O_TRUNC nor O_EXCL is set, the file will be opened as if the O_CREAT flag were not present.

For example, assuming an error condition doesn't arise,

```
fd = open("file", O_WRONLY|O_CREAT|O_APPEND, 0644);
```

will, when file does not exist, create it with permissions 0644. If file does exist, it is opened as normal for writing in append mode. The point here is that, unlike creat, this particular form of open won't truncate an already existing file.

If you do want open to truncate, then the O_TRUNC flag must be used. Interestingly enough, it can be used independently of O_CREAT. As with creat, any file permission argument will be ignored when a file is truncated. The following example use of open combines both O_CREAT and O_TRUNC, and is equivalent to a call to creat:

```
fd = open("file", O_WRONLY|O_CREAT|O_TRUNC, 0644);
```

The third flag value in this group, O_EXCL, cannot be used alone. However, if set with O_CREAT, it will cause open to fail (that is, return −1) when the file exists. In other words,

```
fd = open("lock", O_WRONLY|O_CREAT|O_EXCL, 0644);
```

means: create file lock if it doesn't already exist, otherwise fail (and so return −1). This is useful in circumstances where several concurrent processes may attempt to create the same file, since it prevents the accidental destruction of that file.

Exercise 2.13 Write a routine `fileopen` which takes two arguments; the first is a pointer to a filename, the second a pointer to a string which can take the following values:

`r`	open a file read only
`w`	open a file write only
`rw`	open a file read and write
`a`	open a file for appending data

`fileopen` should return a file descriptor or the error code −1.

2.1.13 The `fcntl` system call

At the same time the extended form of `open` appeared, a call named `fcntl` was also introduced to provide a degree of control over already-open file descriptors. It is a rather strange beast that performs a variety of functions instead of having a single, well defined role.

Usage

```
#include <fcntl.h>
/*
 *NB: type of 'args' can vary
 */
int status, cmd, filedes, args;
  .
  .
  .
status = fcntl(filedes, cmd, args);
```

`fcntl` acts on the open file identified by the file descriptor `filedes`. The programmer selects a particular function by choosing a value for the integer `cmd` parameter from the header file `fcntl.h`. The type of `args` depends upon the value of the `cmd` parameter.

Some of these functions are concerned with the interaction of files and processes and we will not look at them here; however there are two that are of immediate interest, identified by the `cmd` values `F_GETFL` and `F_SETFL`.

`F_GETFL` instructs `fcntl` to return the current file status flags as set by `open`. The following function `filestatus` uses `fcntl` in this way to display the current state of an open file.

```
/*filestate  - describe current state of file*/
#include <fcntl.h>

int filestate(filedes)
int filedes;
{
        int  arg1, dummy;
```

```
        if((arg1 = fcntl(filedes, F_GETFL, dummy)) == -1){
            printf("filestate failed\n");
            return(-1);
        }

        printf("File descriptor %d: ",filedes);

        /*
         *test using bitwise AND
         */
        if(arg1 & O_WRONLY)
            printf("write only");
        else if(arg1 & O_RDWR)
            printf("read-write");
        else
            printf("read only");

        if(arg1 & O_APPEND)
            printf(" - append flag set");

        printf("\n");
        return(0);
}
```

Notice how we test whether a particular bit is set in the file status flags held in `arg1` by using the bitwise AND operator, denoted by the single & symbol. (There is a good reason why we haven't tested `arg1` against `O_RDONLY`. Can you see what it is? Hint: examine the file `/usr/include/fcntl.h`. Can you a devise a better bitwise test than we have used?)

`F_SETFL` is used to re-set the file status flags associated with a file. The new flags are given in `arg`, the third argument for `fcntl`. Only certain flags can be set in this way; you can't for example suddenly turn a file open for reading only into a file open for both reading and writing. (Why?) However, you can ensure that all future writes will append to the end of file with a call of the following form:

```
if( fcntl(filedes, F_SETFL, O_APPEND) < 0)
    printf("fcntl error\n");
```

2.2 Standard input, standard output and standard error

2.2.1 Basic concepts

A UNIX system automatically opens three files for any executing program. These are called **standard input**, **standard output** and **standard error**.

Within a program, they are always identified by the file descriptors 0, 1 and 2, respectively. Because of the similar sounding names, don't confuse them with the Standard I/O Library package.

By default, a read from standard input will cause a program to accept data from the keyboard. Similarly, writing to either standard output or standard error will, by default, cause a message to be displayed on the terminal screen. This, in fact, provides our first example of the way the file access primitives can be used for all types of I/O and not just that involving ordinary disk files.

A program that uses these standard channels is by no means committed to using the terminal however. Each channel can be separately reassigned when the program is invoked using the redirection features provided by the UNIX shell (the UNIX command processor). For example the command,

```
$ prog_name < infile
```

will cause the program to accept data from `infile` when it reads from file descriptor 0, rather than the terminal, the normal source for standard input.

Any data written to standard output can similarly be redirected to an output file. For example,

```
$ prog_name > outfile
```

Most useful of all perhaps, the standard output of one program can be made the standard input of another using the UNIX pipe facility. The following shell command means that anything written by `prog_1` on its standard output becomes the standard input of `prog_2`:

```
$ prog_1|prog_2
```

These standard input and output channels offer the chance to build flexible, consistent programs. A program can be developed as a general tool that is able, for example, to accept input direct from the user, from a file or even the output of another program, as required. In each case the program simply reads from standard input using file descriptor 0 and the final decision of the source of input is left until runtime.

2.2.2 The `io` example

As an extremely simple example of the use of the standard channels, the program `io` uses the system calls `read`, `write` and the file descriptors 0 and 1 to copy its standard input to its standard output. It is in essence a cut-down version of the UNIX `cat` program. Notice the absence of any calls to `open` or `creat`.

```
/*io  -- copy std input to std output*/

#define SIZE 512

main()
{
        int nread;
        char buf[512];

        while( (nread = read(0, buf, SIZE)) > 0)
            write(1, buf, nread);
        exit(0);

}
```

Suppose this program is contained in the source file `io.c` and is compiled to give the executable binary `io`:

```
$ cc -o io io.c
```

If `io` is now invoked simply by typing its name, it will wait for input from the terminal. If the user types a line of data then presses the RETURN or ENTER key, `io` will simply redisplay the line typed, i.e. it writes the input line to standard output. The actual dialogue might look something like:

```
$ io                        (user types io, followed by return)
This is line 1              (user types this, followed by return)
This is line 1              (io redisplays line)
 .
 .
 .
```

After redisplaying the line, `io` will be waiting for more input. The user can keep on typing indefinitely. `io` will obediently redisplay each line as RETURN or ENTER is typed.

To terminate the program, the user can type the system's *end of file* character on a line by itself. This is typically ^D, i.e. CTRL-D, sent by pressing the CTRL and D keys simultaneously. This action will cause `read` to return 0, indicating that the end of the data has been reached. The complete dialogue might therefore look like:

```
$ io
This is line 1
This is line 1
This is line 2
This is line 2
<CTRL-D>                (user types CTRL-D)
$
```

The more perceptive of you might have noticed that io is not behaving as we might immediately expect. Instead of reading in a full 512 characters before printing them , as the program logic seems to suggest, it prints each line as the RETURN key is pressed. This is because read, when used to accept data from a terminal, returns after each newline character – clearly an aid to meaningful interaction. To be even more precise, this is true only for a common terminal setting. Terminals can also be set into other modes, allowing, for example, single character input. More about this can be found in Chapter 8.

Since io does use the standard channels, it can be used in conjunction with the shell's redirection and piping facilities. For example, the command

```
$ io < /etc/motd > message
```

will cause io to copy the contents of the message of the day file /etc/motd to the file message, while the command line

```
$ io < /etc/motd | wc
```

will cause the standard output of io to be piped into the UNIX word-count utility wc. Since the standard output of io will in fact be identical to the contents of /etc/motd, this is a cumbersome way of counting the words, lines and characters in what is the system's message of the day file.

Exercise 2.14 Write a version of io that checks to see if there are any command line arguments. If any exist, the program should treat each argument as a file name and copy the contents of each file to its standard output. If there are no command line arguments, input should be taken from standard input. How should the new io deal with files it cannot open?

Exercise 2.15 Sometimes data in a file will accumulate slowly over a lengthy period. Write a version of io called watch that will read up to the end of file on standard input, echoing the data on standard output. When it reaches the end of its input, watch should pause for five seconds. It should then restart reading its standard input to see if any more data has arrived, without re-opening the file or adjusting the read-write pointer. To put the process to rest for a set time, you can use the standard library subroutine sleep which takes a single argument, an integer giving the number of seconds to wait. For example,

```
sleep(5);
```

tells a process to sleep for five seconds. watch is similar to a program called readslow that is found in some versions of UNIX. Also, see your manual entry for the tail command.

2.2.3 Using standard error

Standard error is a rather special output channel which is normally reserved for error and warning messages. Having an additional channel for this purpose is useful because it allows a program to display error messages on the terminal while standard output is being written to a file. However, if required, standard error can also be redirected in a manner similar to standard output. For example, the shell command

```
$ make > log.out 2> log.err
```

causes error messages from the `make` program to be sent to the file `log.err`. Standard output is sent to `log.out`.

A programmer could make use of standard error in a program by using the `write` system call and file descriptor 2:

```
char msg[6]="boob\n";
 .
 .
 .
write(2, msg, 5);
```

This however is rather crude and cumbersome. We will provide a better solution in the next section.

2.3 The Standard I/O Library: a look ahead

The file access system calls ultimately provide the basis for all input and output by UNIX programs. However, these calls are true primitives and handle data only in the form of simple sequences of bytes, leaving everything else up to the programmer. Efficiency considerations also fall into the lap of the developer.

To make life a little easier, UNIX offers the Standard I/O Library, which offers many more facilities than the system calls we have so far described. Since this book is mostly concerned with the system call interface to the kernel, we have delayed a full treatment of the Standard I/O Library until Chapter 9. However, for comparative purposes it is worth briefly investigating Standard I/O here.

Perhaps the most obvious difference between Standard I/O and the system call primitives lies in the way files are described. Instead of integer file descriptors, the Standard I/O routines work, implicitly or explicitly, with entities called **streams**. Rather confusingly, streams are represented by a structure type called `FILE`. (Even more confusingly, the term 'streams' has two very distinct meanings in UNIX System V.3. See Chapter 8 for more details.) The next example shows how a file is associated with a stream by the `fopen` routine:

```
#include <stdio.h>

main()
{
   FILE *stream;
```

```
    if((stream = fopen("junk", "r")) == NULL){
        printf("Could not open file junk\n");
        exit(1);
    }
    .
    .
    .
}
```

The first line of the example:

```
#include <stdio.h>
```

includes the Standard I/O Library header file `stdio.h`. This file contains, among many other things, the definition of `FILE`, `NULL` and `extern` declarations for functions such as `fopen`. The real meat of the example is contained in the statement:

```
if((stream = fopen("junk", "r")) == NULL){
  .
  .
  .
}
```

Here, `junk` is a file name, while the string `"r"` means that the file is to be opened read-only. The string `"w"` could be used to open the file for writing. If successful, `fopen` will initialize a `FILE` structure and return its address into `stream`. The pointer `stream` can then be passed to other routines in the library. It is important to realize that somewhere within the body of `fopen`, a call to our old friend `open` is made. As a corollary, somewhere within a `FILE` structure, there is an integer file descriptor which ties that structure to the file. The essential point is that Standard I/O routines are written around the system call primitives. The main function of the library is to provide a more programmer-friendly interface.

Once a stream has been opened, many Standard I/O routines are available to access it. One such is `getc`, which reads a single character; another is `putc`, which writes a single character. They are used along the following lines:

```
#include <stdio.h>

int c;
FILE *istream;
  .
  .
  .
c = getc(istream); /*read c from istream*/
```

and

```
#include <stdio.h>


int c ;
FILE *ostream;
  .
  .
  .
putc(c, ostream); /*place c onto ostream*/
```

Notice how `c` is defined as `int` in both cases.

Both routines can be placed into a loop to copy one file to another:

```
while((c = getc(istream)) != EOF)
        putc(c, ostream);
```

`EOF` is again defined in `stdio.h`. It is returned by `getc` when it reaches end of file. The actual value of `EOF` is −1.

At first sight, `getc` and `putc` look worrying because they process single characters, and, as we have seen, this is extremely inefficient for system calls. Standard I/O avoids inefficiency by an elegant buffering mechanism, which works along the following lines: the first call to `getc` results in `BUFSIZ` characters being read from the file, via the system call `read` (as we saw in Section 2.1.5, `BUFSIZ` is a constant defined in `stdio.h`). The data is kept in a buffer set up by the library (but still in the user's address space). Only the first character will be returned via `getc`. All the other internal workings are kept well away from the calling program. Successive calls to `getc` return characters in order from the buffer. When `BUFSIZ` characters have been passed to the program via `getc`, and another `getc` call is made, the next buffer-full is read in from the file. A similar, outward mechanism is provided for `putc`.

This technique is very useful since it absolves the programmer of worrying about efficiency. However it also means that data is only written out in large chunks, and files will lag behind programs somewhat (special arrangements are made for terminals). It is very unwise therefore to mix Standard I/O routines and system calls for the same file. Unless you know exactly what you are doing, chaos could result. On the other hand, it is perfectly all right to mix system calls and Standard I/O routines for separate files.

Besides the buffering mechanism, Standard I/O provides formatting and conversion utilities; for example, `printf` offers output formatting as in

```
printf("An integer %d\n", ival);
```

This should be familiar to most readers of this book. (`printf`, by the way, implicitly writes to a stream called `stdout`, which corresponds to standard output.)

Writing error messages with `fprintf`

`printf` can be used for displaying diagnostic messages. Unfortunately, it writes to standard output, not standard error. However, we can use `fprintf`, a generalization of `printf`, to do this. The following program fragment shows how:

```
#include <stdio.h>  /*for stderr definition*/
 .
 .
 .
fprintf(stderr, "error number %d\n", errno);
```

The only difference between this use of `fprintf` and a call to `printf` is the `stderr` parameter. This is a pointer to standard stream which is automatically associated with standard error.

The following routine extends the use of `fprintf` to a more general-purpose error routine:

```
/*notfound -- print file error then exit*/

#include <stdio.h>

notfound(progname,filename)
char *progname, *filename;
{
        fprintf(stderr, "%s: file %s not found\n",
            progname,filename);
        exit(1);
}
```

In later examples we will use `fprintf` for error messages, rather than `printf`. This ensures consistency with most commands and programs, which use standard error for diagnostics.

2.4 The `errno` variable and system calls

As we have seen, all the file access system calls so far described can fail in some way. This is universally indicated by a return value of −1. To help the program gain more information when such an exception occurs, UNIX provides a globally accessible integer variable which contains an error code number. This records the last type of error that occurred during a system call.

The name of the error variable is `errno`. A programmer can use `errno` within a C program by declaring it as an `extern` variable of integer type:

```
extern int errno;
```

The following program calls `open` and if this fails, the program will use `fprintf` to display the value of `errno`:

```
/* err1.c -- open a file with error handling*/

#include <stdio.h>
#include <fcntl.h>

extern int errno;

main()
{
        if(open("nonesuch", O_RDONLY) == -1)
              fprintf(stderr,"error %d\n", errno);
}
```

If, for example, the file `nonesuch` does not exist, the error code displayed on a standard UNIX implementation will be 2. Like all of the possible values of `errno`, this code is also given a symbolic name; in this case `ENOENT` which simply means 'no such file or directory'. You can make direct use of these symbolic names by including the system header file `errno.h` in your program, where they are defined using the preprocessor directive `#define`.

Care should be exercised when using `errno` since it is not reset when a new system call is made. It is therefore only valid to use `errno` immediately after a system call has been made and has failed.

If you want more information, a description of each of the possible system call errors defined in the AT&T *System V Interface Definition* can be found in Appendix A.

2.4.1 The `perror` subroutine

As well as `errno`, UNIX provides a routine (not a system call) called `perror`. This takes a single string argument. When called it will produce a message on standard error consisting of the string argument passed to the routine, a colon and then an additional message associated with the current value of the `errno` variable. Usefully, the error message is printed on standard error, not standard output.

In the example above, the line containing the `printf` call could be replaced with

```
perror("error opening nonesuch");
```

If `nonesuch` is non-existent then `perror` would display the message:

```
error opening nonesuch: No such file or directory
```

Exercise 2.16 Write routines that mimic the file access primitives described in this chapter, but call `perror` when an exception or error occurs.

Chapter 3 The File in Context

Files are not completely specified simply by the data they contain. Each UNIX file also possesses a number of additional primitive properties necessary for the administration of what is a complex, multi-user system. It is these additional properties, and the system calls that manipulate them, that we will study in this chapter.

3.1 Files in a multi-user environment

3.1.1 Users and ownerships

Every file on a UNIX system is *owned* by one of that system's users, who is normally the user who created the file. The owner's actual identity is represented by a non-negative integer called the **user-id** (sometimes abbreviated to **uid**) which is stored by the system when the file is created.

The user-id associated with a particular user-name can be found in the third field of the user's entry in the password file, i.e. the line in the file `/etc/passwd` that identifies a user to the system. The typical entry

```
keith::35:10::/usr/keith:/bin/sh
```

indicates that user `keith` has a user-id of 35.

(The fields in a password file entry are separated by colons. The first gives the username, the second the password. In the example no password has been set. As we have seen the third field contains the user-id. Field four contains the user's default **group-id**, explained in more detail in a moment. Field five is an optional comment field. Field six gives the user's **home directory**. The last field is the pathname of the program started after the user has logged in. Usually this is `/bin/sh`, the standard UNIX shell.)

In fact, as far as UNIX is concerned, it is the user-id that is really important in identifying a user. Each UNIX process is normally associated with the user-id of the user who started that process. (Remember, a process is simply an execution of a program.) The actual user-name is really just a mnemonic convenience for human beings. When a file is created, the system establishes ownership by referring to the user-id of the creating process.

The ownership of a file can be later changed, but only by either the system's privileged superuser or the file's owner. It is worth noting that the superuser usually has username **root** and always has user-id 0.

As well as individual users, files are also associated with **groups**; a group being simply an arbitrary collection of users which offers a straightforward method of controlling projects involving several people. Each user belongs to at least one group, possibly more.

Groups are defined in the file `/etc/group`; each group being identified by a **group-id**, which like the user-id is a non-negative integer. A user's default group is indicated by the fourth field of his or her password file entry.

As with user-ids, the group-id of a user is inherited by the processes that user initiates. So, when a file is created, the group-id associated with the creating process is stored along with the user-id.

Effective group- and user-ids

To be a little more precise, we should actually describe file creation in relation to the **effective user-id** associated with a process. This is because, although a process may be started by one user (`keith` say), it can under certain very specific circumstances acquire the file system privileges of another user (`ben` say). Just how this is done we shall see very shortly. The user-id of the user who actually initiated a process is described as the **real user-id** of that process. In most cases of course, the *effective* and *real* user-ids coincide.

For similar reasons, it is the **effective group-id** of a process that establishes the group associated with the file.

3.1.2 Permissions and file modes

Like any kind of ownership, file ownership gives certain privileges to the owner. In particular, the owner can choose the **permissions** associated with a file. Permissions determine how different users can access a file. Three types of user are affected:

1. The file's owner.
2. Anyone who belongs to the same group as the one associated with the file. Note that, as far as the file's owner is concerned, the permissions for category (1) override the permissions for the file's group.
3. Anyone who is not covered by categories (1) or (2).

For each category of user, there are three basic types of file permission. These specify whether a member of a particular category can:

1. Read the file.
2. Write to the file.

3. Attempt to execute the file. (In this case the file will normally contain a program or a list of shell commands.)

Superuser, as always, is a special case and is able to manipulate any file regardless of the read or write permissions associated with it.

The system stores the permissions associated with a file as a bit pattern within an integer called the **file mode**. A suitable bit pattern can be constructed by adding together some of the octal constants shown in Table 3.1. Each value listed is a power of two and so specifies a particular bit within a variable of type integer. For example, 001 indicates the first bit, 002 the second bit, 004 the third bit, 0010 the fourth bit and so on. Each permission therefore corresponds to a particular bit within the file mode. On a more general level, using octal values in this way is a painless method of manipulating program objects at bit level and something you will meet in many other contexts throughout UNIX. Remember that in C octal constants are always indicated by a preceding 0, otherwise the compiler will assume you are speaking decimal.

Table 3.1 Octal values for constructing file permissions.

Octal value	*Meaning*
0400	Read allowed by owner
0200	Write allowed by owner
0100	Owner can execute file
0040	Read allowed by group
0020	Write allowed by group
0010	Group member can execute file
0004	Other types of user can read file
0002	Other types of user can write file
0001	Other types of user can execute file

It is easy to see that we can make a file readable by all types of user by adding 0400 (read permission for the owner), 040 (read permission for members of the file's group) and 04 (read permission for all other users). This gives a final file mode of 0444. Since none of the other values from the table are involved, this particular mode also means that no user is able to write or execute the file, including the owner.

To circumvent this, it is possible to use more than one of the octal values relating to one category of user. For example, adding together 0400, 0200 and 0100 to give the value 0700 means that the file's owner is allowed to read, write or execute the file.

The more likely mode value:

0700 + 050 + 05 = 0755

means the owner can read, write or execute the file, while members of the file's group and any other type of user are restricted to just reading or executing the file.

Symbolic representation

Permissions can also be represented in a standard symbolic form, as used by the `ls` program. This notation represents permissions as a string of nine characters. The first group of three characters describes permissions for the file owner, the second for the file's group and the third for the 'anyone else' category.

Within each of these triplets of characters, the first character is set to `'r'` if read permission for that type of user is on, the second to `'w'` if write permission is on and the third to `'x'` if execute permission is on. If a permission bit is not set then the corresponding character is set to a hyphen (`'-'`).

This can be made plainer with the following example string:

```
rwxr-xr--
```

which reads more clearly if written:

```
rwx  r-x  r--
```

It means that the file's owner can read, write and execute the relevant file (indicated by the first triplet of characters); members of the same group as the file can read or execute the file (indicated by the middle three characters); other users are only allowed to read the file (indicated by the final triplet of characters).

This isn't the whole permission story. In the next sub-section we will see how three other types of permission affect files containing executable programs. Perhaps more important as far as file access goes, each UNIX directory also has a set of access permissions much like an ordinary file; this affects the accessibility of files within the directory. We will discuss this issue in detail in Chapter 4.

Exercise 3.1 What do the following permission values mean: 0761, 0777, 0555, 0007 and 0707?

Exercise 3.2 Translate the octal values in Exercise 3.1 into their symbolic equivalents.

Exercise 3.3 Write a routine `symoct` which translates a symbolic set of permissions into its octal equivalent. Then write its inverse `octsym`.

3.1.3 Extra permissions for executable files

There are three other types of file permission, which specify special attributes relevant when a file contains an executable program. The appropriate octal values, which again correspond to specific bits within the file mode, and their meanings are:

04000	Set user-id on execution
02000	Set group-id on execution
01000	Save text image on execution

Note that *Issue 2* of the *SVID* identifies bit 01000 simply as 'reserved': **save text image** is its usual meaning.

If the **set-user-id** permission is set, then when the program contained in the file is started, the system gives the resulting process an **effective user-id** taken from the *file owner* rather than that of the user who started the process (the latter case being the normal state of affairs). The process then assumes the file system privileges of the file owner, not the user who started the process.

This mechanism can be used to control access to sensitive data; the delicate information can be protected from public gaze or manipulation by use of the standard read-write-execute permissions. The owner of the file can then create a program that accesses the file in a specific, tightly defined manner. When the program is complete, its set-user-id permission can be set, allowing other users access to the file through that program only. Of course, the program must be carefully written to avoid any temporary privilege being abused.

The classic example of this technique is the `passwd` program. A system supervisor is asking for trouble if any user can write to the password file at whim. However, all users must write to this file sometimes in order to change their password. The `passwd` program circumvents this problem because it is owned by superuser and has the set-user-id bit set.

Perhaps rather less usefully, the **set-group-id** permission does the same thing for the file's group-id. If it is set then, when the file is started, the resulting process acquires the group-id of the file, not the user who started up the program.

The **save-text-image** permission, more usually known by its nickname, the **sticky bit**, is designed to save time in accessing commonly used programs. To explain it fully we must first introduce the idea of a sharable program.

A sharable program is one that is separated into an invariant **text** portion, containing program instructions, and a **data** portion which can be altered while the program is running. The text part of the program will be identical for all users running that program, but each user will have their own, unique data part.

The system need therefore keep only one copy of the text part of a program in memory, even when it is being run concurrently by several users. This can considerably reduce the system's administrative overhead and so speed up response times. In some implementations of UNIX, programs are sharable by default. However, in other variants, programs must be explicitly made sharable by giving a special option to the linker: `ld`. You should refer to your manual for details specific to your system.

If the save-text-image permission of a sharable program is set, then, when it is executed, its program-text part will remain in the system's **swap area** until the system is halted. So, when the program is next invoked, the system doesn't hunt for it through the system's directory structure but instead simply (and quickly) **swaps** it into memory. This might be useful in the case of very commonly used programs such as an editor or compiler.

Be warned, over-zealous use of the sticky bit can cause the swap area to fill up and halt your system. It should be used very sparingly or avoided.

Exercise 3.4 The following examples show how `ls` represents the set-user-id, set-group-id and save-text-image permissions respectively:

```
r-sr-xr-x
r-xr-sr-x
r-xr-xr-t
```

Using the command `ls -l`, examine the contents of `/bin`, `/etc` and `/usr/bin` for files with unusual permissions of this type. The more experienced should be able to speed things up by using the `grep` program. If you do find any files with strange permissions, explain why.

3.1.4 `open` and `creat` revisited

As we very briefly saw in Chapter 2, the initial permissions of a file are set when the file is created via a call to either `creat` or `open` in its extended mode. For example the statement

```
filedes = creat("datafile",0644);
```

should, assuming `datafile` doesn't already exist, cause it to be created with permissions 0644. In addition the file's owner-id will be set to the effective user-id associated with the calling process. As a result, the creator (and therefore owner) of the file will be able to read and write the file, while others will only be able to read it.

But what happens if the file already exists? When the process attempts to create the file, the system will check the user-id and group-id associated with the process against the set of permissions associated with the file. The system does this to ensure that the process can write to the file.

For example, if the process's user-id doesn't match the user-id of the file's owner, but both process and file share the same group-id, then the system will check to see whether the group permissions for the file allow writing, i.e. whether permission bit 0020 is set.

If the file's permissions do allow the process to write to the file, then it will be truncated and its original permissions and ownership left unchanged. Otherwise the call will fail and `creat` will return the error code −1. The special error indication variable `errno` will also contain the value `EACCES`. (Remember that `errno` must be declared as an external integer if it is to be used.)

As a trivial example, the following program will, if `sillyfile` doesn't already exist, abort at the second call to `creat` because the first call denies the owner write access. However, note that both calls to `creat` will succeed if the user is the privileged superuser.

```
#include <stdio.h>
#define PERMISSION 0444     /*read only - owner included*/

main()
{
    int filedes;

    if((filedes = creat("sillyfile",PERMISSION)) < 0){
        fprintf(stderr,"1st creat failed\n");
        exit(1);
    }

    close(filedes); /*leave file empty*/

    if((filedes = creat("sillyfile",PERMISSION)) < 0){
        fprintf(stderr,"2nd creat failed\n");
        exit(1);
    }

    printf(
    "This should not appear unless you are root\n");
    printf(
    "or the file already exists and allows writing\n");
    exit(0);
}
```

It is important to note that whatever permissions are used, if a call to `creat` succeeds in creating a file then the calling process can write to that file until it is closed. This is true even if the permissions used would later deny the owner write access.

`open` and file permissions

The `open` system call's interaction with file permissions is more complex. If it is used to open an existing file for reading or writing, then the system checks whether the mode of access requested by the process (read only, write only or read-write) is allowed by the file's permissions. If it is not, `open` will return −1 indicating failure and `errno` will again contain the error code `EACCES`.

When open is used in its extended mode to create a file, it will behave very similarly to creat. The O_CREAT, O_TRUNC and O_EXCL flags do mean however that the treatment of existing files is more flexible with open. Example uses of open with file permissions are:

```
filedes = open(pathname,O_WRONLY|O_CREAT|O_TRUNC,0600);
```

and

```
filedes = open(pathname,O_WRONLY|O_CREAT|O_EXCL,0600);
```

In the first example, open will behave identically to creat and the file in question will be truncated if it exists, providing file permissions allow the calling process write access. In the second the call to open will fail if the file exists, whatever its permissions.

Exercise 3.5

(a) Suppose a process has effective user-id 100 and effective group-id 200. File XXX is owned by user 101 and has a group-id of 200. For each possible mode of access (read only, write only and read-write) state whether a call to open would succeed when XXX has the following permissions:

```
rwxr-xrwx    r-xrwxr-x    rwx--x---    rwsrw-r--
--s--s--x    ---rwx---    ---r-x--x
```

(b) For which of the above cases could a call to creat truncate XXX?

(c) What would happen if the process also had *real* user-id 101 and *real* group-id 201?

3.1.5 Determining file accessibility with access

access is a useful system call that determines whether or not a process can access a file, according to the *real* user-id of the process, rather than the current *effective* user-id. It provides another level of security in a process which has gained powers via the set-uid bit.

Usage

```
int result, amode;
char *pathname;

  .
  .
  .

result = access(pathname,amode);
```

As we have seen there are several ways of accessing a file, so to give more information to the system the parameter amode contains a value indicating the required method of access. This value is constructed rather like an ordinary file mode from the following octal values:

04 Has calling process read access?
02 Has calling process write access?
01 Can calling process execute the file?

There is just one set of values for `amode` because we are concerned with only the ability of one user, identified by the real user-id of the calling process, to access the file. `amode` can also take the value 0. This causes `access` to check for the file's existence only.

The other parameter `pathname` gives, rather unsurprisingly, the name of the file.

The return value from `access` is either 0 (indicating that the user identified by the process's real user-id can access the file in the manner indicated by `amode`) or −1 (indicating that he or she cannot). In the latter case, `errno` will contain a value indicating the reason why. A value of `EACCES`, for example, means the file's permissions don't allow the required access, while `ENOENT` means that the file simply does not exist.

The following skeleton program uses `access` to check if its user can read a file, whatever the set-uid bit setting:

```
/*example use of access*/

#include <stdio.h>

char filename[]="afile";

main()
{

        if(access(filename,04) == -1){
            fprintf(stderr,"User cannot read file %s\n",filename);
            exit(1);
        }

        printf("%s readable, proceeding\n",filename);

        /*rest of program ... */
}
```

Exercise 3.6 Write a program `whatable` which tells you whether you can read, write or execute a file. When a type of access is not available, then `whatable` should say why (use `perror`).

3.1.6 Changing file permissions with `chmod`

Usage

```
int retval, newmode;
char *pathname;
  .
  .
  .
retval = chmod(pathname, newmode);
```

The `chmod` system call is used to alter the permissions of an existing file. It can be used on a file only by the file's owner or superuser.

The `pathname` parameter points to the filename. The integer `newmode` contains the new file mode, constructed in the way described in the first part of this chapter.

An example use of `chmod` is:

```
if(chmod(pathname,0644) < 0)
        perror("call to chmod failed");
```

Exercise 3.7 Write a program `setperm` that takes two command line arguments. The first is a filename, the second the octal or symbolic specification for a set of permissions. If the file exists, then `setperm` should attempt to reset the file's permissions to the value given. Use the routine `symoct` you developed in Exercise 3.3.

3.1.7 Changing ownership with `chown`

`chown` is used to alter both the owner and group of a file.

Usage

```
int retval, owner_id, group_id;
char *pathname;
  .
  .
  .
retval = chown(pathname, owner_id, group_id);
```

As you can see, it has three arguments: `pathname`, which points to the file's pathname, the integer `owner_id` which indicates the new owner and the integer `group_id` which gives the new group. The return value in `retval` is either 0 on success or −1 on error.

`chown` can only be used by either the current file owner or superuser. It is therefore possible for an ordinary user to give a file of theirs away. However, once done this cannot be undone since the user's id and the new user-id of the file will no longer match! Note also, that to prevent the unscrupulous using `chown` to steal file system privileges, the set-user-id and set-group-id permissions are turned off when the ownership of a file is altered. (What could happen if this wasn't the case?)

3.1.8 The file creation mask and the `umask` system call

Associated with each process is an integer called the **file creation mask**. This is used to turn off permission bits automatically whenever a file is created, whatever the mode given within the appropriate `creat` or `open` call. It is useful in safeguarding all files created during the existence of a process because it prevents the specified permissions from being accidentally turned on.

The basic idea is straightfoward: if a permission bit is set in the file creation mask, then it is always turned off when a file is created. The bits in the mask can be set using the same octal constants as described previously for file modes, although only the basic read, write and execute permissions can be used. The more exotic permissions such as *set-user-id* have no significance in a file creation mask.

In programming terms the statement

```
filedes = creat(pathname,mode);
```

is therefore actually equivalent to

```
filedes =  creat(pathname, (~mask)&mode);
```

where `mask` holds the current value of the file creation mask, `~` is the C bitwise negation operator and `&` the bitwise AND operator.

For example, if the value of the mask is 04+02+01=07 then the permissions normally indicated by these values are turned off whenever a file is created. So, with this value in effect, a file created with the statement

```
fd = creat(pathname,0644);
```

will actually be given a mode of 0640. This means that the file owner and members of the group associated with the file will be able to use the file in some way, but other types of user will be denied any access at all.

A process's file creation mask can be changed with the `umask` system call, which should be used as follows:

```
int oldmask, newmask;
  .
  .
  .
oldmask = umask(newmask);
```

The integer parameter `newmask` is the new value for the file creation mask. After the call, `oldmask` will hold the mask's previous value.

As a corollary of all this, if you want to make absolutely sure that files are created with the mode exactly as given in an `open` or `creat` call, then you should first call `umask` with an argument of zero. Since all permission bits in the file creation mask will now be zero, none of the bits in a later file mode will be masked. The following example subroutine uses this idea to create a file with a guaranteed mode, then restores the old file creation mask. It returns the file descriptor from `creat`.

```
int specialcreat(pathname,mode)
char *pathname;
int mode;
{
        int oldu, filedes;

        /*set file creation mask to zero*/
        oldu = umask(0);

        /*create the file*/
        if((filedes = creat(pathname, mode)) < 0)
             perror("specialcreat");

        /*restore the old file mode*/
        umask(oldu);

        /*return file descriptor*/
        return(filedes);
}
```

3.2 Files with multiple names

Any UNIX file can be identified by more than one name. In other words, the same *physical* collection of data can be associated with several UNIX pathnames without the need for the file to be duplicated. This may seem strange at first, but it can be very useful in terms of saving disk space or ensuring a number of people all make use of the same file.

Each such name is referred to as a **link.** The number of links associated with a file is called the **link count** of that file.

A new link is created with the `link` system call, and an existing link can be removed with our old friend, the `unlink` system call.

3.2.1 The `link` system call

Usage

```
int retval;
char *path1, *path2;
```

```
.
.
.
retval = link(path1,path2);
```

`path1` is a character pointer that points to a UNIX pathname. It must identify an existing link to a file, i.e. an existing name for the file. `path2` points to the new name or link for the file. (Note that `path2` may not already exist as a file.)

The return value in `retval` is 0 if the call is successful or −1 if an error occurs. In the latter case no new link will be created.

For example, the statement

```
link("/usr/keith/chap.2","/usr/ben/2.chap");
```

will create a link called `/usr/ben/2.chap` to the existing file `/usr/keith/chap.2`. The file can now be referred to using either name. As you can see links do not have to be in the same directory.

There is an important limitation to use of the `link` call. It is not possible to link a file across different **file systems**, which are the fundamental components of the overall UNIX file structure. This topic will be explored in more detail in Chapter 4.

3.2.2 The `unlink` system call revisited

In Chapter 2 (actually Section 2.1.11) we introduced the `unlink` system call as a simple way of removing a file from the system. For example,

```
unlink("/tmp/scratch");
```

will remove `/tmp/scratch`.

In fact, the `unlink` system call removes just the link named, and reduces the file's link count by one. Only if the link count is reduced to zero, and no program currently has the file open, is the data in the file irredeemably lost from the system. In this latter case, the disk blocks previously allocated to the file are added to a list of free blocks maintained by the system. Although the data may for a time remain in physical existence, it is not recoverable. Since most files have only one link, this is the usual result of a call to `unlink`. Conversely, if the link count isn't reduced to zero, the file data is left untouched and can be accessed through the file's other links.

The following short program renames a file by first linking it to the new desired pathname and if this is successful, unlinking the old pathname. It is a simplified version of the standard UNIX `mv` command.

```
/*move -- move a file from one pathname to another*/

#include <stdio.h>
char usage[]="usage:move file1 file2\n";
```

```
/*main uses args passed from command line in
 *standard manner
 */

main(argc,argv)
int argc;
char *argv[];
{
        if(argc != 3){
            fprintf(stderr, usage);
            exit(1);
        }

        if(link(argv[1],argv[2]) < 0){
             perror("link failed");
             exit(1);
        }

        if(unlink(argv[1]) < 0){
             perror("unlink failed");
             unlink(argv[2]);
             exit(1);
        }

        printf("succeeded\n");
        exit(0);
}
```

Before proceeding, one final point. So far we have not mentioned the interaction of `unlink` and the permissions associated with its filename argument. This is because `unlink` is simply not affected by these permissions. The success or failure of a call to `unlink` is instead determined by the permissions of the *directory* containing the file. Again, this is a topic we will explore in Chapter 4.

Exercise 3.8 Using `unlink` write your own version of the `rm` command. Your program should check that the user has write permission on the file with `access`. If not, it should ask for confirmation before attempting to unlink the file. (Why?) Be careful while testing it!

3.3 Obtaining file information: `stat` and `fstat`

So far we have seen only how to set or change the basic properties associated with files. The two system calls `stat` and `fstat` enable a program to discover the values of these properties for an existing file.

Usage

```
#include <sys/types.h>
#include <sys/stat.h>

int retval, filedes;
char *pathname;
struct stat buf;
  .
  .
  .
retval = stat(pathname, &buf);

retval = fstat(filedes, &buf);
```

`stat` is given two arguments; `pathname` as usual points to the pathname that identifies the file. The second (`&buf` above) is a pointer to a `stat` structure. This structure will hold the information associated with the file.

If the call to `stat` is successful, `retval` will be set to 0 and the structure `buf` will be updated.

The `fstat` system call is more or less identical in function to the `stat` system call. The only difference is that, instead of a pathname, `fstat` expects a file descriptor `filedes`. `fstat` can therefore only be used with an open file.

The definition of the structure template `stat` is found in the system header file `stat.h`, and, under System V, takes the form:

```
struct stat {
        dev_t     st_dev;
        ino_t     st_ino;
        ushort    st_mode;
        short     st_nlink;
        ushort    st_uid;
        ushort    st_gid;
        dev_t     st_rdev;
        off_t     st_size;
        time_t    st_atime;
        time_t    st_mtime;
        time_t    st_ctime;
};
```

The `short` data type in the left-hand column should already be familiar as a standard C data type. The others, such as `ushort` or `time_t`, are probably unfamiliar. They are implementation-dependent and describe types used internally by the system. The standard C types to which these defined types reduce can be found in the system header file `types.h` (in some flavours of UNIX the file `param.h` is also involved). For example, on the system on which this text was prepared, `time_t` is equivalent to `long`, and `ushort` is equivalent to `unsigned short`.

The members of the `stat` structure template itself have the following meanings:

1. `st_dev, st_ino` The first of these structure members describes the logical device on which the file resides and the second gives the *inode number* of the file. This, in conjunction with `st_dev`, identifies a file uniquely. In fact, both `st_dev` and `st_ino` are concerned with the underlying management of the UNIX file structure. We will explain these ideas in the next chapter. For the moment, you can safely ignore both these members.
2. `st_mode` This gives the file mode and enables a programmer to calculate the permissions associated with the file. A word of caution is due here. The value contained in `st_mode` also gives information on the type of file, and only the lowest 12 bits are concerned with permissions. This will become clearer in Chapter 4.
3. `st_nlink` The number of links (in other words, the number of different pathnames) associated with the file. This value will be updated with each call of the `link` and `unlink` system calls.
4. `st_uid, st_gid` The user-id and group-id of the file. Altered by the `chown` system call. Initially set by `creat` or `open`.
5. `st_rdev` This is meaningful only when the file entry is used to describe a device. Again you can safely ignore this member for the time being.
6. `st_size` The current *logical* size of the file in bytes. This is changed after each write to the end of the file.
7. `st_atime` This records the last time the data in the file was read (although the initial `creat` will also set this value).
8. `st_mtime` This records the time the data in the file was in any way modified and is reset with each write to the file.
9. `st_ctime` This records the time since any of the information returned in the `stat` structure itself was altered. System calls which change this include `link` (because of `st_nlink`), `chmod` (because of `st_mode`) and `write` (because of `st_mtime` and possibly `st_size`).

The following example subroutine `filedata` displays details associated with a file identified by `pathname`. The information printed out consists of the file size, the user and group ids of the file, and the file's read-write-execute permissions.

To help translate the file permissions into a readable form like that produced by `ls`, we have used an array of short integers `octarray`, which contains the values for the basic permissions, and a character array `perms`, which holds the symbolic equivalent.

Notice how we must include the header files `types.h` and `stat.h` at the top of the subroutine. The prefix `sys` in `<sys/types.h>` means that `types.h` inhabits the directory `/usr/include/sys` rather than the normal directory for header files: `/usr/include`.

```
/*filedata -- display information about a file*/

/*header files from directory /usr/include/sys*/

#include <stdio.h>
#include <sys/types.h>
#include <sys/stat.h>

/*use octarray for determining
 *if permission bits set
 */
static short octarray[9]={
        0400,0200,0100,0040,0020,0010,
        0004,0002,0001
};

/*mnemonic codes for file permissions,
 *10 chars long  because of terminating null
 */
static char  perms[]= "rwxrwxrwx";

filedata(pathname)
char *pathname;     /*pathname identifies file*/
{

        struct stat statbuf;
        char descrip[9];
        int j;

        if(stat(pathname, &statbuf) < 0){
             fprintf(stderr, "Couldn't stat %s\n",pathname);
             return(-1);
        }

        /*put permissions into readable form*/

        for(j = 0;j < 9;j++){
             /*
              *test whether permission set
              *using bitwise AND
              */
            if(statbuf.st_mode & octarray[j] )
               descrip[j] = perms[j];
            else
```

```
                descrip[j] = '-';
        }
        descrip[9] = '\0'; /*make sure we've a string*/

        /*display file information*/

        printf("\nFile %s:\n", pathname);
        printf("Size %ld bytes\n", statbuf.st_size);
        printf("User-id %d, Group-id %d\n\n",
            statbuf.st_uid,statbuf.st_gid);
        printf("Permissions: %s\n",descrip);
        return(0);
}
```

The following program `lookout` is a more useful tool. Given a list of filenames, it checks once a minute to see if any file in the list has changed. It does this by monitoring the modification time of each file (`st_mtime`). It is a utility intended to be run as a background process.

```
/*lookout -- print message when file changes*/

#include <stdio.h>
#include <sys/types.h>
#include <sys/stat.h>

#define MFILE 10

struct stat sb;

main(argc,argv)
int argc;
char *argv[];
{
        int j;
        time_t last_time[MFILE+1];


        if(argc < 2){
            fprintf(stderr, "usage: lookout filename ...\n");
            exit(1);
        }

        if(--argc > MFILE){
            fprintf(stderr, "lookout: too many file names\n");
            exit(1);
        }

        /*initialization*/
```

```
        for(j=1; j <= argc; j++){
            if(stat(argv[j], &sb) < 0){
                fprintf(stderr, "lookout: couldn't stat %s\n",
                  argv[j]);
                exit(1);
            }
            last_time[j] = sb.st_mtime;
        }

        /*loop until file changes*/
        for(;;){
            for(j=1;j <= argc; j++)
                cmp(argv[j], last_time[j]);

            /*rest for 60 seconds.
             *"sleep" is a standard
             *UNIX library routine.
             */
            sleep(60);
        }

}

cmp(name, last)
char *name;
time_t last;
{
      if(stat(name, &sb) < 0 || sb.st_mtime != last){
           fprintf(stderr,"lookout: %s changed\n", name);
           exit(0);
      }
}
```

Exercise 3.9 Write a program which monitors, and records, the alterations in the size of a file over one hour. At end, it should produce a simple histogram showing any variation over time.

Exercise 3.10 Write a program `slowwatch` which periodically monitors the modification time of a named file (it should not fail if the file does not initially exist). When the file changes, `slowwatch` should copy it to its standard output. How can you ensure (or guess) that the file is fully updated before it is copied?

3.3.1 `chmod` revisited

`stat` and `fstat` enhance the use of `chmod` because, since the mode of a file can now be obtained, a program can modify file permissions instead of merely resetting them unconditionally.

The following program x demonstrates this. It first calls stat to obtain the current file mode of a file named in the program's argument list. If successful, it then modifies the existing permissions so that the file is executable by its owner. This might be useful if the file contained a 'shell script'.

```
/*x -- add execute permission to file*/

#include <stdio.h>
#include <sys/types.h>
#include <sys/stat.h>

#define  XPERM 0100 /*Execute permission for owner*/

main(argc,argv)
int argc;
char *argv[];
{
        int k;
        struct stat statbuf;

        /*loop for all files in arg list*/
        for(k = 1; k < argc; k++){

            /*get current file mode*/
            if(stat(argv[k], &statbuf) < 0){
                fprintf(stderr, "x: couldn't stat %s\n",argv[k]);
                continue;
            }

            /*attempt to add execute permission*/
            /*by using bitwise OR operator     */

            statbuf.st_mode  = (statbuf.st_mode|XPERM);
            if(chmod(argv[k], statbuf.st_mode) < 0)
                fprintf(stderr,
                  "x: couldn't change mode for %s\n",argv[k]);

        }/*end for loop*/

        exit(0);
}
```

The most interesting point here is the way the file mode is modified by using the bitwise OR operator. This ensures that the bit described by XPERM is set. In fact we could have shortened this statement to

```
statbuf.st_mode |= XPERM;
```

We used the longer form for clarity.

Exercise 3.11 This example is, for the task it performs, over-complex. If you know how, write an equivalent using the shell.

Exercise 3.12 Using your UNIX manual as a specification, write your own version of the `chmod` command.

Chapter 4 Directories, File Systems and Special Files

4.1 Introduction

In the previous two chapters we concentrated on the basic component of the UNIX file structure – the ordinary disk file. This chapter will examine the other components of the file structure, namely:

Directories Directories act as repositories for file names and, consequently, allow users to create arbitrary collections of files. The notion of directories will be familiar to most users of UNIX, and many refugees from other operating systems. As we shall see, UNIX directories can be nested and this gives the file structure a hierarchical, tree-like form.

File systems File systems are collections of directories and files. They represent complete sub-sections of the hierarchical tree of directories and files that makes up a UNIX file structure. Typically, file systems correspond to physical sections ('partitions') of a disk. They are, for most purposes, invisible to the user.

Special files UNIX extends the file concept to cover the peripheral devices connected to a system. These peripheral devices, such as printers, disk units and even main memory, are represented by file names in the file structure. A file which stands for a device in this way is called a **special file**. They can be accessed via the file access system calls discussed in Chapters 2 and 3 (for example, `open`, `read`, and `write`). Each such call activates the device driver code within the kernel responsible for controlling the particular device. However, the program need not know anything about this; the system ensures that special files can be treated almost identically to ordinary files.

4.2 Directories and the AT&T *System V Interface Definition*

Traditionally, UNIX programmers have had to know how directories are implemented in order to write programs that manipulate them directly. This means programs get tied to details of a particular implementation, limiting their portability. AT&T's *System V Interface Definition (SVID)* does not actually define the format of a UNIX directory, but it does introduce two subroutines named `ftw` and `getcwd` in an attempt to generalize directory manipulation. We will discuss them later in this chapter. In terms of System V UNIX they will guarantee portability for application programs, but unfortunately neither is available in earlier versions of UNIX.

In practice most UNIX systems have used the same method of implementing directories (Berkeley UNIX is a notable exception). Indeed, much commercial and academic UNIX software assumes this structure. For this reason, and also to give a better understanding of the general file structure, we have included a discussion of the most common form of directory implementation in this chapter. Read it to gain insight, but remember – your programs should not really make assumptions about the actual format of a directory. Similar comments apply to the discussion on special files and file systems later in the chapter.

4.3 Directories: the user view

Even a casual user of UNIX will have some notion of how its directory structure appears at command level. However, for completeness we will briefly review the way the user views the layout of files and directories.

In essence, directories are just collections of file names, which provide a means of dividing files into logically related groups. For example, each user is usually provided with his or her own **home directory**, where they are 'placed' at login, and are allowed to create and manipulate files. This makes obvious sense, since it keeps the files owned by different users separate. Public programs, such as `cat` or `ls`, are similarly kept together in just a handful of directories which have names such as `/bin` and `/usr/bin`. To use a common metaphor, directories can be compared to the drawers within filing cabinets that are used to group paper files.

However, directories do have some advantages over filing cabinets. As well as containing files, they can also contain other directories, called **sub-directories**, and so allow further levels of grouping. Sub-directories may in turn contain their own sub-directories, and this nesting can continue to any depth.

In fact, the UNIX file structure can be represented as an inverted, hierarchical, tree-like structure. A simplified directory tree is shown in Figure 4.1. Any real-life system would, of course, have a more complex layout.

At the top of our example tree, and indeed any complete UNIX directory tree, there is a single directory called the **root directory.** This is given the rather terse name '`/`'. The non-terminal nodes within the tree, such as `keith` or `ben`, are always directories. The terminal nodes, such as

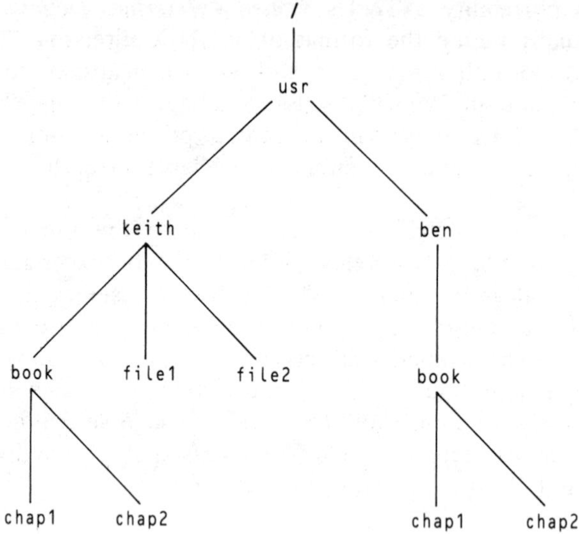

Figure 4.1 Example directory tree.

file1 or file2, are either ordinary files, or empty directories. The names of directories, like files, are limited to 14 characters in length in a standard UNIX implementation.

In our example, keith and ben are sub-directories of their **parent directory** called usr. In the directory called keith are three entries: two ordinary files called file1 and file2, and a sub-directory called book. From the viewpoint of book, it is keith that is the parent directory. book in its turn contains two files, chap1 and chap2. As Chapter 1 shows, the location of a file within the hierarchy can be specified using a **pathname**. For example, the full pathname of the chap2 file contained within keith is /usr/keith/book/chap2. In a similar manner, directories themselves can also be identified by pathnames. The pathname for the ben directory is /usr/ben.

Notice that the directory /usr/ben/book also contains two files called chap1 and chap2. These bear no necessary relation to their namesakes in the /usr/keith/book directory, since it is only the full pathname that uniquely identifies a file. The fact that files in different directories can have the same name means it is unnecessary for users continually to invent weird, wonderful and unique file names.

The current directory

A logged-on user will find him or herself working at a particular place in the file structure called the **current working directory** or sometimes just the **current directory**. This is, for example, the directory from where the ls command will list files, when run without arguments. The initial setting for a user's current directory is that user's home directory, as identified in the system password file. It can be changed using the `cd` command. For example,

```
$ cd /usr/keith
```

changes the current directory to `/usr/keith`. When you need to know, the `pwd` command (the name `pwd` stands for 'print working directory') will print out the name of the current directory explicitly.

```
$ pwd
/usr/keith
```

As far as the system is concerned, the defining characteristic of the current directory is that it is the directory from where the system starts relative pathname searches, i.e. searches involving pathnames that do not begin with a '/'. For example, if the current directory is `/usr/keith`, the command

```
$ cat book/chap1
```

is equivalent to

```
$ cat /usr/keith/book/chap1
```

and the command

```
$ cat file1
```

is equivalent to

```
$ cat /usr/keith/file1
```

4.4 The implementation of a directory

UNIX directories are, in fact, nothing more than files. In many respects they are treated by the system in the same way as ordinary files. They have an owner, group owner, a size and associated access permissions. Many of the system calls used for file manipulation we covered in previous chapters may be used to manipulate directories. For example, directories may be opened for reading using the `open` system call and the returned file descriptor may be used in subsequent calls to `read`, `lseek`, `fstat` and `close`.

There are some important differences, however, between directories and ordinary files that are imposed by the system. Directories may not be created using the `creat` primitive. Nor will `open` work on a directory when either of the `O_WRONLY` or `O_RDWR` flags is set. It will instead fail and return an error code of `EISDIR` via the `errno` variable. These limitations make it impossible to update a directory using `write`. As we shall see, special system calls must be used to create and alter directories.

Structurally, directories on most current UNIX systems consist of a series of 16-byte entries, one for each file or sub-directory contained within them (this is where we start to go beyond the confines of the *SVID*). Each 16-byte slot consists of a positive integer, which takes up two bytes, called the file's **inode number**, and a 14-character field which contains the file's name.

A partial slice of a directory containing three files might look something like Figure 4.2. This directory contains the names of three files (which could be sub-directories) called `fred`, `bookmark` and `abc`. These have inode numbers of 120, 207 and 235, respectively.

.
.
.

120	f	r	e	d	\0									
207	b	o	o	k	m	a	r	k	\0					
235	a	b	c	\0										

.
.
.

Figure 4.2 Partial slice of directory.

The inode number uniquely identifies a file (actually, inode numbers are really only unique within a file system, but more of that later). The inode number is used by the operating system to locate a disk-based data structure, called the inode structure, which contains all the administrative information for the file: size, owner's user-id, group-id, permissions, date of creation, last modified date and the disk addresses of the blocks on disk that hold the file data. Most of the information supplied by the `stat` and `fstat` calls described in the previous chapter is, in fact, obtained directly from the inode structure. We will explain inode structures in more detail in Section 4.6.

It is important to realize that our representation of a directory is only a logical picture. The two-byte inode is in reality stored using the machine's binary representation of a small integer. Consequently, these two bytes will often contain two non-printable, even non-ASCII, values. Printing the contents of a directory using the `cat` command can result in garbage being output on the terminal screen. A better way to examine a directory is to use the octal dump command `od` with the *-c* option. For example, to view the contents of the current directory, try

```
$ od -c .
```

The '.' in this command is the standard way of referring to the current directory.

4.4.1 `link` and `unlink` revisited

In the previous chapter we saw how the `link` system call was used to create different names that referred to the same physical file. It should now be clear how this actually works. Each link simply results in a new directory slot with the same inode number as the original, and with a new name.

In the directory in Figure 4.2, if we created a link to the file `abc` called `xyz` with the following call:

```
link("abc", "xyz");
```

our partial directory slice might look like Figure 4.3. When a link is removed using the `unlink` system call, the appropriate directory slot is freed for re-use. If this slot represented the last link to the file, the entire inode structure is cleared. The associated disk blocks, which contained the actual file data, are added to a free list maintained by the system and become available for re-use.

120	f	r	e	d	\0									
207	b	o	o	k	m	a	r	k	\0					
235	a	b	c	\0										
235	x	y	z	\0										

Figure 4.3 Example directory with new file.

To be more precise, when a file is deleted from a directory, the 16-byte directory slot is not actually removed. The inode number is merely set to a value of zero to indicate that the file has been removed and that the slot is now invalid. Do not be surprised, therefore, when looking at a directory using the `od` command, to see the names of files that have been previously removed. Of course, since the inode number of such files has been set to zero, there is no way of identifying the disk blocks that previously contained the deleted file data. Files cannot be 'undeleted'.

Conversely, whenever a new file is created in a directory, the system searches through the directory file for the first available 16-byte slot identified by a zero in the inode field. It then overwrites this slot with the inode and name of the newly created file. If an empty slot does not exist the name of the file is added to the end of the directory, which means the directory itself is extended.

This technique produces the rather curious effect that directories never shrink in size. Presumably the overhead of directories being slightly larger than they need to be is outweighed by the ease of implementation of the file deletion and addition algorithms.

4.4.2 Dot and double-dot

Two strange file names are always present in every directory. These are '.' and '..' (that is, dot and double-dot). The single dot is the standard UNIX method of referring to the current directory as in

```
$ cat ./fred
```

which will type the file `fred` from the current directory, or

```
$ ls .
```

which will list the files in the current directory. The double-dot is the standard method of referring to the parent directory of the current directory, i.e. the directory that contains the current directory. So the command

```
$ cd ..
```

moves the user one level up the directory tree.

In fact, '.' and '..' are simply links to the current directory and parent directory, respectively, and every UNIX directory contains these two names in its first two slots. To put it another way, every directory, when created, automatically contains two names.

We can make things clearer by looking at the example section of the directory tree shown in Figure 4.4. If we were to examine each of the

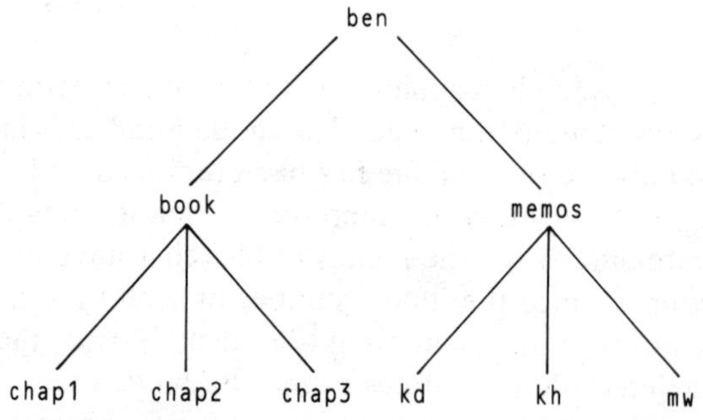

Figure 4.4 Example section of directory tree.

directories `ben`, `book` and `memos` we would see something like Figure 4.5. Notice how in the directory `book`, '.' has an inode number of 260 and '..' has an inode number of 123 which corresponds to the entries `book` and '.' in the parent directory, `ben`. Similarly '.' and '..' in `memos` (401 and 123) correspond to `memos` and '.' in `ben`.

4.4.3 Directory permissions

Like ordinary files, directories have access permissions associated with them controlling the way different users can access them.

Directory permissions are organized in exactly the same way as ordinary file permissions with the three groups of '`rwx`' bits specifying the privileges of the directory owner, users in the owner's group and all other

Directory `ben`

123	.	\0				
247	.	.	\0			
260	b	o	o	k	\0	
401	m	e	m	o	s	\0

Directory `book`

260	.	\0				
123	.	.	\0			
566	c	h	a	p	1	\0
567	c	h	a	p	2	\0
590	c	h	a	p	3	\0

Directory `memos`

401	.	\0	
123	.	.	\0
800	k	h	\0
810	k	d	\0
077	m	w	\0

Figure 4.5 Directories `ben`, `book` and `memos`.

system users. However, even though the permissions are represented in exactly the same way, they are interpreted rather differently.

- Read permission on a directory means that the appropriate class of users is able to list the names of files and sub-directories contained within the directory. This does not mean that the users are able to read the information contained in the files themselves – permission for that is controlled by the access permissions of the individual files.

- Write permission on a directory enables a user to create new files and remove existing files in that directory. Again, it does not permit a user to modify the contents of existing files unless the individual file permissions say so. It would, however, be possible to remove an existing file and create a new one with the same name, which really amounts to the same thing.
- Execute permission (also called **search permission**) on a directory allows a user to 'move into' the directory using the `cd` command, or the `chdir` system call within a program (we discuss the latter below). In addition, to open a file, or execute a program, a user must have execute permission on all directories leading to the file as specified in the file's pathname, which means the actual pathname used, even if it is relative.

At shell command level, the permissions associated with directories can be examined using the *-l* option to the `ls` command. Sub-directories will be identified by a letter 'd' in the first character position of the listing. For example:

```
$ ls -l
  total 168
  -rw-r-----  1 ben    other    39846 Oct 12 21:21 dir_t
  drwxr-x---  2 ben    other       32 Oct 12 22:02 expenses
  -rw-r-----  1 ben    other    46245 Sep 13 10:34 new
  -rw-r-----  1 ben    other     3789 Sep  2 18:40 pwd_text
  -rw-r-----  1 ben    other     1310 Sep 13 10:38 test.c
```

Here the line describing sub-directory `expenses` is tagged with a leading letter 'd'. It shows that the directory has access permissions of read, write and execute (search) for its owner (user `ben`), read and execute permissions for users in the file's group (called `other`), and no access permissions at all for other users.

If you want to obtain listing information about the current directory you can give the *-d* option to `ls` as well as the *-l* option. For example:

```
$ ls -ld
drwxr-x--- 3 ben     other      128 Oct 12 22:02 .
```

Remember that the name '.' at the end of the listing is used to refer to the current directory.

4.5 Programming with directories

The standard operating system header file /usr/include/sys/dir.h contains a data structure which defines the exact, system-specific, format of a directory entry. For most common versions of UNIX it will contain something like:

```
#define DIRSIZ 14

struct direct{
        ino_t        d_ino;
        char         d_name[DIRSIZ];
};
```

The data type ino_t is defined in the header file /usr/include/sys/types (as a corollary, this file must be included in all programs that use the direct structure). ino_t is typically equivalent to unsigned short, and so the total size of a direct structure is normally 16 bytes, matching the usual size of a directory slot on disk.

The fields in the direct structure match the layout of a directory slot on disk. So, for each directory slot, the d_ino field contains the file inode number and the d_name field contains the file name. The file name will be null-terminated, except when the name uses up all 14 characters available. Because of this last point, you should avoid using string functions from the C library on the d_name field; the name it holds might not always be a valid, null-terminated string.

In the following example, the function my_ls will list the names of all the files in a given directory. Additionally, my_ls will print a count of the number of files. It accepts a pointer to a directory name as a parameter, and returns −1 on error. Notice how the directory is opened just like an ordinary file, and also how the address of the direct structure d is passed as a parameter to read. The standard C operator sizeof is used to tell read the size of the structure.

```
#include <sys/types.h>
#include <sys/dir.h>
#include <fcntl.h>

my_ls(name)
char *name;
{
    struct direct d;
    int count = 0;
    int fd;

    if((fd = open(name, O_RDONLY)) < 0)
      return(-1);
```

```
    while(read(fd, (char *)&d, sizeof(d)) == sizeof(d))
      /*ignore empty slots*/
      if(d.d_ino != 0){
          printf("%.14s\n",d.d_name);
          count++;
      }

    printf("Total of %d files\n", count);
    close(fd);
    return(0);

}
```

Because of the algorithm used by the system for filling directory slots, the order of the file names printed by the `my_ls` subroutine will reflect the order in which the files were placed in the directory. If `my_ls` is executed in a directory containing the three files `abc`, `bookmark` and `fred` the output might appear as follows:

```
.
..
fred
bookmark
abc
Total of 5 files
```

A second example: `find_entry`

The next example routine `find_entry` will search through a directory looking for the next occurrence of a file (or sub-directory) ending with a specified suffix. The subroutine takes three parameters: a directory name to be searched, the suffix string and a flag indicating whether the directory should be searched from the start, or whether the search should continue from the last slot found. If a suitable name is found, a pointer to the name is returned, otherwise a null pointer is returned.

`find_entry` uses a string-matching routine called `match` to check whether a particular file name ends with the desired suffix. `match` in turn calls two standard routines from the C library found on all UNIX systems: `strlen` which returns the length of a string in characters, and `strcmp` which compares two strings, returning zero if they match exactly.

```
#include <sys/types.h>
#include <sys/dir.h>
#include <fcntl.h>

#define BEGINNING   1
#define FIRST_TIME (-1)
```

```
char *find_entry(dir, suffix, cont)
char *dir, *suffix;
int cont;
{
      static int fd = FIRST_TIME;
      static char tmp[DIRSIZ+1];
      int i;
      struct direct d;

      /*first time through?*/
      if(fd == FIRST_TIME || cont == BEGINNING){
            if(fd != FIRST_TIME)
                  close(fd);
            if((fd = open(dir, O_RDONLY)) < 0)
                  return( (char *) 0);
      }
      while(read(fd, (char *)&d, sizeof(d)) == sizeof(d)){
         if(d.d_ino == 0)
                  continue;
         /*make a real string*/
         for(i = 0; d.d_name[i] != '\0' && i < DIRSIZ; i++)
                  tmp[i] = d.d_name[i];
         tmp[i] = '\0';

         if(match(tmp, suffix))
                  return(tmp);
      }
      close(fd);
      fd = FIRST_TIME;
      return( (char *)0 );
}
match(s1, s2)
char s1[], s2[];
{
      if(strlen(s1) < strlen(s2))
         return(0); /*FALSE*/

      if(strcmp(&s1[strlen(s1) - strlen(s2)] , s2) == 0)
         return(1); /*TRUE*/
      else
         return(0); /*FALSE*/
}
```

Exercise 4.1 Modify the `my_ls` subroutine from the earlier example to accept a second parameter – an integer called `skip`. When `skip` is set to 0, `my_ls` should perform as before. When `skip` is set to 1, `my_ls` should skip any files with names that begin with a dot '.'.

Exercise 4.2 The subroutine `my_ls` is not particularly efficient in the way it reads from disk since it only reads one `direct` structure at a time (normally 16 bytes). Modify the routine to read in an entire disk block on every call to `read`. Use the `BUFSIZ` parameter from `stdio.h` to get your system's block size (you can be assured that it will contain a whole number of `direct` structures). Declare an array of `direct` structures to read the data into. Use the UNIX `time` command to compare the execution speed of this new version of the routine against the old one. Run both using a large directory such as `/bin` to see the difference between them.

4.5.1 The current directory

As we saw in Section 4.3, each logged-in user works within a current working directory. In fact each UNIX process, i.e. each program execution, has its own current directory. This is used as the starting point for all relative pathname searches in `open` calls and the like. The current directory apparently associated with a user is actually the current directory associated with the shell process that interprets his or her commands.

Initially, the current directory of a process is set to the directory from which the process was started. However, it is possible for a process to change directories via the system call called `chdir`.

4.5.2 Changing directories with `chdir`

Usage

```
char *path;
int retval;

retval = chdir(path);
```

The `chdir` system call causes `path` to become the new current working directory of the calling process. It is important to note that this change applies only to the process that makes the `chdir` call. In particular, a program that changes directory won't disturb the shell that started the program. So, when a program exits, the user will find the shell in the place where it started, regardless of the wanderings of the program.

`chdir` will fail, and consequently return a value of −1, if `path` does not define a valid directory or if execute permission does not exist at every component directory along the path for the calling process.

`chdir` can be usefully invoked when a program needs to access a number of files in a given directory. Changing directory and using file names relative to this new directory will be more efficient than using absolute file names. This is because the system has to scan each directory in a pathname in turn until the final filename is located, so reducing the number of components in a pathname saves time. For example, instead of using the following program fragment

```
fd1 = open("/usr/ben/abc", O_RDONLY);
fd2 = open("/usr/ben/xyz", O_RDWR);
```

a programmer could use

```
chdir("/usr/ben");
fd1 = open("abc", O_RDONLY);
fd2 = open("xyz", O_RDWR);
```

4.5.3 Creating directories

As previously mentioned, directories cannot be created using the `creat` system call. A special system call, `mknod`, is available for this task. `mknod` has a number of other functions; for example, it is used for creating the special files that represent peripheral devices. It can also be used for creating interprocess communications channels known as FIFOs.

Access to `mknod` is limited, and only superuser can use it to create directories. That said, a superuser program can call it as follows:

Usage

```
int retval, mode;
char *path;

retval = mknod(path, mode);
```

`path` points to a character string which contains the pathname of the directory to be created. For our current purposes, `mode` should consist of the octal value 040000 added to the desired directory access permissions. It is the value of 040000 that tells `mknod` that we wish to create a directory. Interestingly enough, the header file `stat.h` defines a constant `S_IFDIR` to represent this value. However, the *SVID* uses the numeric rather than symbolic constant in its `mknod` definition.

Example values for `mode` include:

- 040777 which would create a directory with read, write and search permissions for all users.
- 040755 which would create a directory with read, write and search permission for the owner, but only read and search permission for others, i.e. no-one but the owner can create files in this directory.

You will not be surprised to learn that a successful call to `mknod` will return 0, an unsuccessful call −1. Much more importantly, you should note that `mknod` will not place the two links '.' and '..' into the newly created directory and this must be done by the calling program to produce a valid UNIX directory. If these two did not exist, the entry would be unusable as a directory.

In the next example, the routine `make_dir` uses `mknod` to create a valid UNIX directory. It accepts two parameters, a path name and a set of access permissions, and creates a valid UNIX directory with the required name and access modes. It returns 0 on success and −1 on failure.

The example makes use of several subroutines from the C library. `strlen` has already been encountered. `strcpy` is new. It is used to copy a string into a `char` array. For example,

```
char buf[100];
  .
  .
  .
strcpy(buf, "pearls");
```

copies the string `"pearls"` into `buf`. `strcat` is another newcomer. It concatenates one string to the end of another, for example,

```
char string1[100] = "hello ";
  .
  .
  .
strcat(string1,"world\n");
```

would cause the array `string1` to contain the character string

```
hello world<newline>
```

The final new subroutine is `strrchr`; this will search a string for the last occurrence of a specified character and return a pointer to that character in the string. `strrchr` will return a null pointer if the character does not appear in the string at all. The following call

```
char *p;
  .
  .
  .
p = strrchr("hello world", 'l');
```

would set `p` to point to the character ‘l’ in the word ‘world’.

Let’s get back to `make_dir`.

```
#include <stdio.h>

#define DIRFLAG 040000
#define NAMESZ  100

extern char *strrchr();

make_dir(name, mode)
char *name;
int mode;
{
```

```
    char path1[NAMESZ+4], path2[NAMESZ+4], *p;

    /*check length of name*/
    if(strlen(name) >= NAMESZ)
    {
        fprintf(stderr,"dir name too long in make_dir\n");
        return(-1);
    }

    /*make "empty" directory*/
    if(mknod(name, DIRFLAG|mode) != 0)
    {
        fprintf(stderr, "cannot create %s\n", name);
        return(-1);
    }


    /*creat "." link*/
    strcpy(path1, name);
    strcat(path1, "/.");
    link(name, path1);

    /*now create ".." link*/
    strcat(path1, ".");
    strcpy(path2, name);

    if((p = strrchr(path2, '/')) == (char *)0)
        link(".", path1);
    else{
        *p = '\0';
        link(path2, path1);
    }

    return(0);
}
```

This technique seems overly awkward, and in any case only superuser can create directories this way. Lesser mortals are intended to create directories with the `mkdir` command, which adds the two required links automatically. For example,

```
$ mkdir dname
```

will create the directory `dname`.

Exercise 4.3 The C library subroutine `system` accepts a string as an argument and passes that string to the shell for execution exactly as if the string had been typed at a terminal. system will wait for the resultant process to terminate before returning. For example,

```
system("date > today");
```

would cause the date program to be executed, with output sent to a file called today. Use this subroutine to create a directory by executing the mkdir command. Generalize the method to give a subroutine which takes a directory name as argument, and attempts to create it. (Hint: use some of the string manipulation routines we have introduced to create the command string.)

Exercise 4.4 In the previous chapter, we introduced the stat and fstat system calls as a means of obtaining file information. The stat structure returned by stat and fstat contains a field called st_mode, which contains the file mode. This is made up of the file permissions bitwise ORed with a constant that determines whether the data structure represents an ordinary file, a directory, a special file or a FIFO communications channel. You won't be surprised to learn that the value that indicates a directory is octal 040000, or S_IFDIR in symbolic form. The best way to test whether a file is a directory is as follows:

```
/*buf comes from a call to stat*/
if((buf.st_mode & S_IFMT) == S_IFDIR)
        printf("It's a directory\n");
else
        printf("It's not\n");
```

S_IFMT is a special bit mask which is defined in stat.h and masks off the permission bits. (It is worth noting that this technique is general. It can be used with other types of file as we shall see in Section 4.7.2.) Modify the my_ls routine so that it calls stat for every file found, and prints an asterisk after every file name that refers to a directory.

4.5.4 Changing the root directory

As we saw in Section 4.3, the top of the UNIX file system is called the root directory and is represented by the '/' character. Whenever a path name is supplied to a system call, the root directory is the starting point for searches for all files or directories with names that begin with a '/'.

UNIX provides a system call for changing a process's idea of where the start of the file system hierarchy is. This system call is called chroot. You will almost certainly never need to use it.

Usage

```
int retval;
char *path;

retval = chroot(path);
```

`path` points to a pathname naming a directory. If `chroot` succeeds, `path` will become the starting point for those file searches that begin with a '/' (for the calling process only, the system as a whole is not affected). `chroot` returns −1 and the root directory remains unchanged if the call fails. This call is only available to superuser.

4.5.5 Finding the name of the current directory

UNIX System V defines a subroutine (not a system call) called `getcwd` which returns the name of the current working directory. Strangely enough, this routine is not available in earlier releases of the operating system, although many programmers have probably spent long hours searching for something like it. Its implementation isn't as straightforward as you might at first think, and it achieves its result by actually running the `pwd` program.

Usage

```
int size;
char *buf, *ret, *getcwd();

ret = getcwd(buf,size);
```

`getcwd` returns a pointer to the current directory pathname. For some strange reason, the `size` argument must be at least two greater than the length of the pathname to be returned. A largish number will do. If `buf` is a null pointer, `getcwd` will allocate `size` bytes of dynamic memory. Otherwise the directory name is copied into the array pointed to by `buf`. `getcwd` will fail if `size` is not sufficiently big, or if insufficient dynamic memory space is available for creating the buffer. In such circumstances, it returns a null value.

An example: `my_pwd`

This short program imitates the `pwd` command:

```
/*my_pwd - print working directory*/

#include <stdio.h>
#define VERYBIG 200


main()
{
        my_pwd();
}

extern char *getcwd();
```

```
my_pwd()
{
        char *dirname;

        if((dirname = getcwd((char *)0, VERYBIG)) == (char *)0)
            fprintf(stderr, "getcwd error, increase VERYBIG\n");
        else
            printf("%s\n", dirname);
}
```

In this example, space for storing the pathname is automatically allocated by the `getcwd` routine.

Exercise 4.5 Rewrite `my_pwd` so that it uses a buffer passed to it from the program.

4.5.6 Walking a directory tree

Sometimes it is necessary to perform an operation on a directory hierarchy, beginning at some starting directory, and working down through all files and sub-directories. To this end, UNIX System V provides a routine called `ftw` which performs a directory tree walk starting at any directory and calls a user-defined routine for each directory entry found. Like `getcwd`, this is a recent innovation and is not available in earlier releases of the operating system.

Usage

```
#include <ftw.h>
char *path;
int func();
int depth,ret;

ret = ftw(path, func, depth);
```

`path` defines the directory pathname at which the recursive tree walk should begin. `func` is a user-defined function that will be called for every file or directory found in the hierarchy that starts at `path`. As can be seen in the usage description, `func` is passed to the `ftw` routine as a function pointer. It needs, therefore, to be declared prior to the call to `ftw`.

The `depth` parameter is a rather strange beast that controls the number of different file descriptors used by `ftw`. The larger the value of `depth`, the less reopenings of directories have to be performed, increasing its speed. Clearly, its value must not be greater than the number of file descriptors available, and the safest value is one, especially in a general-purpose subroutine. In any case, only one file descriptor will be used at each level in the tree.

At each call, `func` will be called with three arguments: a null-terminated string holding the object name; a pointer to a `stat` structure containing data about the object, and an integer code. `func` should therefore be constructed as follows:

```
int func(name, statptr, type)
char *name;
struct stat *statptr;
int type;
{
        /*body of function*/
}
```

The integer argument (`type` above) contains one of several possible values (all defined in the header file `ftw.h`) which describe the object encountered. These values are:

`FTW_F`	The object is a file.
`FTW_D`	The object is a directory.
`FTW_DNR`	The object is a directory that could not be read.
`FTW_NS`	The object is one for which stat could not be executed successfully.

If the object was a directory that could not be read (`FTW_DNR`), then descendants of that directory will not be processed. If the `stat` function could not be executed successfully (`FTW_NS`), then the `stat` structure passed to the user-defined structure will not be valid.

The tree walk continues until the bottom of the tree is reached or an error is encountered in `ftw`. The walk can also be terminated if the user-defined function returns a non-zero value. At this point, `ftw` halts execution and returns the value returned to it by the user function. Errors within `ftw` cause a value of -1 to be returned and the error type is set in `errno`.

The next example uses `ftw` to descend a directory hierarchy, printing out the name of the files it encounters on the way along with their access permissions, and indicating which files are directories by appending an asterisk to their name.

First, let's look at the function `list` that will be passed as an argument to `ftw`.

```
#include <sys/types.h>
#include <sys/stat.h>
#include <ftw.h>

int list(name, status, type)
char *name;
struct stat *status;
int type;
{
```

```
        /*if the stat call failed, just return*/
        if(type == FTW_NS)
                return(0);

        /*
         *otherwise print object name,
         *permissions and "*" postfix
         *if object is a directory
         */
        if(type == FTW_F)
                printf("%-30s\t0%3o\n", name,
                 status->st_mode&0777);
        else
                printf("%-30s*\t0%3o\n", name,
                 status->st_mode&0777);

        return(0);
}
```

The next task is to write a main program that accepts a pathname as an argument and uses it as the starting point for the tree walk. If no argument is supplied, the walk will begin at the current directory.

```
main(argc,argv)
int argc;
char **argv;
{
   int list();

   if(argc <= 1)
      ftw(".", list, 1);
   else
      ftw(argv[1], list, 1);
   exit(0);
}
```

The output from our `list` program might look something like:

```
$ list
 .                                  *  0755
 ./list                             *  0755
 ./file1                               0644
 ./subdir                           *  0777
 ./subdir/another                      0644
 ./subdir/subdir2                   *  0755
 ./subdir/yetanother                   0644
```

for a simple directory hierarchy. Notice the order in which directories are processed.

4.6 UNIX file systems

We have seen that files may be organized into groups called directories and that directories form part of an overall hierarchical tree structure. Directories may themselves be grouped together into an object called a **file system**. File systems are generally only of concern to the UNIX System Administrator. They allow the directory structure to be accommodated across several distinct, physical disks or disk partitions, while retaining the uniform user view of the structure.

Each file system starts at a directory node within the hierarchy tree. This facility allows system administrators to divide up a UNIX file hierarchy and allocate parts of it to specific areas of a disk or indeed to split a complete file structure across several physical disk devices. The physical division into separate file systems is, for the most part, invisible to users.

File systems are also called **demountable volumes** because it is possible to dynamically introduce complete subsections of the hierarchy anywhere into the tree structure. More to the point, it is also possible to dynamically disconnect, or unmount, a complete file system from the hierarchy and, therefore, make it temporarily inaccessible to users. At any given moment in time several file systems may be on-line, but not all of them will necessarily be visible as part of the tree-structured hierarchy.

The information contained in a file system resides on a disk partition that is identified by an entity called a UNIX **special file**, the idea of which is discussed in detail below. For the time being, just note that file systems are in some way uniquely identified by UNIX file names.

The actual low-level layout of the data held in a file system is completely different from the high-level hierarchical view of directories presented to the user. In addition, this layout is not part of the *SVID* and a variety of alternative forms exist. We will take the same approach we did with directories, and consider the most common and traditional form.

This type of file system is divided into a number of logical blocks. Under UNIX System V these blocks are, typically, 1024 bytes in size, though System V does support 512-byte file systems for compatibility with older versions of UNIX. Every such file system contains four distinct sections: a **bootstrap** area, a file system **super block**, a number of blocks reserved for file system inode structures and the area reserved for the data blocks that make up the files on that particular file system. Pictorially, this layout is as shown in Figure 4.6. The first of these blocks (logical block 0 in the file system but physically wherever the disk partition begins) is reserved for use as the bootstrap block. That is, it may contain a hardware-specific boot program that is used to load UNIX at system startup time.

Logical block 1 on the file system is called the file system super block. It contains all the vital information about the file system, for example the total file system size (r blocks in the diagram), the number of blocks reserved for inodes ($n - 2$), and the date and time that the file system was last updated.

The super block also contains two lists. The first holds part of a chain of free data block numbers and the second, part of a chain of free inode numbers for fast access when allocating new disk blocks for data or creating a new directory slot. The super block for a mounted file system is kept in memory to give fast access into the free block and free inode lists. The in-memory lists are replenished from disk when they become exhausted.

Inode structures are 64-bytes in size and consequently 16 fit into each of the $n - 2$ blocks allocated for inodes, assuming a 1024-byte block size. Inodes are numbered sequentially from 1 onwards, and so a simple

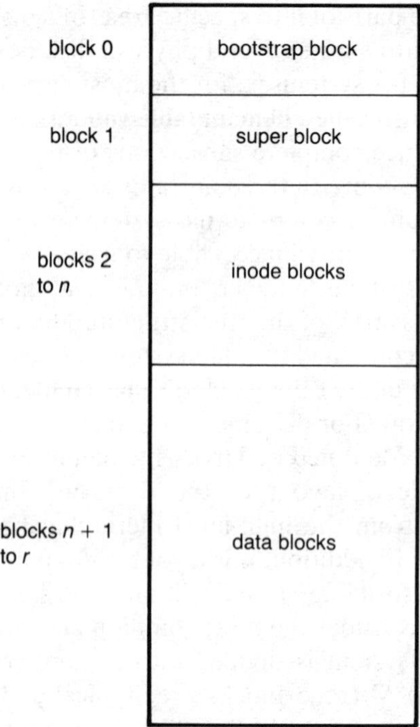

Figure 4.6 File system layout.

algorithm is used to determine the location of an inode structure given the inode number that is extracted from a directory slot.

File systems are created using the `mkfs` program and it is when this program is executed that the sizes of the inode areas and data areas for the file system must be specified. These sizes cannot be changed dynamically and it is possible to run out of space on a file system in two ways. Firstly, all the data blocks may be used up (even though there may still be available inode numbers). Secondly, it is possible to use up all the inode numbers (by creating lots of small files) and consequently not be able to create any new files on the file system but still have data blocks free. The ratio between the inode area and data blocks can be crucial and should be varied depending on the characteristics of the files stored on the file system.

You should be able to see from this discussion that inode numbers are only unique within a file system and that it is impossible, therefore, to link files across file systems. This is a great pity, and is the only flaw in the otherwise apparently totally homogeneous tree hierarchy that is presented to users.

Berkeley UNIX 4.2bsd provides a mechanism called symbolic links which does permit the creation of links across file systems. These links are implemented by storing the name of the file which is being linked to rather than its inode number. It is possible, therefore, for a runtime error to be generated when accessing the link if the original file is not available (because its file system is not mounted).

4.6.1 System calls for manipulating file systems

UNIX provides two fundamental system calls for manipulating file systems: `mount` which makes a file system available for use, and `umount` which unmounts a file system, removing it from the public gaze. Neither of these calls is particularly useful for programmers; their actions are usually performed via the `mount` and `umount` commands. For completeness, however, we will briefly discuss them here.

4.6.2 Mounting file systems: the `mount` call

Usage

```
char *partition, *dir;
int rwflag;

mount(partition, dir, rwflag);
```

`mount` will mount the file system volume that resides on the disk partition identified by the filename `partition` onto the directory called `dir`. Conventionally, `partition` will have a name of the form `/dev/name`, where `name` is more or less arbitrary. The `/dev` part is the name of the directory where **special files** are stored. As we shall see very shortly, special files are used to describe peripheral devices. In this case, the special file `partition` identifies an area on the physical disk.

After mounting, the directory hierarchy held on `partition` is reached via the directory `dir`. For example, if the file system contained a file called `bin/more`, and was mounted onto directory `/usr`, the file could be accessed with the pathname `/usr/bin/more`.

If the `rwflag` parameter has a low-order bit set to 1 (setting it equal to 1 will do) the file system will be mounted read-only, and it will be impossible to write to any of the files or directories that form part of the newly mounted file system. This could be useful for mounting backup copies of a file system (on a removable disk pack say) in order to extract deleted files.

`mount` may be called by the superuser only and will return −1 on failure, 0 on success.

4.6.3 Unmounting file systems: the `umount` call

Usage

```
char *partition;

umount(partition);
```

`umount` will cause the previously mounted file system that resides on disk partition `partition` to be removed from the directory hierarchy. The files and directories on this file system will now no longer be accessible.

`umount` may only be invoked by the superuser. It returns −1 on failure and 0 on success. It will fail when any user is currently accessing files on the file system, or has a directory on the file system as his or her current directory.

Cacheing and the `sync` call

For efficiency reasons, copies of the super blocks of mounted file systems are kept in a UNIX machine's main memory. Updates to these super blocks can then occur quickly without the need to access the disk directly. Similarly, all transfers from memory to disk, i.e. writes, are cached in the operating system's data space instead of being written out to disk immediately. Reads as well are buffered within the cache. At any given moment, therefore, the actual data on disk may be out of date with respect to the cache stored in main memory. UNIX provides a system call called `sync` to flush out all main memory buffers to disk, making sure things are up to date.

Usage

```
sync();
```

`sync` is typically called by programs that need to examine a file system at a low level via the file system's special file name, or programs that want to preserve data integrity across a machine crash.

In order to ensure that file systems are not out of date for too long, UNIX employs a utility program called `update` that runs continually while the system is in multi-user mode, and repeatedly calls `sync`, pausing for a specified period of time between each call. Typically, this period is 30 seconds, though on UNIX System V the time interval is a configurable parameter under the control of the system administrator.

4.6.4 File systems and the future

The area of file systems is one undergoing considerable change. For example, UNIX System V.3 will introduce a **file system switch** allowing the kernel to support file systems with different layouts concurrently, something not possible in previous releases of UNIX. The user's view of things is not affected.

More exciting perhaps is the emergence of distributed file systems, where users on several machines have simultaneous access to the same files. One utility to do this is called RFS (for Remote File Sharing) which again is part of System V.3. It allows directory hierarchies on remote machines to be 'mounted' onto a directory on the local system, and so make remote files accessible to local users. The mechanism is transparent which means that programs do not need changing to use remote files.

4.7 UNIX special files

The peripheral devices attached to UNIX systems (disks, terminals, printers, tape units and so on) are represented by file names in the file system. These files are called special files. The disk partitions corresponding to file systems are among the objects represented by special files.

Unlike ordinary disk files, reads and writes to these special files cause data to be transferred directly between the system and the appropriate peripheral device.

Typically, these special files are stored in a directory called `/dev`. So, for example

```
/dev/tty00
/dev/tty01
/dev/tty02
```

could be the names given to three of a system's terminal ports, and

```
/dev/lp
/dev/rmt0
```

could refer to a line printer and magnetic tape unit respectively.

Names for disk partitions are much more variable. Possibilities include:

```
/dev/dk0
/dev/dk1
```

Special files may be used at command level or within programs just like ordinary files. For example,

```
$ cat fred > /dev/lp
$ cat fred > /dev/rmt0
```

would cause the file called `fred` to be written to the line printer and magnetic tape unit, respectively (access permissions permitting). It is obviously madness to try to manipulate disk partitions containing file systems directly in this way. Much valuable information could be accidentally destroyed with a careless command. In addition, if the permissions on such a special file are too permissive, then it is possible for sophisticated users to bypass the permissions of files held on the file system. System administrators should always ensure that this is impossible, by setting the access permissions on the special file names representing disk partitions appropriately.

From within a program, `open`, `close`, `read` and `write` can all be used on special files. For example,

```
#include <fcntl.h>

main()
{
        int i,fd;

        fd = open("/dev/tty00", O_WRONLY);

        for(i = 0; i < 100; i++)
                write(fd,"x", 1);

        close(fd);
}
```

would cause 100 `x`s to be written to terminal port `tty00`. Terminal handling is obviously an important topic and we will go into this in very much greater detail in Chapter 8.

4.7.1 Block and character special files

UNIX special files are divided into two categories: **block devices** and **character devices**.

1. *Block special files* include devices such as disk or magnetic tape units. The transfer of data between these devices and the kernel (normally) occurs in standard-sized blocks, a typical block size being 1024 bytes. All block devices will support random access. Inside the kernel, access to these devices is controlled by a highly structured set of kernel data structures and routines. This common interface to block devices means that, typically, block device drivers are very similar, varying only in their low-level control over the device in question.
2. *Character special files* include devices such as terminal lines, modem lines and printer devices that do not share this structured transfer

mechanism. Random access may, or may not, be supported. Data transfer is not done in fixed size blocks, but in terms of byte streams of arbitrary length. Some block devices have associated character devices for fast access.

It is important to note that file systems can only exist on block devices.

UNIX uses two operating system configuration tables called the **block device** and **character device tables** to associate a peripheral device with the device-specific code to drive the particular peripheral. These tables and the device-specific code are held within the kernel itself. Both tables are indexed using an integer called the **major device number** which is stored in the special file's inode. The sequence for transmitting data to or from a peripheral device is as follows:

1. `read` or `write` system calls access the special file's inode in the normal way.
2. The systems checks a flag within the inode structure to see whether the device is a block or a character device. The major number is also extracted.
3. The major number is used to index into the appropriate device configuration table and the device specific driver routine is called to perform the data transfer.

In this way accesses to peripheral devices can be entirely consistent with accesses to normal disk files.

Apart from the major device number, a second integer value called the **minor device number** is also stored in the inode and is passed to the device driver routines in order to identify exactly which port is being accessed on those devices which support more than one peripheral port. For example, on an 8-line terminal board each terminal line would share the same major number (and consequently the same set of device driver routines), but would each have their own unique minor number in the range 0 to 7 to identify the particular line being accessed.

4.7.2 The `stat` structure revisited

In the `stat` structure we first discussed in Chapter 3 there is provision for storing special file information in two fields.

`st_mode` In the case of a special file, this contains the file's permissions added to a value of octal 060000 for block devices or 020000 for character devices. There are symbolic constants defined in `stat.h` which can be used instead of these actual numbers, namely: `S_IFBLK` and `S_IFCHR`.

`st_rdev` This contains the major and minor device numbers.

This information can be displayed by using the ls command with the -l option. For example:

```
$ ls -l /dev/tty3
  crw--w--w- 1 ben     other    8,  3 Sep 13 10:19 /dev/tty3
```

Notice the letter 'c' in the first column of the output which specifies that /dev/tty3 is a character special file. The integer values 8 and 3 represent the major and minor device numbers, respectively.

Within a program, st_mode can be tested using the technique introduced in Exercise 4.4:

```
if((buf.st_mode & S_IFMT) == S_IFCHR)
        printf("It's a character device\n");
else
        printf("It's not\n");
```

Remember that S_IFMT is a special bit mask which is defined in stat.h.

For devices that hold file systems, one important use of the st_rdev member of a stat structure is as an argument to the ustat routine. ustat obtains basic file system information such as the total number of free disk blocks and the number of free inodes. It is invoked as follows:

Usage

```
#include <sys/types.h>
#include <ustat.h>

int dev, ret;
struct ustat buf;

ret = ustat(dev, &buf);
```

Here dev contains the major and minor device numbers taken from the st_rdev part of a stat structure. The buf parameter is an occurrence of the ustat structure type which is defined in the ustat.h header file. The ustat structure has the following definition:

```
struct ustat {
        daddr_t f_tfree;
        ino_t   f_tinode;
        char    f_fname[6];
        char    f_fpack[6];
}
```

f_tfree will contain the total number of free disk blocks on the file system specified by dev. f_tinode will contain the number of free inodes on this file system. f_fname and f_fpack will contain a system-administrator-defined file system name and pack name, respectively. They may not contain meaningful information on all systems. In this case, f_fname and f_fpack will contain zero-length strings. Note that the two types `daddr_t` and `ino_t` are implementation-dependent; again, the basic C types they reduce to are defined in `sys/types.h`.

Our final example in this chapter parallels the standard `df` command. It uses `ustat` to print the number of free blocks and free inodes on a file system. It makes some (reasonable) assumptions about the types of the `f_tfree` and `f_inode` members.

```
/*us: print file system information.
 *the file system name is passed in as an argument
 *in the form /dev/xxxx
 */
#include <sys/types.h>
#include <sys/stat.h>
#include <ustat.h>
#include <stdio.h>

main(argc, argv)
int argc;
char **argv;
{
    struct stat sbuf;
    struct ustat buf;

    if(argc != 2){
       fprintf(stderr, "usage: us filesys-name\n");
       exit(1);
    }

    if(stat(argv[1], &sbuf) < 0){
       fprintf(stderr, "us: stat error\n");
       exit(2);
    }else{
       if(ustat(sbuf.st_rdev, &buf) < 0)
       {
          fprintf(stderr,"ustat error\n");
          exit(2);
       }
       printf("%s:\tfree blocks %d\tfree inodes %d\n",
              argv[1], buf.f_tfree, buf.f_tinode);
    }
    exit(0);
}
```

Chapter 5 The Process

5.1 Review of the notion of a process

As we saw in Chapter 1, a process in UNIX terms is simply an instance of an executing program, corresponding to the notion of a task in other environments. Each process incorporates program code, the data values within program variables, and more exotic items such as the values held in hardware registers, the program stack and so on.

The shell creates a new process each time it starts up a program in response to a command. For example, the command line

```
$ cat file1 file2
```

results in the shell creating a process especially to run the `cat` command. The slightly more complex command line

```
$ ls | wc -l
```

results in *two* processes being created to run the commands `ls` and `wc` concurrently. (In addition the output of the directory listing `ls` is piped into the word count program `wc`.)

Because a process corresponds to an execution of a program, processes should not be confused with the programs they run; indeed several processes can concurrently run the same program, something that often happens with commonly used utilities. For example, several users may be running the same editor program simultaneously, each invocation of the one program counting as a separate process.

Any UNIX process may in turn start other processes. This gives the UNIX process environment a hierarchical structure paralleling the directory tree of the file system. At the top of the process tree is a single controlling process, an execution of an extremely important program called `init`, which is ultimately the ancestor of all user processes.

For the programmer, UNIX provides a handful of system calls for process creation and manipulation. Excluding the various facilities for interprocess communication, the most important of these are:

`fork` Used to create a new process by duplicating the calling process. `fork` is the basic process creation primitive.

`exec` A family of system calls, each of which performs the same function: the transformation of a process by overlaying its memory space with a new program. The differences between `exec` calls lie mainly in the way their argument lists are constructed.

`wait` This call provides rudimentary process synchronization. It allows one process to wait until another related process finishes.

`exit` Used to terminate a process.

In the rest of this chapter we will discuss the UNIX process in general and these four important calls in particular.

5.2 Creating processes

5.2.1 The `fork` system call

The fundamental process creation primitive is the `fork` system call. It is the mechanism which transforms UNIX into a multitasking system.

Usage

```
int pid;

pid = fork();
```

A successful call to `fork` causes the kernel to create a new process which is a (more or less) exact duplicate of the calling process. In other words the new process runs a copy of the same program as its creator, the variables within this having the same values as those within the calling process, with a single important exception which we shall discuss shortly.

The newly created process is described as the **child process**, the one that called `fork` in the first place is called, not unnaturally, its **parent**.

After the call the parent process and its newly created offspring execute concurrently, both processes resuming execution at the statement immediately after the call to `fork`.

For those used to a purely sequential programming environment, the idea of `fork` can be a little difficult at first. Figure 5.1 demonstrates the notion more clearly. The diagram centres around three lines of code, consisting of a call to `printf`, followed by a call to `fork` and then another call to `printf`.

There are two sections to the diagram: *BEFORE* and *AFTER*. The *BEFORE* section shows things prior to the invocation of `fork`. There is a single process labelled *A* (we are using the label *A* purely for convenience; it means nothing to the system). The arrow labelled *PC* (for program counter) shows the statement currently being executed. Since it points to the first `printf`, the result of this state is that the rather trivial message *One* is displayed on standard output.

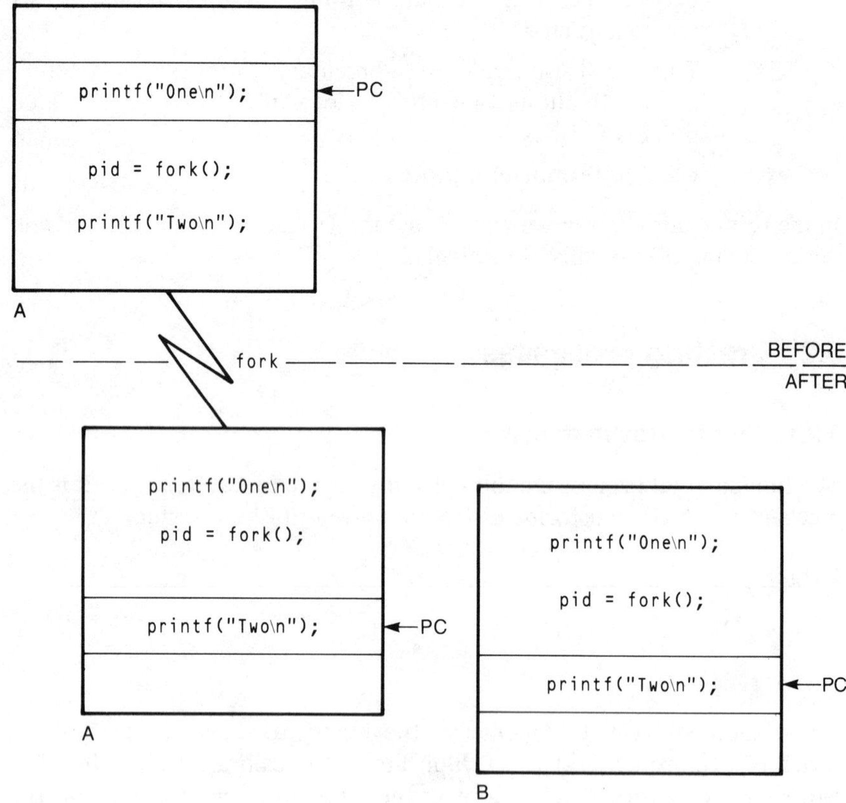

Figure 5.1 The `fork` call.

The *AFTER* section shows the situation immediately following the call to `fork`. There are now *two* processes *A* and *B* running together. Process *A* is the same as in the *BEFORE* part of the diagram. *B* is the new process spawned by the call to `fork`. It is an exact copy of *A* and is executing the same program as *A*, hence the duplication of the three lines of source code in the diagram. Using the terminology we introduced above, *A* is the parent process while *B* is its child.

The two *PC* arrows in this part of the diagram show that the next statement executed by both parent and child after the `fork` invocation is a call to `printf`. In other words, both *A* and *B* pick up at the same point in the program code, even though *B* is new to the system. The result of this state is therefore that the message *Two* is displayed twice.

Process-ids

As you can see from the usage description at the beginning of this section, `fork` is called without arguments and returns an integer `pid`:

```
pid = fork();
```

It is the value of `pid` that distinguishes child and parent. In the parent, `pid` is set to a non-zero, positive integer. In the child it is set to zero. Because the return value in parent and child differs, the programmer is able to specify different actions for the two processes.

The number returned to the parent in `pid` is called the **process-id** of the child process. It is this number that identifies the new process to the system, rather like a user-id identifies a user. Since all processes are born through a call to `fork`, every UNIX process has its own process-id, which at any one time is unique to that process. A process-id can therefore best be thought of as the identifying signature of its process.

The following short program demonstrates the action of `fork`, and the use of the process-id, perhaps a little more clearly:

```
/*spawn -- demonstrate fork*/

main()
{
      int pid; /*hold process-id in parent*/


      printf("Just one process so far\n");
      printf("Calling fork ...\n");

      pid = fork(); /*create new process*/

      if(pid == 0)
          printf("I'm the child\n");
      else if (pid > 0)
          printf("I'm the parent, child has pid %d\n",pid);
      else
          printf("Fork returned error code, no child\n");
}
```

There are three branches to the `if` statement after the `fork`. The first specifies the action for the child process, corresponding to a zero value for the variable `pid`. The second gives the action for the parent process, corresponding to a positive value for `pid`. The third branch deals, implicitly, with a negative value (in fact −1) for `pid`, which can arise when `fork` has failed to create a child. This can indicate that the calling process has tried to breach one of two limits; the first is a system-wide limit on the number of processes; the second restricts the number of processes an individual user may run simultaneously. In both circumstances, the error variable `errno` contains the error code `EAGAIN`. Also notice that, since the two processes generated by the example program will run concurrently and without synchronization, there is no guarantee that the output from parent and child will not become confusingly intermingled.

Before we move on, it is worth discussing why `fork` is a useful call, since it may seem a little pointless in isolation. The essential point is that `fork` becomes valuable when combined with other UNIX facilities. For example, it is possible to have a child and parent process perform different but related tasks, cooperating by using one of the UNIX interprocess communication mechanisms such as signals or pipes (described in the next chapter). Another facility often used in combination with `fork` is the `exec` system call which we shall discuss in the next section.

Exercise 5.1 A program can call `fork` several times. Similarly, each child process can use `fork` to spawn children of its own. To prove this write a program which creates two subprocesses. Each of these should then create one subprocess of its own. After each `fork`, each parent process should use `printf` to display the process-ids of its offspring.

5.3 Running new programs with `exec`

5.3.1 The `exec` family

If `fork` was the only process creation primitive available to the programmer, UNIX would be a little boring since only copies of the same program could be created. Thankfully, a member of the `exec` family of system calls can be used to initiate the execution of a new program. The following usage description shows the simplest members of the family.

Usage

```
char *path, *file;
char *arg0, *arg1, ..., *argn;
char *argv[];
int ret;
 .
 .
 .
ret = execl(path, arg0, arg1, ..., argn, (char *)0);

ret = execv(path, argv);

ret = execlp(file, arg0, arg1, ..., argn, (char *)0);

ret = execvp(file, argv);
```

All varieties of exec perform the same function: they transform the calling process by loading a new program into its memory space. If the exec is successful the calling program is completely overlaid by the new program, which is then started from its beginning. The result can be regarded as a new process, but one that is given the same process-id as the calling process.

It is important to stress that exec does *not* create a new subprocess to run concurrently with the calling process. Instead the old program is obliterated by the new. So, unlike fork there is no return from a successful call to exec.

To simplify matters, we will spotlight just one of the exec calls, namely execl.

All parameters for execl are character pointers. The first, path in the usage description, gives the name of the file containing the program to be executed; with execl this must be a valid pathname, absolute or relative. The file itself must also contain a true program; execl (and for that matter execv) cannot be used to run a file of shell commands. (The system tells whether a file contains a program by looking at its first two bytes or so. If these contain a special value, called a **magic number**, then the system treats the file as a program.) The second parameter arg0 is, by convention, the name of the program or command stripped of any preceding pathname element. This and the remaining variable number of arguments (arg1 to argn) are available to the invoked program, corresponding to command line arguments within the shell. Indeed the shell itself invokes commands by using one of the exec calls. Because the argument list is of arbitrary length, it must be terminated by a null pointer to mark the end of the list.

As always a short example is worth a thousand words, and the following program uses execl to run the directory listing program ls:

```
/*runls -- use "execl" to run ls*/

main()
{
        printf("executing ls\n");

        execl("/bin/ls", "ls", "-l", (char *)0);

        /*If execl returns, the call has failed, so...*/
        perror("execl failed to run ls");
        exit(1);

}
```

The action of this example program is represented in Figure 5.2. The *BEFORE* section shows the process immediately before the call to execl. The *AFTER* section shows the transformed process, which now runs the ls program. The program counter *PC* points at the first line of `ls`, indicating that `execl` causes the new program to start from its beginning.

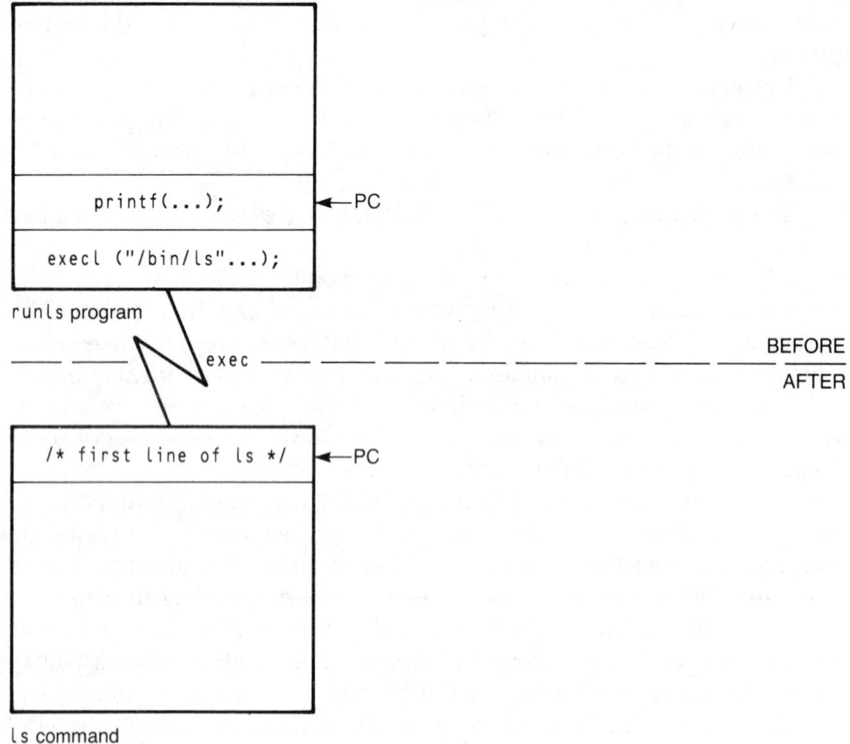

Figure 5.2 The `exec` call.

Notice that in the example, the call to `execl` is followed by an unconditional call to the library routine `perror`. This reflects the way a successful call to `execl` (and for that matter all its relations) obliterates the calling program. If the calling program does survive and `execl` returns, then an error must have occurred. As a corollary of this, when `execl` and its relatives do return, they will always return −1.

`execv`, `execlp` and `execvp`

The other forms of `exec` give the programmer flexibility in the construction of parameter lists. `execv` takes just two arguments: the first (`path` in the usage description above) points to a string containing the pathname of the program to be executed. The second (`argv`) is an array of character pointers, declared as

```
char *argv[];
```

The first member of this array points, again purely by convention, to the name of the program to be executed (excluding any pathname prefix). The remaining members point to any additional arguments for the program. Since this list is of indeterminate length, it must always be terminated by a null pointer.

The next example uses `execv` to run the same `ls` command as the previous example:

```
/*runls2 -- use execv to run ls*/

main()
{
        char *av[3];

        av[0] = "ls";
        av[1] = "-l";
        av[2] = (char *)0;

        execv("/bin/ls", av);

        /*again - getting this far implies error*/
        perror("execv failed");
        exit(1);
}
```

`execlp` and `execvp` are almost identical to `execl` and `execv`. The main difference is that the first argument for both `execlp` and `execvp` points to a simple file name, not a pathname. The path prefix for this filename is found by a search of the directories denoted by the shell environment variable `PATH`. `PATH` of course can be simply set at shell level with a sequence of commands such as:

```
$ PATH=/bin:/usr/bin:/usr/keith/mybin
$ export PATH
```

This means that both the shell and `execvp` will hunt down commands first in `/bin`, then `/usr/bin` and finally `/usr/keith/mybin`. An additional property of `execlp` and `execvp` is that they can be used to run shell scripts, not just ordinary programs.

Exercise 5.2 In what circumstances would you use `execv` instead of `execl`?

Exercise 5.3 `execvp` and `execlp` do not appear in some earlier versions of UNIX. Write subroutine equivalents using `execl` and `execv`. The parameters for these routines should consist of a list of directories and a set of command line arguments.

5.3.2 Accessing arguments passed with `exec`

Any program can gain access to the arguments in the `exec` call that invoked it through parameters passed to the `main` function of the program. These parameters can be used by defining the program's `main` function as follows:

```
main(argc, argv)
int argc;
char **argv;
{
        /*body of program*/
}
```

This should look familiar to many of you, since the same technique is used for accessing arguments from the command line that started a program, another indication that the shell itself uses `exec` to start processes. (We have, not unreasonably, assumed a knowledge of command line parameters in a few of the preceding examples and exercises. This section should therefore clarify things for those who had any problems with these.)

In the `main` function declaration above, `argc` is an integer count of the number of arguments. `argv` points to the array of arguments themselves. So, if a program is executed through a call to `execvp` as follows,

```
char *argin[4];

argin[0] = "command";
argin[1] = "with";
argin[2] = "arguments";
argin[3] = (char *)0;

execvp("prog", argin);
```

then within `prog` we would find the following conditions holding true:

```
argc == 3

argv[0] == "command"

argv[1] == "with"

argv[2] == "arguments"

argv[3] == (char *)0
```

As a simple demonstration of this technique, consider the next program which prints its arguments, excluding its first, on standard output:

```
/*myecho -- echo command line arguments*/

main(argc,argv)
int argc;
char **argv;
{

      while(--argc >0)
          printf("%s ",*++argv);

      printf("\n");
}
```

If this program is invoked with the following program fragment:

```
char *argin[4];

argin[0] = "myecho";
argin[1] = "hello";
argin[2] = "world";
argin[3] = (char *)0;

execvp(argin[0],argin);
```

then `argc` in `myecho` would be set to 3, and the following output would result:

```
hello world
```

which is the same result as would be obtained by the shell command

```
$ myecho hello world
```

Exercise 5.4 Write `waitcmd` , a program which, when a file changes, executes an arbitrary command. It should pick up both the name of the file to watch and the command to execute from its command line arguments. The calls `stat` and `fstat` can be used to monitor the file. The program should not unnecessarily waste system resources; therefore use the standard `sleep` subroutine (introduced in Exercise 2.15) to make `waitcmd` pause for a decent interval after it has examined the file. How should it cope if the file doesn't initially exist?

5.4 Using `exec` and `fork` together

`fork` and `exec` combined offer the programmer a powerful tool. By forking, then using `exec` within the child, a program can run another program within a subprocess and without obliterating itself. The following example shows how. In it we also introduce a simple error routine called `fatal` and, rather prematurely, the system call `wait`.

```
/*runls3 -- run ls in a subprocess*/

main()
{
        int pid;

        pid = fork();

        /*if parent, use wait to suspend execution
         *until child finishes
         */
        if(pid > 0){
            wait((int *)0);
            printf("ls completed\n");
            exit(0);
        }

        /*if child then exec ls*/
        if(pid == 0){
            execl("/bin/ls", "ls", "-l", (char *)0);
            fatal("execl failed");
        }

        /*getting here means pid is negative,
         *so error has occurred
         */
        fatal("fork failed");

}
```

`fatal` simply uses `perror` to display a message, then exits. It is implemented as follows:

```
fatal(s) /*print error message and die*/
char *s;
{
        perror(s);
        exit(1);
}
```

In the example `wait` is invoked immediately after it has created a child through a call to `fork`. The system will respond to this by putting the parent to sleep until the child terminates. `wait` therefore allows the programmer to synchronize process execution in a fairly rudimentary manner. We will discuss it in more detail below.

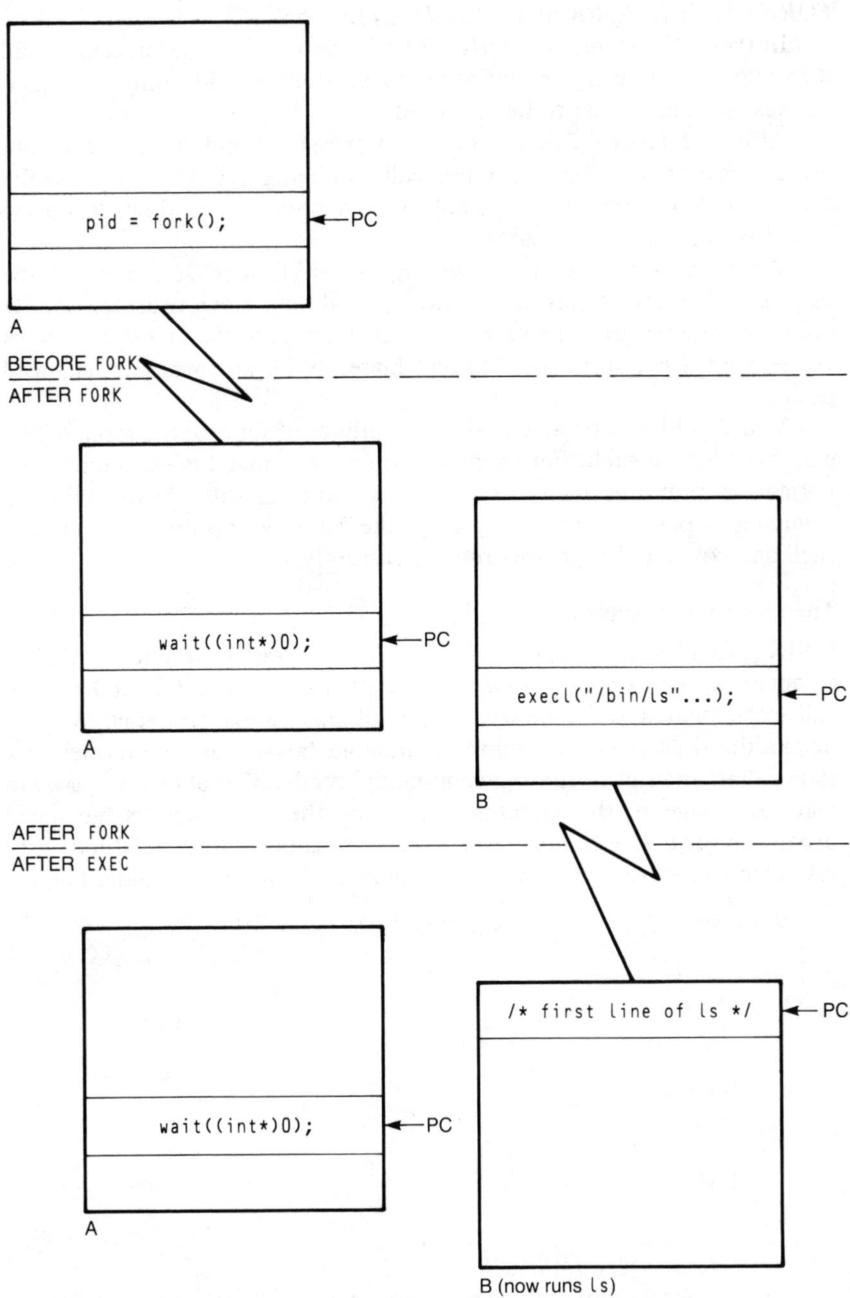

Figure 5.3 The fork and exec calls combined.

Again we will use a diagram for clarity in explaining the program's action, in this case Figure 5.3. This is divided into three parts: *BEFORE FORK*, *AFTER FORK* and *AFTER EXEC*.

In the initial state, *BEFORE FORK*, there is a single process *A* and the program counter *PC* points at the `fork` statement, indicating that this is the next statement due to be executed.

After the `fork` call, there are two processes *A* and *B*. *A*, the parent process, is executing the `wait` system call. All being well, this will cause the execution of *A* to be suspended until *B* terminates. Meanwhile, *B* is using `execl` to load the `ls` command.

What happens next is shown in the *AFTER EXEC* part of the diagram. Process *B* has been transformed and now executes the `ls` program. The program counter for *B* has been set to the first statement of `ls`. Because *A* is waiting for *B* to terminate, its *PC* arrow has not changed position.

You should now be able to see the outlines of some of the mechanisms employed by the shell. For example, when a command is executed in the normal fashion the shell uses `fork`, `exec` and `wait` as above. When a command is placed in the background the call to `wait` is omitted and both shell and command processes run concurrently.

The `docommand` example

UNIX provides a library routine called `system` which allows a shell command to be executed from within a program. Using `fork` and `exec` we will implement a rudimentary version of this called `docommand`. We will invoke the shell (identified by the pathname `/bin/sh`) as an intermediary, rather than attempt to run the command directly. This allows `docommand` to take advantage of the features offered by the shell such as file name expansion. The `-c` argument used in the invocation of the shell tells it to take commands from the next string argument, rather than standard input.

```
/*docommand -- run shell command, first version*/

docommand(command)
char *command;
{

    int pid;


    if((pid = fork()) < 0)
        return(-1);

    if(pid == 0){ /*child*/
        execl("/bin/sh", "sh", "-c", command, (char *)0);
        exit(127);
    }
```

```
    /*code for parent
     *wait until process pid exits
     */

     wait((int *)0);
}
```

This, it must be said, is only a first approximation to the proper library routine `system`. For example, if the end user of the program hit the interrupt key (usually `DEL`) while the shell command was running, then both the command and the calling program would be stopped. There are ways to circumvent this, but we will delay discussing these until the next chapter.

5.5 Inherited data and file descriptors

5.5.1 `fork`, files and data

A child process created with `fork` is an almost perfect copy of its parent. In particular all variables within the child will retain the values they held in the parent (the one exception is the return value from `fork` itself). Since the data available to the child is a *copy* of that available to the parent, and occupies a different absolute place in memory, it is important to realize that subsequent changes in one process will not affect the variables in the other.

Similarly, all the files open in the parent are also open in the child; the child maintaining its own copy of the file descriptor associated with each file. However, files kept open across a call to `fork` remains intimately connected in child and parent. This is because the read-write pointer for each file is shared between child and parent. This is possible because the read-write pointer is maintained by the system; it is not embedded explicitly within the program itself. Consequently, when a child process moves forward in a file, the parent process will also find itself at the new position. The following short program demonstrates this. In it we will use the routine `fatal` introduced above, and a new routine called `printpos`. In addition, we are assuming the existence of a file called `data` which is at least 20 characters in length.

```
/*proc_file  - show how files are handled across*/
/*forks assumes "data" is at least 20 chars long*/

#include <fcntl.h>


main()
{
    int fd;          /*file descriptor*/
```

```
        int pid;          /*process-id*/
        char buf[10];     /*buffer to hold file data*/

        if( (fd = open("data", O_RDONLY)) < 0)
             fatal("open failed");

        read(fd, buf, 10);   /*advance file pointer*/

        printpos("Before fork", fd);

        /*now create two processes*/
        if( (pid = fork()) < 0)

             fatal("fork failed");

        else if (pid == 0){ /*child*/

             printpos("Child before read", fd);
             read(fd, buf, 10);
             printpos("Child after read", fd);

        }else{ /*parent*/

              /*wait until child finished*/
              wait( (int *)0 );
              printpos("Parent after wait", fd);
        }
}
```

`printpos` simply displays the current position within a file together with a short message. It can be implemented as follows:

```
printpos(string, filedes) /*print pos'n  in file*/
char *string;
int filedes;
{
        long pos, lseek();

        if( (pos = lseek(filedes, 0L, 1)) < 0L)
            fatal("lseek failed");
        printf("%s:%ld\n", string, pos);
}
```

When we ran this example we obtained the following results, fairly conclusive proof that the read-write pointer is shared by both processes:

```
Before fork:10
Child before read:10
Child after read:20
Parent after wait:20
```

Exercise 5.5 Write a program that demonstrates that program variables in a parent and child process have the same initial values but are independent of each other.

Exercise 5.6 Discover what happens within a parent process when a child closes a file descriptor inherited across a fork. In other words, does the file remain open in the parent, or is it also closed there?

5.5.2 `exec` and open files

Normally open file descriptors are also passed across calls to `exec`. That is, files open in the original program are kept open when an entirely new program is started through `exec`. The read-write pointers for such files are unchanged by the `exec` call. (It obviously makes no sense to talk about the values of variables being preserved across an `exec` call, since the original and newly loaded programs will in general be entirely different.)

However, the all-purpose, all-weather routine `fcntl` can be used to set the **close-on-exec** flag associated with a file. If this is on (the default is off) then the file is closed when any member of the `exec` family is invoked. The following code fragment shows how the close-on-exec flag is enabled:

```
#include <fcntl.h>
  .
  .
  .
int fd;

fd = open("file", O_RDONLY);
  .
  .
  .
/*set close-on-exec flag on*/
fcntl(fd, F_SETFD, 1);
```

The close-on-exec flag can be turned off with

```
fcntl(fd, F_SETFD, 0);
```

Its value can be obtained as follows:

```
res = fcntl(fd, F_GETFD, 0);
```

The integer `res` will be 1 if the close-on-exec flag is on for the file descriptor `fd`, 0 otherwise.

5.6 The exit system call

Usage

```
int status;

exit(status);
```

exit is an old friend, but we can now place it into its proper context. It is used to terminate a process, although a process will also stop when it runs out of program by reaching the end of the main function, or when main executes a return statement.

As well as stopping the calling process, exit has a number of other consequences: most importantly, all open file descriptors are closed. If the parent process has executed a wait call, as in the last example, it will be restarted. exit will also in some circumstances perform what are described vaguely in the UNIX Programmer's Manual as clean-up actions. These can, for example, be concerned with the buffering in the Standard I/O Library. Details of this are deliberately hidden from the user.

The single, integer argument to exit is called the process's **exit status**, the low-order eight bits of which are available to the parent process, providing it has executed a wait (more details of this in the next section). The value returned through exit in this way is normally used to indicate the success or failure of the task performed by the process. By convention a process returns zero on normal termination, some non-zero value if something has gone wrong.

For completeness, we should also mention the system call _exit(), which is distinguished from exit by the leading underscore in its name. This is used in exactly the same way as exit. However, it circumvents those mysterious clean-up actions we described earlier. The _exit call should be avoided by most programmers.

Exercise 5.7 The exit status of a program can be obtained by using the '$?' variable within the shell, for example:

```
$ ls nonesuch
nonesuch not found
$ echo $?
2
```

Write a program called fake which uses the integer value of its first argument as its exit status. Using the method outlined above, try out fake using a variety of arguments, including negative and large values. Is fake a useful program?

5.7 Synchronizing processes with `wait`

Usage

```
int retval, status;

retval = wait(&status);
```

or

```
retval = wait( (int *)0 );
```

As we have already seen briefly, `wait` temporarily suspends the execution of a process while a child process is running. Once the child has finished, the waiting parent is restarted. If more than one child is running then `wait` returns the first time one of the parent's offspring exits.

`wait` is often called by a parent process just after a call to `fork`. For example:

```
pid = fork();    /*create new process*/

if(pid ==  0 ){

        /*child            */
        /*do something ....*/

}else{

        /*parent, so wait for child*/
        wait( (int *)0);
}
```

This combination of `fork` and `wait` is seen when the child process is intended to run a completely different program through `exec`.

The return value from `wait` is normally the process-id of the exiting child. If `wait` returns −1, it can mean that no child exists and in this case `errno` will contain the error code `ECHILD`.

`wait` takes one argument. This can either be a pointer to an integer or a null pointer. If a null pointer is used, it is simply ignored. If however `wait` is passed a valid pointer, then the integer this describes will contain useful status information when `wait` returns. Normally this information will be the exit-status of the child passed through `exit`. The following program `status` demonstrates how `wait` is used in these circumstances:

```
/*status -- how to get hold of a child's exit status*/

main()
{
   int pid, status, exit_status;
```

```
    if((pid = fork()) < 0)
         fatal("fork failed");

    if(pid ==  0){   /*this is the child*/

        /*now call the library routine sleep
         *to suspend execution for 4 seconds
         */
        sleep(4);
        exit(5);    /*exit with non-zero value*/
    }

    /*getting this far means this is the parent*/
    /*so wait for child*/

    if(wait(&status) < 0){
        perror("wait failed");
        exit(1);
    }

    /*test low-order bits using bitwise AND*/
    /*Note: 0xFF is hex for 255*/

    if((status & 0xFF) != 0)
        printf("Some low-order bits not zero\n");
    else{
        /*shift high-order bits rightwards*/
        /*using the ">>" operator         */

        exit_status = status >> 8;

        /*mask off unwanted  bits*/
        exit_status &= 0xFF;

        printf("Exit status from %d was %d\n",
              pid, exit_status);
     }

     exit(0);
}
```

Although this might look a little complex at first the basic idea is straightforward: the value returned to the parent via `exit` is stored in the high-order bits of `exit_status`. For these to be meaningful the low-order eight bits must be zero, hence the test with the bitwise AND operator (the `&` symbol) after the return from `wait`. If they aren't zero then the child was stopped in its tracks by another process, using a communication method called a **signal**. Signals will be discussed in Chapter 6.

Exercise 5.8 Adapt the `docommand` routine so that it returns the `exit` status of the command it executes. What should happen if the `wait` call involved returns −1?

5.8 Zombies and premature exits

So far, we have assumed that `exit` and `wait` are used in an orderly fashion, where each subprocess is waited for. However, there are two other situations worth discussing.

1. A child exits when its parent is not currently executing a `wait`.
2. A parent exits while one or more children are still running.

In case (1), the exiting process is placed into a kind of limbo and becomes a **zombie**. A zombie process is one that occupies a slot in a table maintained in the kernel for process control, but uses no other kernel resources. It will be finally put to rest if its parent claims the child by executing a `wait`. The zombie will then be deleted from the system and the parent will gain access to its exit status. In case (2), the parent is allowed to exit normally. The children (including zombies) of the parent process are adopted by the system's initialization process.

5.9 `smallsh`: a command processor

In this section we will construct a simple command processor called `smallsh`. This project has two advantages. The first is that it develops the concepts we have introduced in this chapter. The second is that it demonstrates that there is really nothing special about standard UNIX facilities. In particular it shows that the shell is just an ordinary program that happens to be invoked when you login.

The initial demands that we shall make of `smallsh` are straightforward. The program should assemble commands and execute them, either in the background or foreground. It should also be able to deal with lines consisting of several commands, separated by semicolons. Other facilities, such as filename expansion or I/O redirection, can be added later.

The basic logic is clear:

```
while(EOF not typed){
     get command line from user
     assemble command args and execute
}
```

We shall give the *get command line* function the name `userin`. `userin` should print a prompt, then wait for a line of input from the keyboard. Any input it does receive it should place into a program buffer. We have implemented `userin` as follows:

```
#include "smallsh.h" /*include file for example*/

/*program buffers and work pointers*/
static char inpbuf[MAXBUF], tokbuf[2*MAXBUF],
            *ptr = inpbuf,  *tok = tokbuf;


userin(p) /*print prompt and read a line*/
char *p;
{
   int c, count;

   /*initialization for later routines*/
   ptr = inpbuf;
   tok = tokbuf;

   /*display prompt*/
   printf("%s ",p);

   for(count = 0;;){

       if((c = getchar()) == EOF)
          return(EOF);

       if(count < MAXBUF)
          inpbuf[count++] = c;

       if(c == '\n' && count < MAXBUF){
          inpbuf[count] = '\0';
          return(count);
       }

       /*if line too long restart*/
       if(c == '\n'){
          printf("smallsh:input line too long\n");
          count = 0;
          printf("%s ",p);
       }


   }

}
```

Some of the initialization detail you can ignore for now. The essential point is that `userin` first prints a prompt (which is passed as a parameter), then reads a character at a time from the user, exiting when it encounters a newline or end of file (the latter case denoted by the symbol `EOF`).

The basic input routine we have used is `getchar`. `getchar` is actually a **macro** taken from the Standard I/O Library (and consequently a relative of `printf`). It reads a single character from the program's standard input, which normally corresponds to the keyboard. `userin` places each new character (where possible) into the character array `inpbuf`. When it terminates `userin` returns either a count of the number of the characters read or `EOF` to signify end of file. Note that newlines are added to `inpbuf` and not discarded.

The include file `smallsh.h` referenced within `userin` contains definitions for some useful constants (such as `MAXBUF`). Its actual contents are:

```
/*smallsh.h - defs for smallsh command processor*/

#include <stdio.h>

#define  EOL 1              /*end of line*/
#define  ARG 2              /*normal argument*/
#define  AMPERSAND 3
#define  SEMICOLON 4

#define  MAXARG  512        /*max. no. command args*/
#define  MAXBUF  512        /*max. length input line*/

#define  FOREGROUND 0
#define  BACKGROUND 1
```

The other constants not referenced within `userin` we will meet in later routines.

`smallsh.h` also includes the standard header file `stdio.h`. This gives us the definition of `getchar` and the constant `EOF`.

The next routine we shall look at is `gettok`. This extracts individual **tokens** from a command line constructed by `userin`. (A token is a lexical unit such as a command name or argument.) `gettok` is invoked as follows:

```
toktype = gettok(&tptr);
```

`toktype` is an integer which will contain a value denoting the type of the token. The range of possible values is taken from `smallsh.h` and includes `EOL` (for end of line), `SEMICOLON`, etc. `tptr` is a character pointer which will point to the actual token itself after the call to `gettok`. Because `gettok` will allocate its own storage for the token string we must pass the address of `tptr` rather than its value.

The source code for `gettok` follows. Note that since it references the character pointers `tok` and `ptr`, it must be included in the same source file as userin. (You should now also be able to see the reason for the initialization of tok and ptr at the beginning of userin.)

```
gettok(outptr) /*get token and place into tokbuf*/
char **outptr;
{
      int type;


      *outptr =  tok;

      /*strip white space*/
      for(;*ptr == ' ' || *ptr == '\t'; ptr++)
          ;


      *tok++ = *ptr;

      switch(*ptr++){
         case '\n':
          type = EOL; break;
         case '&':
          type = AMPERSAND; break;
         case ';':
          type = SEMICOLON; break;
         default:
          type = ARG;
          while(inarg(*ptr))
             *tok++ = *ptr++;
      }

      *tok++ = '\0';
      return(type);
}
```

inarg is used for determining whether a character can be part of an 'ordinary' argument. For the present, we need just check whether the character is special to smallsh or not:

```
static char special[]=
{' ', '\t', '&', ';', '\n', '\0'};

inarg(c) /*are we in an ordinary argument*/
char c;
{

      char *wrk;
```

```
    for(wrk = special;*wrk != '\0';wrk++)
        if(c == *wrk)
            return(0);

    return(1);
}
```

We are now ready to introduce the function that does the real work. `procline` will parse a command line using `gettok`, constructing an argument list in the process. When it encounters a newline or semicolon it invokes a routine called `runcommand` to execute the command. It assumes that an input line has already been read with `userin`.

```
#include "smallsh.h"

procline() /*process input line*/
{
   char *arg[MAXARG+1];      /*pointer array for runcommand*/
   int toktype;              /*type of token in command*/
   int narg;                 /*number of arguments so far*/
   int type;                 /*FOREGROUND or BACKGROUND?*/


   for(narg = 0;;){ /*loop FOREVER*/


      /*take action according to token type*/

      switch(toktype = gettok(&arg[narg])){

        case ARG:

          if(narg < MAXARG)
             narg++;
          break;

        case EOL:
        case SEMICOLON:
        case AMPERSAND:

          type = (toktype == AMPERSAND) ?
          BACKGROUND : FOREGROUND;

          if(narg != 0){
             arg[narg] = NULL;
             runcommand(arg, type);
          }

          if(toktype == EOL)
             return;
```

```
                narg = 0;
                break;
            }
        }
    }
```

The next stage is to specify the `runcommand` routine, which actually starts any command processes. `runcommand` is essentially an adaptation of the routine `docommand` we met earlier. It has an extra integer parameter called `where`. If `where` is set to the value `BACKGROUND` as defined in `smallsh.h`, then the `wait` call is omitted and `runcommand` simply prints the process-id and returns.

```
#include "smallsh.h"

/*execute a command with optional wait*/
runcommand(cline,where)
char **cline;
int where;
{

    int pid, exitstat, ret;


    if((pid = fork()) < 0){
        perror("smallsh");
        return(-1);
    }

    if(pid == 0){ /*child*/
        execvp(*cline, cline);
        perror(*cline);
        exit(127);
    }

    /*code for parent*/
    /*if background process print pid and exit*/

    if(where == BACKGROUND){
        printf("[Process id %d]\n",pid);
        return(0);
    }


    /*wait until process pid exits*/

    while( (ret=wait(&exitstat)) != pid && ret != -1)
        ;

    return(ret == -1 ? -1 : exitstat);
}
```

Notice that the simple `wait` call of `docommand` has been replaced with the more complex loop

```
while( (ret=wait(&exitstat)) != pid && ret != -1)
        ;
```

This ensures that `runcommand` exits only when the child it last started terminates and avoids problems with background commands that terminate in the interim. (If this seems unclear, remember that `wait` returns the process-id of the first child process to exit, not the last to be started.)

`runcommand` also makes use of the `execvp` system call. This ensures that the program identified by a command is hunted for along the string of directories in the current `PATH`, although, unlike a real shell, `smallsh` doesn't have any means of manipulating `PATH`.

The last step is to write the `main` function which ties everything together. This is a trivial exercise:

```
/*smallsh -- simple command processor*/

#include "smallsh.h"

char *prompt = "Command>";      /*prompt*/

main()
{
        while(userin(prompt) != EOF)
            procline();

}
```

This routine completes the first version of `smallsh`. Again, it must be stressed that it is only a skeleton of any finished solution. As with `docommand`, the behaviour of `smallsh` is less than ideal when the user types the current interrupt character, since this causes `smallsh` to terminate. We will see how to make `smallsh` more robust in the next chapter.

Exercise 5.9 Add to `smallsh` a mechanism for escaping special characters such as ampersand and semicolon so that they can be included within program arguments. Also make it correctly interpret comments, as indicated by a leading hash (`#`) character. What should happen to the prompt when a newline is escaped?

Exercise 5.10 The `fnctl` routine can be used to duplicate an open file descriptor. In this context, it is called as follows:

```
newfdes = fnctl(filedes, F_DUPFD, reqvalue);
```

`filedes` is the original file descriptor for the open file. The constant `F_DUPFD` is taken from the system include file `fcntl.h`. `reqvalue` should be a small integer. After a successful call `newfdes` will contain a file descriptor which refers to the same file as `filedes` and has the same numeric value as `reqvalue` (assuming `reqvalue` isn't already a file descriptor). The following program fragment shows how to reassign standard input, i.e. file descriptor 0.

```
close(0);
fd1 = open("somefile", O_RDONLY);
fd2 = fcntl(fd1, F_DUPFD, 0);
```

After this call the value of `fd2` will be 0.

Using this call in conjunction with the `open` and `close` system calls, adapt `smallsh` so that it supports redirection of standard input and standard output using the same notation as the conventional UNIX shell. Remember that standard input and output correspond to file descriptors 0 and 1, respectively.

Note that on some elderly versions of UNIX, this method of duplicating file descriptors is provided by the now obsolete `dup2` system call. (A close relative called `dup` is still available in System V.)

5.10 Process attributes

Each UNIX process is associated with a number of attributes which help the system control the running and scheduling of processes, maintain the security of the file system and so on. One attribute we have already met is the process-id, an integer which uniquely identifies a current process. Other attributes range from the environment, which is a collection of strings maintained outside the data areas defined by the programmer, to the effective user-id which determines the file system privileges of the process. In the rest of this chapter we will look at the more important process attributes.

5.10.1 The process-id

As we saw at the beginning of this chapter, the system gives each process a non-negative, identifying integer called a process-id. At any one time a process-id is unique although it may eventually be re-used when the process has terminated. The system reserves the process-ids 0 and 1 for special processes. Process 0 is the scheduler. Process 1 is the initialization process which is actually an execution of the program `/etc/init`. Process 1 is, directly or indirectly, the ancestor of every other process on a UNIX system and is the ultimate controller of the process structure.

A program can obtain its own process-id by using the following system call:

```
pid = getpid();
```

Similarly the `getppid` call gets the process-id of the calling process's parent:

```
ppid = getppid();
```

The following example routine `gentemp` uses `getpid` to generate a unique, temporary file name. This name has the form:

```
/tmp/tmp<pid>.<no>
```

The suffix number is incremented on each call to `gentemp`. The routine also calls `access` to check if the file already exists:

```
static int num = 0;

static char namebuf[20];
static char prefix[] = "/tmp/tmp";

char *gentemp()
{
      /*standard string-handling routines*/
      char *strcpy(), *strcat();

      int length, pid;

      pid = getpid(); /*get process-id*/

      strcpy(namebuf, prefix);
      length = strlen(namebuf);

      /*add pid to file name*/
      itoa(pid, &namebuf[length]);

      strcat(namebuf, ".");
      length = strlen(namebuf);

      do{
           /*add suffix number*/
           itoa(num++, &namebuf[length]);

      }while (access(namebuf, 0) != -1);

      return namebuf;
}
```

The routine `itoa` simply converts an integer into its string equivalent:

```
/*itoa -- convert int to string*/

itoa(i, string)
int i;
char *string;
{
        int power, j;

        j = i;
```

```
        for( power = 1; j >= 10; j /= 10)
                power *= 10;

        for( ; power >0; power /= 10){
                *string++ = '0' + i/power;
                i %= power;
        }

        *string = '\0';
}
```

Notice the way we convert a digit into its character equivalent with the first statement inside the second `for` loop.

Exercise 5.11 Adapt `gentemp` so that it takes a stem for the temporary file name as an argument.

5.10.2 Process groups and process group-ids

UNIX also allows processes to be usefully placed into groups. Each **process group** is denoted by an integer called the **process group-id.** Initially a process inherits its process group-id across a `fork` or `exec`. A process can however place itself in a new group by invoking the `setpgrp` system call:

```
newpg = setpgrp();
```

The return value `newpg` is the new process group-id, which will in fact be equal to the process-id of the calling process. The calling process becomes the **process group leader** for the new group. Any processes it creates will inherit the process group-id held in `newpg`.

Conversely, a process can obtain its current process group-id with the `getpgrp` system call:

```
pgid = getpgrp();
```

With programs that leave their process group-ids untouched, the value of `pgid` will be the process-id of the ancestral shell process.

Process groups are most useful in conjunction with a type of process intercommunication system called signals. We will explore signals in the next chapter. However, there is one application that we can discuss now. Normally, when a user logs out, all processes started by the shell process concerned are forcibly terminated (**killed** in UNIX terminology). Processes are chosen for termination on the basis of their process group-ids. If a process has the same process group as its ancestral shell process, then it too is doomed when the user logs out. If, on the other hand, a process changes its process group, then it prolongs its life beyond logout, which is useful for long-running background tasks. The following example program demonstrates this approach, although you should normally use the 'no hangup' program `nohup` to achieve the same effect:

```
/*remain.c -- can live beyond logout*/

main()
{
        int newpgid;

        /*change process group*/
        newpgid = setpgrp();

        /*body of program*/
}
```

5.10.3 The environment

The **environment** of a process is simply a collection of null-terminated strings, represented within a program as a null-terminated array of character pointers. By convention, each environment string has the form:

```
name=something
```

A programmer can make direct use of the environment of a process by adding an extra parameter `envp` to the parameter list of the `main` function within a program. The following program fragment shows the type of `envp`:

```
main(argc, argv, envp)
int argc;
char **argv, **envp;
{
        /*do something*/
}
```

As a trivial example, the next program simply prints out its environment and exits:

```
/*showmyenv.c -- show environment*/

main(argc,argv,envp)
int argc;
char **argv,**envp;
{
        while(*envp != (char *)0)
            printf("%s\n",*envp++);
}
```

Running this program on one machine produced the following results:

```
CDPATH=:..:/
HOME=/
LOGNAME=keith
MORE=-h -s
PATH=/bin:/etc:/usr/bin:/usr/cbin:/usr/lbin
SHELL=/bin/sh
TERM=vt100
TZ=GMT0BST
```

This layout may well look familiar to you. It is the environment of the shell process that invoked the `showmyenv` program and includes important variables used by the shell such as `HOME` and `PATH`.

What this example shows is that the default environment of a process is the same as the process that created it through a call to `exec` or `fork`. Since the environment is passed on in this way, it allows information to recorded semi-permanently which would otherwise have to be respecified for each new process. The `TERM` environment variable, which stores the current terminal type, is a good example of how useful this can be.

To actually specify a new environment for the process you must use one of two new members of the `exec` family: `execle` and `execve`. These are called as follows:

```
execle(path, arg0, arg1, ..argn, (char *)0, envp);
```

and

```
execve(path,argv, envp);
```

These duplicate, respectively, the actions of the system calls `execv` and `execl`. The one difference is the addition of the `envp` parameter which is a null-terminated array of character pointers that specifies the environment for the new program. The next example uses `execle` to pass a new environment to the `showmyenv` program:

```
/*setmyenv.c -- set environment for program*/

main()
{
      char *argv[2], *envp[3];

      argv[0] = "showmyenv";
      argv[1] = (char *)0;

      envp[0] = "foo=bar";
      envp[1] = "bar=foo";
      envp[2] = (char *)0;

      execve("./showmyenv", argv, envp);

      perror("execve failed");
}
```

As well as using the parameters passed to the main function, a process can also gain access to its environment through the global cell:

```
extern char **environ;
```

We can use this external object to construct a general-purpose routine `findenv`. Given a string `name`, `findenv` will scan the environment for a string of the form `name=string`. If successful `findenv` will return a pointer to the `value` part of the string, otherwise it returns a null pointer.

```
/*findenv -- search for "name=string" in env*/

extern char **environ;

char *findenv(name)
char *name;
{
        int l;
        char **p;

        for(p = environ; *p != (char *)0; p++)
            if( (l = pcmp(name,*p)) >= 0 &&
                *(*p+l) == '=')
               return(*p+l+1);

        return((char *)0);
}

/*pcmp - partially match s1 against s2*/
/*return length s1 if match*/

pcmp(s1,s2)
char *s1,*s2;
{

        int i=0;

        while(*s1 != '\0'){
            i++;
            if(*s1++ != *s2++)
               return(-1);
        }

        return(i);
}
```

There is a standard UNIX library routine `getenv` that performs the same function as `findenv`. It is called in exactly the same way. A companion routine `putenv` is also provided to change or extend the environment. It is called along the following lines:

```
putenv("NEWVARIABLE=value");
```

`putenv` returns zero if it was successful. It alters the environment pointed to by `environ`, but it cannot affect the third argument to `main`.

5.10.4 The current working directory

As we saw in Chapter 4, each process is associated with a current working directory. The initial setting for the current directory is inherited across the `fork` or `exec` that started the process. To put it another way, a process is initially placed in the same directory as its parent.

The fact that the current directory is a per-process attribute is important. If a child process changes position by calling `chdir`, the current directory in the parent process is unchanged. For this reason the standard `cd` command is actually a 'built-in' command within the shell itself and does not correspond to a program. (It is amusing to note that when multitasking was first added to UNIX, the effect on the change directory command, then implemented as an ordinary program, wasn't anticipated and caused some confusion. See the article by Ritchie in the October 84 *Bell Labs Technical Journal* for this and other historical anecdotes.)

In a similar manner, each process is associated with a root directory used in absolute pathname searches. As with the current directory, the root directory of a process is initially determined by that of its parent. However, as we saw in Chapter 4, a process's idea of the root directory can be changed with the `chroot` system call. Like `chdir`, a call to `chroot` does not affect any ancestral processes.

Exercise 5.12 Add the `cd` command to the `smallsh` command processor.

5.10.5 User- and group-ids

Each process is associated with a real user-id and a real group-id. These are always the user and current group-ids of the user who invoked the process.

Perhaps more important, because they are used to determine whether a user can access a file, are the effective user- and group-ids. More often than not, these are the same as the real user- and group-ids. However, as process or one of its ancestors had its set-user-id or set-group-id permission bit set. For example, if the program file's set-user-id bit is set, then when the program is invoked through a call to `exec`, the effective user-id of the process becomes that of the file owner, not the user who started the process.

There are several system calls available for obtaining the user- and group-ids associated with a process. The following program fragment demonstrates these:

```
int uid, euid, gid, egid;

/*get real user-id*/
uid = getuid();

/*get effective user-id*/
euid = geteuid();

/*get real group-id*/
gid = getgid();

/*get effective group-id*/
egid = getegid();
```

Two calls are also available for setting the effective user- and group-ids of a process:

```
int status, newuid, newgid;
.
.
.
/*set effective user-id*/
status = setuid(newuid);

/*set effective group-id*/
status = setgid(newgid);
```

A process invoked by a non-privileged user (that is anybody who is not superuser) can only reset its effective user- and group-ids back to their real counterparts. Superuser as usual is allowed free rein. The return value from both routines is 0 on successful completion, −1 otherwise.

Exercise 5.13 Write a routine that obtains the real user- and group-ids of the calling process, then writes the ASCII equivalents of these onto the end of a log file.

5.10.6 File size limits: `ulimit`

In System V there is a per-process limit on the size of a file that can be created with the `write` system call. This limit also covers the situation where a pre-existing file, shorter than the limit, is extended.

The file size limit can be manipulated with the `ulimit` system call.

Usage

```
long retval, newlimit, ulimit();
int cmd;
  .
  .
  .
retval = ulimit(cmd, newlimit);
```

To obtain the current file size limit, a programmer can call `ulimit` with the parameter `cmd` set to 1. The value returned into `retval` is in units of 512-byte blocks.

To change the file size limit, a programmer should set `cmd` to 2 and place the new file size limit, again in 512-byte blocks, into `newlimit`. For example

```
if(ulimit(2, newlimit) < 0)
        perror("ulimit failed");
```

Only superuser can actually increase a file size limit in this way. Processes that have the effective user-ids of other users are, however, allowed to decrease their limit.

5.10.7 Process priorities: `nice`

The system decides the proportion of cpu time a particular process is allocated partly on the basis of an integer **nice** value. Nice values range from 0 to to a system-dependent maximum (typically 39). The higher the number the lower the process's priority. Socially aware processes can lower their priority, and thus allocate more resources to other processes, by using the `nice` system call. This takes one argument, a positive increment to be added to the current nice value; for example

```
nice(5);
```

Superuser (and only superuser) processes can increase their priority by using a negative value as the `nice` call parameter. `nice` is a useful call if all you want to do is calculate π to a hundred million places, and not use too many system resources in doing it.

Chapter 6 Interprocess Communications: 1

6.1 Introduction

It is often desirable to construct software systems that consist of several cooperating processes rather than just a single, monolithic program. There are several possible reasons for this: a single program might, for example, be too large for the machine it is running on, either in terms of physical memory or available address space; part of the required functionality may already reside in an existing program; the problem might be best solved with a server process that cooperates with an arbitrary number of client processes, and so on.

Of course, for two or more processes to cooperate in performing a task, they need to share data. One possible method is for processes to share files, since there is nothing to prevent several processes from reading or writing the same file simultaneously. However, this can be inefficient and some care has to be taken to avoid contention problems.

Luckily, UNIX is rich in interprocess communication mechanisms. In this chapter, we will discuss the three most widely used of these facilities: **signals**, **pipes** and **FIFOs**. Together with the newer facilities we highlight in Chapter 7, they offer a wide choice for the software developer who wants to build multi-process systems.

We shall start by looking at signals.

6.2 Signals

6.2.1 Overview

Suppose you are running a UNIX command that seems likely to take a long time:

```
$ cc verybigprog.c
```

Then you realize that something is wrong, and the command will eventually fail. To save time, you can stop the command by hitting the current interrupt key, which is often `DEL` or `CTRL-C`. The command will be terminated, and you will be returned to the shell prompt.

What actually happens is this: the part of the kernel responsible for keyboard input sees the interrupt character. The kernel then sends a signal called SIGINT to all processes that recognize the terminal as their control terminal. This includes the invocation of cc. When cc receives the signal, it performs the default action associated with SIGINT and terminates. It is interesting to note that the shell process associated with the terminal is also sent SIGINT. However, because it has to stay around to interpret later commands it sensibly ignores the signal. As we shall see, programs can also elect to 'catch' SIGINT, which means they perform a special interrupt routine whenever the user presses interrupt.

Signals are also used by the kernel to deal with certain kinds of severe error. For example, supposing a program file has become corrupted in some way and contains illegal machine instructions. When a process executes the program, the kernel will detect the attempt to execute illegal instructions and send the process the signal SIGILL (the ILL here stands for 'illegal') to terminate it. The resulting dialogue could look like:

```
$ badprog
Illegal instruction - core dumped
```

We will explain the phrase core dumped in due course.

As well as being sent from the kernel to a process, signals can be sent from process to process. This is easiest to show with the kill command. For example, suppose a programmer starts off a long running command in the background:

```
$ cc verybigprog.c&
1098
```

then decides to terminate it. kill can then be used to send the signal SIGTERM to the process. Like SIGINT, SIGTERM will terminate a process unless it has made explicit arrangements otherwise. The process-id must be given to the kill command as an argument.

```
$ kill 1098
1098 Terminated
```

Signals, then, provide a simple method for transmitting software interrupts to UNIX processes. If you need a metaphor, think of a signal as a kind of software tap on the shoulder, which interrupts a process whatever it may be doing. Because of their nature, signals tend to be used for handling abnormal conditions rather than the straightforward transmission of data between processes.

Signal names

Signals can't carry information directly, which limits their usefulness as an general interprocess communication mechanism. However, each type of signal is given a mnemonic name – SIGINT is an example – which indicates the purpose for which the signal is normally used. Signal names are defined in the standard header file signal.h with the preprocessor directive

`#define`. As you might expect these names just stand for small, positive integers. For example, `SIGINT` is usually defined as

```
#define    SIGINT   2
```

Most of the signal types provided by UNIX are intended for use by the kernel, although four are provided to be sent from process to process. The complete list of standard signals, as described in the AT&T *System V Interface Definition*, and their meanings follows. (On first reading you can safely skip this list.)

`SIGHUP` The *hangup* signal. This is sent by the kernel to all processes attached to a **control terminal** when that terminal is disconnected. (Normally, a process group's control terminal will be the user's own terminal, although this isn't always the case. The concept is further explored in Chapter 8.) It is also sent to all members of a process group when the process group leader, normally a shell process, exits, providing the process group is associated with a control terminal. This ensures background processes are terminated when a user logs out, unless explicit arrangements have been made otherwise (see Section 5.10.2 for more details).

`SIGINT` *Interrupt*. This is sent by the kernel to all processes associated with a terminal when a user hits the interrupt key. It is the conventional way of halting a running program.

`SIGQUIT` *Quit*. Very similar to `SIGINT`, this is sent by the kernel when the user hits the quit key associated with their terminal. The default value for the quit key is ASCII `FS` or `CTRL-\`. Unlike `SIGINT`, `SIGQUIT` will result in what the *SVID* describes as **abnormal termination**. The actual effect on the UNIX implementations we know is a **core dump**, indicated by the message `Quit - core dumped`, where the process image is dumped into a disk file for debugging purposes. More of this later.

`SIGILL` *Illegal instruction*. This is sent by the operating system when a process attempts to execute an illegal instruction. It is possible that the program has corrupted its own code, but this is unlikely. Other causes, such as an attempt to execute floating-point instructions without the right hardware support, are more probable. Like `SIGQUIT`, `SIGILL` results in abnormal termination.

`SIGTRAP` *Trace trap*. This is a special signal used by debuggers such as `sdb` and `adb`, in conjunction with the `ptrace` system call. Because of its specialized nature, we won't discuss it further. By default, `SIGTRAP` results in abnormal termination.

`SIGFPE` *Floating-point exception*. This is sent by the kernel when a floating-point error occurs (such as overflow or underflow). It causes abnormal termination.

`SIGKILL` *Kill*. This is a rather special signal that is sent from one process to another to terminate the receiver. It is also occasionally sent by the kernel. The distinguishing feature of `SIGKILL` is that it cannot be ignored or 'caught' (that is, handled via a user-defined interrupt routine). Since all the other signals may be ignored or caught, it is important that there exists one signal that is guaranteed to terminate a process *in extremis*. This is it.

`SIGSYS` *Bad argument to a system call.* This is occasionally sent by the kernel when a process passes an invalid argument to a system call that cannot be handled via the normal system call error recovery mechanisms. This is another signal that results in abnormal termination.

`SIGPIPE` *Write on a pipe with no-one to read it.* A pipe is another interprocess communication mechanism which we will discuss in Section 6.3. `SIGPIPE` will be properly examined then.

`SIGALRM` *Alarm clock.* This is normally sent by the kernel to a process after a timer has expired. The timer is actually set by the process itself using the `alarm` system call. We will describe `alarm` in Section 6.2.6.

`SIGTERM` *Software termination signal.* This signal is provided by the system for use by ordinary programs. By convention, it is used to terminate a process (as you might guess from its name!).

`SIGUSR1` and `SIGUSR2` Like `SIGTERM`, these are never sent by the kernel and may be used for whatever purpose a user wishes.

There are a number of other signals that you may encounter which are implementation-dependent and lie outside the *SVID*. Again, most of these are again used by the kernel to indicate error conditions, for example: `SIGEMT` (*emulator trap*) and `SIGSEGV` (*segmentation violation* – often due to a process misusing pointers and making a reference outside its address space).

The most important signal which has been placed into the implementation-dependent group is `SIGCLD`, the *death of a child* signal. This is used by modern versions of UNIX to implement the `exit` and `wait` system calls. When `exit` executes, `SIGCLD` is sent to the process's parent. If the parent has executed a `wait`, it will be woken up. If not, then providing the parent does not deliberately 'catch' `SIGCLD`, the signal has no effect (except that if the parent 'ignores' `SIGCLD`, a child process will be tidied up immediately it exits, rather than entering a 'zombie' state). This mechanism, although interesting, should be of little concern to most UNIX programmers.

Normal and abnormal termination

For most signals **normal termination** occurs when a signal is received. The effect is the same as if the process had executed an impromptu `exit` call. The exit status returned to the parent in this circumstance tells the parent what happened. The low-order eight bits will contain the signal number (which the parent could compare against the names from `signal.h`), and the high-order bits will be zero.

As we saw above, the signals SIGQUIT, SIGILL, SIGTRAP, SIGSYS and SIGFPE cause instead an abnormal termination, and the usual effect of this is a **core dump**. This means that a memory dump of the process is written to a file called core in the process's current directory ('core', of course, is a rather old fashioned way of describing main memory). The core file will include, in binary form, the values of all program variables, hardware registers and control information from the kernel at the moment termination occurred. The exit status of a process that abnormally terminates will be the same as it would be for normal termination by a signal, except that the seventh low-order bit, bit 0200, is set.

The format of a core file is known to the UNIX debuggers sdb and adb, and these programs can be used to examine the state of a process at the point it core dumped. This can be extremely useful since both adb and sdb will allow you to pinpoint the spot where the problem occurred. sdb can go as far as to automatically display the source line that caused the error condition.

It is worth mentioning the abort routine. This is called straightforwardly,

```
abort();
```

abort will send a signal to the calling process, causing abnormal termination, i.e. a core dump. abort is useful as a debugging aid since it allows a process to record its current state when something goes wrong. It also illustrates the fact that a process can send a signal to itself.

6.2.2 Handling signals with the signal system call

All of the signals defined in the *SVID* will, by default, terminate the receiving process. For simple programs this is perfectly adequate. Indeed, it allows the end user to stop a program that goes astray by typing one of the interrupt or quit keys. However, in larger programs, unexpected signals can cause problems. It makes no sense, for example, to allow a program to be halted by a careless press of an interrupt key during an important database update. A programmer might also want to perform clean-up operations, such as removing workfiles, whenever a program exits, whatever the cause.

Fortunately, a process can choose the way it responds when it receives a particular signal with the signal call, which is used to associate a particular action with a named signal. signal is actually rather poorly named; if read as a verb, it seems to suggest the act of sending a signal. A better name might be handlesig. In any case, signal is used as follows.

Usage

```
#include <signal.h>

int func(), (*was)(), sig;
 .
 .
 .
was = signal(sig, func);
```

The first parameter `sig` identifies the signal in question. To have any effect, `signal` must be called before a signal of type `sig` is received. `sig` can be set to any of the signal names defined previously, with the exception of `SIGKILL` which is provided exclusively for terminating processes and cannot be handled in any other way.

`signal`'s second parameter `func` describes the action to be associated with the signal. It can take three values:

1. The address of a function returning `int`. As long as it is declared before `signal` is called, `func` can just be the name of a function. The compiler will assume you mean the function's address. `func` will be executed when a signal of type `sig` is received, `sig` itself being the sole argument passed to `func`. Control will be passed to `func` as soon as the process receives the signal, whatever part of the program it is executing. When `func` returns, control will be passed back to the point at which the process was interrupted. This mechanism will become clearer in our next example.
2. `SIG_IGN` A special symbolic name which simply means 'ignore this signal'. In future, the process will do just that.
3. `SIG_DFL` Another symbolic name which restores the system's default action. For all the standard signals this means either normal, or abnormal, termination.

The definitions of `SIG_IGN` and `SIG_DFL` must, of course, be properly cast to avoid problems. On the machine on which this chapter was prepared the actual definitions in `signal.h` are:

```
#define SIG_DFL (int (*)())0
#define SIG_IGN (int (*)())1
```

The return value from `signal` is a pointer to an `int` function. Hence the tortuous definition of `was` as:

```
int (*was)();
```

If `signal` is successful, `was` will point to the function previously associated with `sig`. This allows a program to temporarily reset an action associated with a signal, then restore its original value (the technique is shown in Example 4 below).

`signal` will fail if passed an illegal signal value or `SIGKILL`. In this case, its return value will be, quite horribly:

```
(int (*)()) -1
```

and `errno` will be set to `EINVAL`, meaning invalid argument. No checking is performed to see if `func` points to a valid function.

Let us now consider some examples.

Example 1: catching `SIGINT`

This example shows how a signal can be caught, and also sheds more light on the underlying signal mechanism. It centres around the program `sigex` which simply associates a function called `catchint` with `SIGINT`, then executes a series of `sleep` and `printf` statements.

```
/*sigex -- shows how signal works*/

#include <signal.h>

main()
{
    /*declare fn to be associated with SIGINT*/
    int catchint();

    /*before signal call, SIGINT will
     *terminate process (default action)
     */

    signal(SIGINT, catchint);

    /*after signal call control will be passed
     *to catchint when SIGINT received
     */

    printf("sleep call #1\n");
    sleep(1);
    printf("sleep call #2\n");
    sleep(1);
    printf("sleep call #3\n");
    sleep(1);
    printf("sleep call #4\n");
    sleep(1);

    printf("Exiting\n");
    exit(0);
}

/*trivial function to handle SIGINT*/
catchint(signo)
int signo;
{
    printf("\nCATCHINT: signo=%d\n", signo);

    printf("CATCHINT: returning\n\n");
}
```

If left alone `sigex` produces the following output:

```
$ sigex
sleep call #1
sleep call #2
sleep call #3
sleep call #4
Exiting
```

The user can, however, interrupt the progress of `sigex` by typing the interrupt key. If typed before `sigex` has had a chance to execute `signal`, the process will simply terminate. If typed after the `signal` call, control will be passed to the function `catchint`.

```
$ sigex
sleep call #1
<DEL>             (user presses interrupt key)

CATCHINT: signo=2
CATCHINT: returning

sleep call #2
sleep call #3
sleep call #4
Exiting
```

Notice how control is passed from the main body of the program to `catchint`. When `catchint` has finished, control is passed back to the point at which the program was interrupted. `sigex` could equally easily be interrupted at a different place:

```
$ sigex

sleep call #1
sleep call #2
<DEL>             (user presses interrupt key)

CATCHINT: signo=2
CATCHINT: returning

sleep call #3
sleep call #4
Exiting
```

Example 2: ignoring `SIGINT`

Suppose we want a process to ignore the interrupt signal `SIGINT`. All we need do is include the following line in the program:

```
signal(SIGINT, SIG_IGN);
```

After this is executed the interrupt key will be ineffective. It can be enabled again with

```
signal(SIGINT, SIG_DFL);
```

It is perfectly possible to ignore several signals simultaneously. For example,

```
signal(SIGINT, SIG_IGN);
signal(SIGQUIT, SIG_IGN);
```

deals with both SIGINT and SIGQUIT. This is useful for programs which are performing sensitive tasks, like updating a database, and need to be protected from interruption in the crucial stages.

The shell uses this technique to ensure that background processes aren't stopped when the user presses the interrupt key. This is possible because signals that are ignored by a process are still ignored after an exec call. The shell can therefore call signal to make sure SIGQUIT and SIGINT are ignored, then exec the new program. Note, however, that signals which are caught in the original process will have their associated actions set to SIG_DFL after an exec. This is because, of course, the old signal handling functions are not part of the new process image.

Example 3: a graceful exit

Suppose a program uses a temporary workfile. The following simple routine removes the file:

```
/*exit from program gracefully*/
#include <stdio.h>

g_exit()
{
        unlink("tempfile");
        fprintf(stderr, "Interrupted -- exiting\n");
        exit(1);
}
```

This could be associated with a particular signal as follows:

```
extern int g_exit();
  .
  .
  .
signal(SIGINT, g_exit);
```

After this call, control will pass automatically to g_exit() when the user presses the interrupt key. The contents of g_exit() could be expanded depending on the number of clean-up operations required.

There is a small problem if you associate a function with either SIGINT or SIGQUIT. As we have seen, if the program is run in the background from the shell, then SIGINT and SIGQUIT are ignored when the program starts. By associating a function with either interrupt, we are making the process again susceptible to one of the interrupt or quit keys. One solution is to use a statement like the following at the beginning of a program:

```
if(signal(SIGINT, SIG_IGN) != SIG_IGN)
        signal(SIGINT, g_exit);
```

The second `signal` call is only executed if `SIGINT` was not previously associated with `SIG_IGN`.

Example 4: restoring a previous action

As we saw above, `signal` returns the *previous* action associated with the named signal. This allows us to save and restore the previous state of the signal as the next example shows:

```
#include <signal.h>

int (*oldptr)(), new();

/*set action for SIGTERM, saving the old one*/
oldptr = signal(SIGTERM, new);

/*do the work here...*/

/*now restore old action*/
signal(SIGTERM, oldptr);
```

Exercise 6.1 Alter `smallsh` from the last chapter so that it handles interrupts more like a real shell. Make sure background processes aren't halted by either `SIGINT` or `SIGQUIT`. Some variants of the shell (namely the *C-shell* and the *Korn shell*) handle background processes by placing them into a different process group. What are the advantages and disadvantages of this approach?

6.2.3 Signals and system calls

In most cases, if a process is sent a signal when it is executing a system call, the signal has no effect until the system call exits. However, a few system calls behave rather differently, and they can be interrupted by a signal. This is true for a `read`, `write`, or `open` on a slow device (such as a terminal, but not a disk file), a `wait`, or a `pause` call (the last one is new, we will discuss it in due course). In all cases, if the process traps the call, the interrupted system call returns −1 and places `EINTR` into `errno`. This sort of situation can be handled with code like:

```
if(write(tfd, buf, SIZE) < 0){
        if(errno == EINTR){
              warn("Write interrupted");
              .
              .
              .
        }
}
```

6.2.4 Resetting signals

The actions associated with most signals (exceptions being `SIGILL` and `SIGTRAP`) are reset immediately after they are caught. This means that the process 'forgets' any function associated with the signal, and next time it receives the signal, the default action `SIG_DFL` will be performed. For the standard signals, this implies, of course, program termination. Let's make things clear with a small example:

```
/*reset -- signal example*/

#include <signal.h>

int interrupt()
{
        printf("Interrupt called\n");
        sleep(10);
}

main()
{

        signal(SIGINT, interrupt);
        printf("Interrupt set for SIGINT\n");
        sleep(10);
}
```

This trivial program first associates the function `interrupt` with the signal `SIGINT`, then prints a message and finally sleeps for ten seconds. If the user presses the interrupt key then control is passed to `interrupt`, another message is printed and `sleep` is called a second time. If however the interrupt key is pressed a second time the process simply terminates. The resulting dialogue will look like:

```
$ reset
Interrupt set for SIGINT
<DEL>                   (user presses interrupt key)
Interrupt called
<DEL>                   (and a second time)
$
```

This, of course, is a problem, especially in interactive programs where users might type the interrupt key repeatedly. The following version of `interrupt` attempts to cope with this problem:

```
#include <signal.h>

int interrupt()
{
        /*turn off effect of SIGINT*/
```

```
        signal(SIGINT, SIG_IGN);
        printf("Interrupt called\n");
          .
          .
          .

        /*associate function with SIGINT again*/
        signal(SIGINT, interrupt);
}
```

This version ignores `SIGINT` for the duration of the function (or at least tries to, it is possible for another `SIGINT` signal to arrive before the `signal` call at the start of `interrupt`). One interesting point here is that `SIGINT` will be ignored until the process explicitly changes things, even if several instances of the `SIGINT` are received. The last action of the function is to re-associate itself with `SIGINT`.

It is important to note that UNIX signals cannot be stacked. To put it another way, there can never be more than one signal of each type outstanding at any moment for a given process, although there can be more than one type of signal outstanding. The *System V Interface Definition* does not define the order in which signals will be received in this latter case.

The fact that signals cannot be stacked makes them an unreliable method of interprocess communication, since a process can never be sure that a signal it has sent has not been 'lost'.

If the `signal` system call is executed for a particular signal when that signal is outstanding, the outstanding signal will be cancelled, unless it is `SIGKILL`.

Exercise 6.2 Make the `g_exit` routine introduced in Section 6.2.2 ignore both `SIGINT` and `SIGQUIT` for the duration of the function.

6.2.5 Sending signals with `kill`

A process calls `signal` to handle signals sent by other processes. The inverse operation of actually sending a signal is performed by the dramatically named `kill` system call (a better name might be `sendsig`). `kill` is used as follows.

Usage

```
#include <signal.h>

int  pid, sig, retval;
 .
 .
 .
retval = kill(pid, sig);
```

The first parameter `pid` determines the processes, or processes, to which the signal `sig` will be sent. Normally `pid` will be a positive integer and in this case it will be taken to be an actual process-id. So the statement

```
kill(1234, SIGTERM);
```

means *send signal* `SIGTERM` *to the process with process-id 1234.* Because the process that calls `kill` needs to know the id of the process it is sending to, `kill` is most often used between closely related processes, e.g. parent and child. It is also worth noting that processes can send signals to themselves.

There are some privilege issues here; in order to send a signal to a process, the real or effective user-id of the sending process must match the real or effective id of the receiver. Super-user processes, naturally enough, can send signals to any other process. If a non-superuser process does try to send to another process which belongs to a different user, then `kill` fails, returns −1 and places `EPERM` into `errno`. (The other possible values for `errno` with `kill` are: `ESRCH` meaning no such process, or `EINVAL` if `sig` is not a valid signal number.)

The `pid` parameter to `kill` can take other values which have special meanings. There are four of these additional meanings:

1. If `pid` is zero, the signal will be sent to all processes that belong to the same process group as the sender. This includes the sender.
2. If `pid` is −1, and the effective user-id of the process is not super-user, then the signal is sent to all processes with a real user-id equal to the effective user-id of the sender. Again this includes the sender.
3. If `pid` is −1, and the sender has an effective user-id of super-user, then the signal will be sent to all processes with the exception of some special system processes (this last prohibition actually applies to all attempts to send a signal to a group of processes, but is most important here).
4. Finally, if `pid` is less than zero but not −1, the signal will be sent to all processes with a process group-id equal to the absolute value of `pid`. This includes the sender if appropriate.

An example is called for; `synchro` will produce two processes. Both will write messages alternately to standard output. They synchronize themselves by using `kill` to send the signal `SIGUSR1` to each other.

```
/*synchro - example for "kill"*/

#include <signal.h>

int ntimes = 0;
```

```
main()
{

    int pid, ppid;
    int p_action(), c_action();

    /*set SIGUSR1 action for parent*/
    signal(SIGUSR1, p_action);

    switch( pid  = fork()){
      case -1:            /*error*/
        perror("synchro");
        exit(1);
      case 0:             /*child*/

        /*set action for child*/
        signal(SIGUSR1, c_action);

        /*get parent process-id*/
        ppid = getppid();

        for(;;){
            sleep(1);
            kill(ppid, SIGUSR1);
            pause();
        }
        /*never exits*/

       default:            /*parent*/

        for(;;){
            pause();
            sleep(1);
            kill(pid, SIGUSR1);
        }
        /*never exits*/
      }
}

p_action()
{
    printf("Parent caught signal #%d\n", ++ntimes);
    signal(SIGUSR1, p_action);
}

c_action()
{
    printf("Child caught signal #%d\n", ++ntimes);
    signal(SIGUSR1, c_action);
}
```

Each process sits in a loop, pausing until it receives a signal from the other. This is done with `pause` which simply suspends execution until a signal arrives (see Section 6.2.7). It then prints a message and takes its turn to send a signal with `kill`. The child process kicks things off (notice the ordering of statements in each loop). Both processes are terminated when the user hits the interrupt key. An example dialogue might look like:

```
$ synchro
Parent caught signal #1
Child caught signal #1
Parent caught signal #2
Child caught signal #2
<DEL>        (user hits interrupt key)
$
```

The `kill` command

We first met the `kill` command in Section 6.1. It can be used to send a signal to a running process, and is essentially just a command level interface to the `kill` system call. By default, the signal sent is `SIGTERM`. Other signals can be specified, but unfortunately you must (currently) give a signal number, rather than a symbolic name. So, since `SIGINT` actually stands for the number 2, the command

```
$ kill -2 1234
```

sends `SIGINT` to process 1234 (user-ids allowing). To get the process-id of a process you can use the `ps` command, which displays information on the processes currently running.

Exercise 6.3 Write a version of the `kill` command which uses symbolic signal names. Make sure it prints adequate diagnostics when the `kill` system call returns −1.

6.2.6 The `alarm` system call

`alarm` is a simple and useful call that sets up a process alarm clock. Signals are used to tell the program the clock's timer has expired.

Usage

```
unsigned int remain, secs;
  .
  .
  .
remain = alarm(secs);
```

Here, `secs` gives the time in seconds to the alarm. When this interval has expired the process will be sent a `SIGALRM` signal. So the call

```
alarm(60);
```

arranges for a `SIGALRM` signal in 60 seconds. Note that `alarm` isn't like `sleep` which suspends process execution; `alarm` instead returns immediately and the process continues execution in the normal manner, or at least until `SIGALRM` is received. In fact an active alarm clock will also continue across an `exec` call (after a `fork`, however, the alarm clock is turned off in the child).

An alarm can be turned off by calling `alarm` with a zero parameter:

```
/* turn alarm clock off */
alarm(0);
```

`alarm` calls aren't stacked: in other words if you call `alarm` twice, the second call supersedes the first. However, the return value from `alarm` does give the time remaining for any previous alarm timer, which can be recorded if necessary.

`alarm` is useful when a programmer needs to place a time limit on some activity. The basic idea is simple: `alarm` is called, and the process carries on with the task. If the task is completed in good time, the alarm clock is turned off. If it takes too long, the process is interrupted by `SIGALRM` and takes corrective action.

The following subroutine `quickreply` uses this approach to force an answer from the user. It takes one argument, a prompt, and returns a pointer to a string containing the input line, or the null pointer if nothing is typed after five retries. Note that each time `quickreply` reminds the user, it sends `CTRL-G` to the terminal. This will ring the bell on most hardware.

`quickreply` calls a routine `gets` which comes from the *Standard I/O Library*. `gets` places the next line from standard input into a `char` array. It returns either a pointer to the array, or a null pointer on end of file or error. Notice how `SIGALRM` is caught by the interrupt routine `catch`. This is important, since the default action associated with `SIGALRM` is, of course, termination. `catch` sets a flag called `timed_out`. `quickreply` checks this within the body of `quickreply` to see if it has indeed been timed out.

```
#include <stdio.h>
#include <signal.h>

#define TIMEOUT   5       /*in seconds*/
#define MAXTRIES  5
#define LINESIZE  100
#define CTRL_G    '\007' /*ASCII*/
#define TRUE      1
#define FALSE     0

/*used to see if timeout has occurred*/
static int timed_out;
```

```
/*will hold input line*/
static char inline[LINESIZE];

extern char *gets();

char *quickreply(prompt)
char *prompt;
{

    int (*was)(), catch(), ntries;
    char *answer;

    /*catch SIGALRM + save previous action*/
    was = signal(SIGALRM, catch);

    for(ntries = 0;ntries < MAXTRIES; ntries++){

        timed_out = FALSE;
        printf("\n%s > ", prompt);

        /*set alarm clock*/
        alarm(TIMEOUT);

        /*get input line*/
        answer = gets(inline);

        /*turn off alarm*/
        alarm(0);

        /*if timed_out TRUE, then no reply*/
        if(!timed_out)
            break;
    }

    /*restore old action*/
    signal(SIGALRM, was);

    /*return appropriate value*/
    return (ntries == MAXTRIES ? ((char *)0) : answer);
}

/*executed when SIGALRM received*/
catch()
{
    /*set timeout flag*/
    timed_out = TRUE;

    /*ring bell*/
    putchar(CTRL_G);
```

```
        /*for next time..*/
        signal(SIGALRM, catch);
    }
```

6.2.7 The `pause` system call

As a companion to `alarm`, UNIX provides the `pause` system call, which is invoked very simply as follows.

Usage

```
int retval;

retval = pause();
```

`pause` suspends the calling process (in such a way that it will not waste system resources) until some kind of signal, e.g. `SIGALRM`, is received. If the signal causes normal termination then that is just what will happen. If the signal is ignored by the process, `pause` ignores it too. If the signal is caught, however, then when the appropriate interrupt routine has finished, `pause` returns −1 and places `EINTR` into `errno` (why?).

The following program `tml` (for 'tell-me-later') uses both `alarm` and `pause` in order to display a message in a given number of minutes. It is called as follows:

```
$ tml #minutes message-text
```

For example:

```
$ tml 10 time to go home
```

The message is preceded with three `CTRL-G`s or bells for dramatic effect. Note how `tml` forks to create a background process to do the work, allowing the user to continue with other tasks.

```
/*tml - tell-me-later program*/

#include <stdio.h>
#include <signal.h>

#define TRUE  1
#define FALSE 0
#define BELLS "\007\007\007"    /*ASCII*/

int alarm_flag = FALSE;

/*routine to handle SIGALRM*/
setflag()
{
    alarm_flag = TRUE;
}
```

```
main(argc, argv)
int argc;
char *argv[];
{
    int nsecs, pid;
    int j;

    if(argc <= 2){
        fprintf(stderr, "Usage: tml #minutes message\n");
        exit(1);
    }

    if((nsecs = atoi(argv[1])*60) <= 0){
        fprintf(stderr, "tml: invalid time\n");
        exit(2);
    }

    /*fork to create background process*/
    switch(pid = fork()){
      case -1:              /*error*/
        perror("tml");
        exit(1);
      case  0:              /*child*/
        break;
      default:              /*parent*/
        printf("tml process-id %d\n", pid);
        exit(0);
    }


    /*set action for alarm*/
    signal(SIGALRM, setflag);

    /*turn on alarm clock*/
    alarm(nsecs);

    /*pause until signal...*/
    pause();

    /*if signal was SIGALRM, print message*/
    if(alarm_flag == TRUE){
        printf(BELLS);
        for(j = 2; j < argc; j++)
            printf("%s ", argv[j]);
        printf("\n");
    }

    exit(0);
}
```

From this example you should get an insight into how the sleep subroutine works by calling first alarm, then pause.

Exercise 6.4 Write your own version of sleep. Make sure it saves the previous state of the alarm clock and restores it when it exits. (Look at your system's manual for a full specification of sleep.)

Exercise 6.5 Rewrite tml using your version of sleep.

6.2.8 setjmp and longjmp

Sometimes it makes sense to jump back to a previous position in a program when a signal is received. You might want, for example, to allow a user to go back to a program's main menu when he or she presses the interrupt key. This can be done using two special subroutines called setjmp and longjmp. setjmp 'saves' the current position in a program (in fact, by saving the stack environment), and longjmp passes control back to a saved position. In a sense longjmp is a kind of long-distance, non-local goto. It is important to realize that longjmp never returns because the stack frames are collapsed back to the point where the position was saved. As we shall see, it is the corresponding setjmp that appears to return.

A program position is saved in an object of type jmp_buf, which is defined in a standard header file called setjmp.h. The following example shows things more clearly:

```
/*example use of setjmp and longjmp*/

#include <signal.h>
#include <setjmp.h>
#include <stdio.h>

jmp_buf position;

main()
{
    int goback();
    .
    .
    .


    /*save current position*/
    setjmp(position);

    signal(SIGINT, goback);

    domenu();
```

```
        .
        .
        .

}

goback()
{
    signal(SIGINT, SIG_IGN);
    fprintf(stderr, "\nInterrupted\n");

    /*go back to saved position*/
    longjmp(position, 1);
}
```

If the user types an interrupt after the `signal` call, control is passed first to `goback`. This in turn calls `longjmp` and control is passed back to where `setjmp` recorded the program position. So program execution continues as if the corresponding call to `setjmp` had just returned. The return value from `setjmp` (which is not used here) is in this case taken from the second `longjmp` parameter.

6.3 Interprocess communications using pipes

Useful though they are for dealing with unusual events or errors, signals are entirely unsuited for transmitting large amounts of information from one process to another. For this purpose, UNIX provides a construct called the **pipe**. A pipe is a one-way communications channel which couples one process to another, and is yet another generalization of the UNIX file concept. As we shall see, a process can send data 'down' the pipe by using the `write` system call, and another process can receive the data by using `read` at the other end.

6.3.1 Pipes at command level

Most UNIX users will have come across pipes at command level. For example,

```
$ pr doc | lp
```

causes the shell to start the commands `pr` and `lp` simultaneously. The '|' symbol in the command line tells the shell to create a pipe to couple the standard output of `pr` to the standard input of `lp`. The final result of this command will be a nicely paginated version of the file *doc* being sent to the line printer.

Let us dissect the command further. The `pr` program on the left-hand side of the pipe symbol does not know that its standard output is being sent to a pipe. It just writes to standard output as normal, making no special arrangements. Similarly, `lp` on the right-hand side reads from the pipe just as if its standard input is coming from the keyboard or ordinary disk file. The overall effect is as if the following sequence had been executed:

```
$ pr doc > tmpfile
$ lp < tmpfile
$ rm tmpfile
```

Flow control along the pipe is handled automatically and invisibly. So if `pr` produces information too quickly, its execution is suspended. It is restarted when `lp` catches up and the amount of data in the pipe falls to an acceptable level.

Pipes are one of the strongest and most distinctive features of UNIX, especially at command level. They allow arbitrary sequences of commands to be simply coupled together. UNIX programs can therefore be developed as general tools which read from their standard input, write to their standard output and perform a single, well defined task. Complex command lines can be built up from these basic building blocks using pipes. For example,

```
$ who | wc -l
```

pipes the output of the `who` into the word count program `wc`, the `-l` option telling `wc` just to count lines. The number finally output by `wc` is a count of the number of logged-on users.

6.3.2 Programming with pipes

Within a program a pipe is created using a system call named `pipe`. If successful, this call returns two file descriptors: one for writing down the pipe, and one for reading from it. `pipe` is called as follows.

Usage

```
int filedes[2], retval;

retval = pipe(filedes);
```

`filedes` is a two-integer array that will hold the file descriptors that will identify the pipe. If the call is successful, `filedes[0]` will be open for reading from the pipe and `filedes[1]` will be open for writing down it.

`pipe` can fail and so return −1. This can happen if the call would cause more file descriptors to be opened than the per process limit (in which case `errno` will contain `EMFILE`), or if the kernel's open file table would overflow (`errno` would then contain `ENFILE`).

Once created, a pipe can be straightforwardly manipulated with `read` and `write`. The following example shows this; it creates a pipe, writes three messages down it, then reads them back:

```
/*first pipe example*/
#include <stdio.h>

/*this figure includes terminating null*/
#define MSGSIZE 16

char *msg1 = "hello, world #1";
char *msg2 = "hello, world #2";
char *msg3 = "hello, world #3";

main()
{
        char inbuf[MSGSIZE];
        int p[2], j;

        /*open pipe*/
        if(pipe(p) < 0){
                perror("pipe call");
                exit(1);
        }

        /*write down pipe*/
        write(p[1], msg1, MSGSIZE);
        write(p[1], msg2, MSGSIZE);
        write(p[1], msg3, MSGSIZE);

        /*read from pipe*/
        for(j = 0; j < 3; j++){
                read(p[0], inbuf, MSGSIZE);
                printf("%s\n", inbuf);
        }

        exit(0);
}
```

The output from this program is

```
hello, world #1
hello, world #2
hello, world #3
```

Notice the way the messages are read in the order in which they were written. Pipes treat data on a *first-in first-out* or *FIFO* basis. In other words, what you place first into a pipe is what is read first at the other end. This order cannot be altered since `lseek` will not work on a pipe.

Although we do so in the example, a process does not have to read from a pipe in the same size chunks as the pipe was written. A pipe could, for example, be written in 512-byte blocks and then read a character at a time, just like an ordinary file. There are advantages in using fixed sized chunks however, as we see in Section 6.4.

The action of the example is shown pictorially in Figure 6.1. This diagram should make it clear that the process is just sending data to itself using the pipe as a kind of loop-back mechanism. This may seem a little pointless, since the process is only talking to itself. A pipe's true value only becomes apparent when it is used in conjunction with the `fork` system call, where the fact that file descriptors remain open across a `fork` can be exploited. The next example shows this. It creates a pipe, and calls `fork`. The parent process then writes a series of messages down to the child.

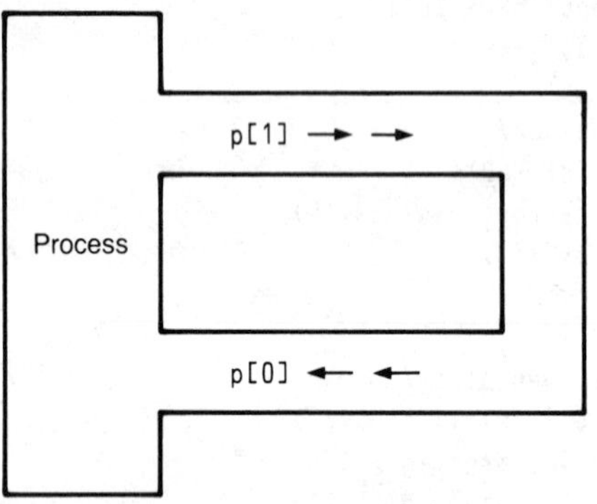

Figure 6.1 First pipe example.

```
/*second pipe example*/
#include <stdio.h>

#define MSGSIZE 16

char *msg1 = "hello, world #1";
char *msg2 = "hello, world #2";
char *msg3 = "hello, world #3";

main()
{
        char inbuf[MSGSIZE];
        int p[2], j, pid;

        /*open pipe*/
        if(pipe(p) < 0){
```

```
                perror("pipe call");
                exit(1);
        }


        if((pid = fork()) < 0){
                perror("fork call");
                exit(2);
        }

        /*if parent then write down pipe*/
        if(pid > 0){
                write(p[1], msg1, MSGSIZE);
                write(p[1], msg2, MSGSIZE);
                write(p[1], msg3, MSGSIZE);
                wait((int *)0);
        }

        /*if child then read from pipe*/
        if(pid == 0){
                for(j = 0; j < 3; j++){
                        read(p[0], inbuf, MSGSIZE);
                        printf("%s\n", inbuf);
                }
        }

        exit(0);
}
```

This example is represented in diagram form in Figure 6.2. It shows how the pipe now connects two processes. As you can see, both parent and child have two open file descriptors, allowing reading and writing on the pipe. So, either process could write down file descriptor `p[1]` and read from file descriptor `p[2]`. There is a problem here. Pipes are intended to be used as unidirectional communication channels. If both processes do freely read and write on the pipe at the same time, confusion will result. To avoid this, it is customary for each process to either just read or just write the pipe and close down the file descriptor it does not need. As a positive side-effect, this also saves one valuable file descriptor per process. In fact, a program really has to do this to avoid problems when the sending process closes its write end – Section 6.3.4 explains why. The examples shown so far only work because the receiving processes know exactly how much data to expect. The next example shows the finished solution:

```
/*third pipe example*/
#include <stdio.h>


#define MSGSIZE 16
```

```
char *msg1 = "hello, world #1";
char *msg2 = "hello, world #2";
char *msg3 = "hello, world #3";

main()
{
        char inbuf[MSGSIZE];
        int p[2], j, pid;

        /*open pipe*/
        if(pipe(p) < 0){
                perror("pipe call");
                exit(1);
        }



        if((pid = fork()) < 0){
                perror("fork call");
                exit(2);
        }

        /*if parent then close read file
         *descriptor and write down pipe
         */
        if(pid > 0){

                close(p[0]);
                write(p[1], msg1, MSGSIZE);
                write(p[1], msg2, MSGSIZE);
                write(p[1], msg3, MSGSIZE);
                wait((int *)0);
        }

        /*if child then close write file
         *descriptor and read from pipe
         */
        if(pid == 0){

                close(p[1]);
                for(j = 0; j < 3; j++){
                        read(p[0], inbuf, MSGSIZE);
                        printf("%s\n", inbuf);
                }
        }

        exit(0);
}
```

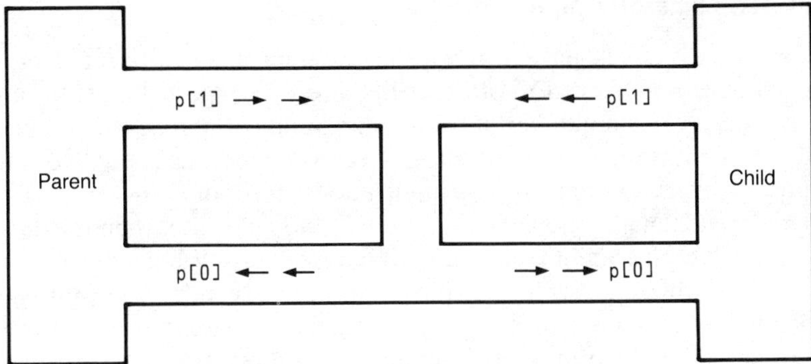

Figure 6.2 Second pipe example.

The end result is a one-way pathway between parent and child. This simplified situation is shown in Figure 6.3.

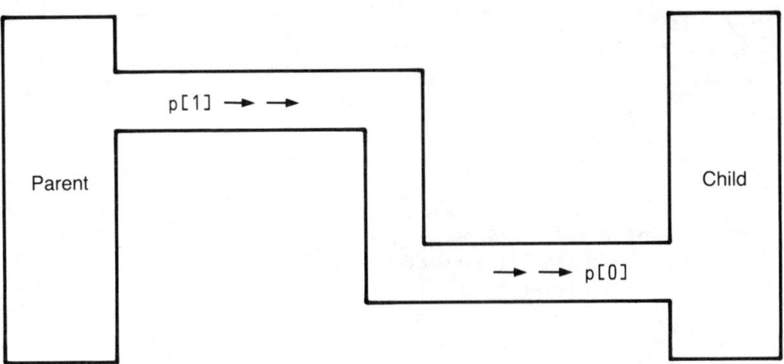

Figure 6.3 Third pipe example.

Exercise 6.6 In the last example, a pipe was used to establish a link between a parent and a child process. In fact, a pipe's file descriptors can be passed across several calls to `fork`. This means that more than one process can read the pipe, and more than one process can write the pipe. To demonstrate this, write a program that creates three processes, two that write down the pipe and one that reads from the pipe. Make the reading process print any messages it receives on its standard output.

Exercise 6.7 To establish two-way communications between processes, two pipes operating in different directions are necessary. Devise a possible conversation between two processes and implement it using pipes in this way.

6.3.3 The size of a pipe

So far our examples have transmitted only small amounts of data. In practice, it is important to note that the size of a pipe is finite. In other words, only a certain number of bytes can remain in the pipe without being read. The limit is typically 5120 bytes. Although generous enough for most purposes, this maximum size has implications for both `write` and `read`.

If a `write` is made on a pipe and there is enough space, then the data is sent down the pipe and the call returns immediately. If however a `write` is made that would overfill the pipe, process execution is (normally) suspended until room is made by another process reading from the pipe.

As an example, the next program writes down a pipe character by character until the `write` call blocks. It uses `alarm` to prevent the process waiting too long after `write` blocks for a `read` that will never happen.

```
/*write down a pipe until we get blocked*/

#include <signal.h>

int count;
int alrm_action();

main()
{
        int p[2];
        char c = 'x';

        if(pipe(p) < 0){
                perror("pipe call");
                exit(1);
        }

        signal(SIGALRM, alrm_action);

        for(count = 0;;){

                /*set alarm*/
                alarm(20);

                /*write down pipe*/
                write(p[1], &c, 1);

                /*reset alarm*/
                alarm(0);

                if((++count % 1024) == 0)
                        printf("%d characters in pipe\n", count);
        }
}
```

```
/*called when SIGALRM received*/
alrm_action()
{
        printf("write blocked after %d characters\n", count);
        exit(0);
}
```

On many systems, this will produce the following output:

```
1024 characters in pipe
2048 characters in pipe
3072 characters in pipe
4096 characters in pipe
5120 characters in pipe
write blocked after 5120 characters
```

Things get a little more complicated when a process attempts a single `write` of more data than the pipe can hold even when empty. In this case, the kernel will first write as much as it can into the pipe. It then suspends execution of the process until room becomes available for the rest of the data. This is important; normally a `write` on a pipe will execute **atomically**, all the data being transferred in a single, uninterrupted kernel operation. If a `write` of more data than the pipe can hold is made, the `write` has to be performed in stages. If several concurrent processes were writing the same pipe in this way, data could get confusingly intermingled.

The interaction of `read` and pipes is simpler. When a `read` call is made, the system checks whether the pipe is empty. If it is empty, the `read` will (normally) block until data is written into the pipe by another process. If there is data waiting in the pipe, then the `read` returns, even if there is less data than the amount requested.

6.3.4 Closing down pipes

What happens if the file descriptor that represents one end of a pipe is closed? There are two cases:

1. *Closing the write-only file descriptor* If there are other processes that still have the pipe open for writing, then nothing will happen. However, if there are no more processes capable of writing to the pipe and the pipe is empty, any processes that attempt to read from the pipe will return no data. Processes that were asleep waiting to read from the pipe will be woken up, their `read` calls again returning zero. The effect for the reading processes is therefore much like reaching the end of an ordinary file.
2. *Closing the read-only file descriptor* If there are still processes that have the pipe open for reading, then again nothing will happen. If no other process is reading the pipe, however, all processes waiting to

write to the pipe are sent the signal SIGPIPE by the kernel. If this signal is not caught, a process will terminate. If it is caught then, after the interrupt routine has completed, write will return −1 and errno will contain EPIPE. Processes that attempt to write to the pipe later will also be sent SIGPIPE.

6.3.5 Non-blocking reads and writes

As we have seen both read and write can block when used on a pipe. Sometimes this isn't desirable. You may want a program, for example, to execute an error routine, or maybe poll through several pipes until it receives data through one of them. Luckily, there are two ways of making sure that a read or write on a pipe won't hang.

The first method is to use fstat on the pipe. The st_size field in the returned stat structure gives the number of characters currently in the pipe. If only one process is reading the pipe, this is fine. However, if several processes are reading the pipe, another process could read from a pipe in the gap between an fstat and read.

The second method is to use fcntl (again!). Among its many roles, it allows a process to set the O_NDELAY flag for a file descriptor. This stops a future read or write on a pipe from blocking. In this context, fcntl can be used as follows:

```
#include <fcntl.h>
  .
  .
  .
if(fcntl(filedes, F_SETFL, O_NDELAY) < 0)
        perror("fcntl");
```

If filedes was the write-only file descriptor for a pipe, then future calls to write would never block if the pipe was full. They would instead return a value of 0 immediately. Similarly, if filedes represented the reading end of a pipe, then the process would immediately return a value of 0 if there was no data in the pipe, rather than sleeping. This situation is actually a pity. In the case of read, it means there is no general way of distinguishing between a pipe which is simply empty, or one where the write end has been closed down. This anomaly is well known; the *SVID* states that, sometime in the future, read will be adjusted so that it returns −1, and places EAGAIN into errno, if a non-blocking read is made on an empty pipe which still has a write end. Similarly, write will be altered so that it returns −1 and places EAGAIN into errno if the pipe is full. Some authorities recommend that you allow for both return values (that is, 0 and −1) in your programs.

The following program demonstrates this variation on the fcntl theme. It creates a pipe, sets the O_NDELAY flag for the read file descriptor, then forks. The child process sends messages to the parent, which sits in a loop polling the pipe to see if any data has arrived. Notice the use of special message to terminate the conversation. As we saw above, a process has no way to distinguish between a pipe which is simply empty, and one where the write end has been closed. The message solves this problem.

```
/*O_NDELAY example*/

#include <fcntl.h>

#define MSGSIZE 6

char *msg1 = "hello";
char *msg2 = "bye!!";

main()
{
     int pfd[2];

     /*open pipe*/
     if(pipe(pfd) < 0)
         fatal("pipe call");

     /*set O_NDELAY flag for p[0]*/
     if(fcntl(pfd[0], F_SETFL, O_NDELAY) < 0)
         fatal("fcntl call");

     switch(fork()){
       case -1:          /*error*/
         fatal("fork call");
       case 0:           /*child*/
          child(pfd);
       default:          /*parent*/
          parent(pfd);
     }
}

parent(p)      /*code for parent*/
int p[2];
{
     int nread;
     char buf[MSGSIZE];

     close(p[1]);

     for(;;){
         switch(nread = read(p[0], buf, MSGSIZE)){
           case -1:
             fatal("read call");
           case 0:
```

```
                printf("(pipe empty)\n");
                sleep(1);
                break;
              default:
                if(strcmp(buf, msg2) == 0){
                   printf("End of conversation\n");
                   exit(0);
                }else
                    printf("MSG=%s\n", buf);
            }
        }
}


child(p)      /*code for child*/
int p[2];
{
        int count;

        close(p[0]);

        for(count = 0; count < 3; count++){
            write(p[1], msg1, MSGSIZE);
            sleep(3);
        }

        /*send final message*/
        write(p[1], msg2, MSGSIZE);
        exit(0);
}
```

The example makes use of an error routine called `fatal`. We introduced this in the previous chapter. To save you looking back, it is implemented as follows:

```
fatal(s) /*print error message and die*/
char *s;
{
        perror(s);
        exit(1);
}
```

The output of the example isn't entirely predictable since the number of 'pipe empty' messages may vary. On one machine however it produced:

```
(pipe empty)
MSG=hello
(pipe empty)
(pipe empty)
(pipe empty)
```

```
MSG=hello
(pipe empty)
(pipe empty)
(pipe empty)
MSG=hello
(pipe empty)
(pipe empty)
(pipe empty)
End of conversation
```

6.3.6 Pipes and the `exec` system call

Remember how a pipe can be set up between two programs at shell level:

```
$ ls | wc
```

How is this achieved? The answer has two parts: first, the shell takes advantage of the fact that open file descriptors are kept open (by default) across `exec` calls. This means that two pipe file descriptors opened prior to a `fork/exec` combination will still be open when the child process begins execution of the new program. Second, before invoking `exec`, the shell couples the standard output of `ls` to the write end of the pipe, and the standard input of `wc` to the read end. This can be done either by using `fcntl` in the way introduced in Exercise 5.10, or, more traditionally, with the `dup` call. `dup` is called as follows:

```
dup(filedes);
```

If successful, it returns a new file descriptor that refers to the same open file as `filedes`. The new file descriptor is the lowest number available. Since standard input, standard output and standard error have values 0, 1 and 2, respectively, a programmer could, for example, couple standard output to another file descriptor as follows (assuming standard input is open):

```
/*close down standard output*/
close(1);

/*dup will now return "1"*/
dup(filedes);
 .
 .
 .
/*program will now write its standard output*/
/*to the file referred to by fildes         */
 .
 .
 .
```

Our next example, `join`, shows the piping mechanism employed by the shell in simplified form. `join` takes two parameters, `com1` and `com2`, each of which describes a command to be run. Both parameters are actually arrays of character pointers that will be passed to `execvp`. `join` will run both programs and pipe the standard output of `com1` into the standard input of `com2`. The action of `join` can be described in pseudo-code form (excluding error-handling) as follows:

```
process forks, parent waits for child
and child continues

child creates a pipe

then forks again

In child created by second fork:
  standard output is coupled to
  write end of pipe using dup

  excess file descriptors are closed

  program described by com1 is exec'ed

In child of first fork:
  standard input is coupled to
  read end of pipe using dup

  excess file descriptors are closed

  program described by com2 is exec'ed
```

The actual implementation of `join` is as follows; again, it uses `fatal`:

```
/*join --  join two commands by pipe*/
int join(com1, com2)
char *com1[], *com2[];
{

     int p[2], status;

     /*create child to run commands*/
     switch(fork()){
       case -1:        /*error*/
          fatal("1st fork call in join");
       case 0:         /*child*/
          break;
       default:        /*parent*/
          wait(&status);
          return(status);
     }

     /*remainder of routine executed by child*/
```

```
        /*make pipe*/
        if(pipe(p) < 0)
            fatal("pipe call in join");

        /*create another process*/
        switch(fork()){
          case -1:        /*error*/

            fatal("2nd fork call in join");

         case 0:

            close(1);     /*close current std. output*/
            dup(p[1]);    /*make std. output go to pipe*/

            close(p[0]); /*save file descriptors*/
            close(p[1]);

            execvp(com1[0], com1);

            /*if execvp returns, error has occurred*/
            fatal("1st execvp call in join");

          default:

            close(0);     /*close current std. input*/
            dup(p[0]);    /*make std. input come from pipe*/

            close(p[0]);
            close(p[1]);
            execvp(com2[0], com2);
            fatal("2nd execvp call in join");
        }
    }
```

This routine can be invoked along the following lines:

```
    main()
    {
        char *one[4], *two[3];
        int ret;

        one[0] = "ls";
        one[1] = "-l";
        one[2] = "/usr/lib";
        one[3] = (char *)0;

        two[0] = "grep";
        two[1] = "^d";
        two[2] = (char *)0;
```

```
        ret = join(one, two);
        printf("join returned %d\n", ret);
        exit(0);
}
```

Exercise 6.8 How can the technique shown in `join` be generalized to couple more than two commands in a pipe line?

Exercise 6.9 Incorporate pipes into the `smallsh` command processor introduced in the previous chapter.

Exercise 6.10 Devise a method where a process creates a child to run a single program, the parent reading the standard output of the child through a pipe. It is worth noting that this idea underlies the `popen` and `pclose` routines which form part of the *Standard I/O Library*. `popen` and `pclose` relieve the programmer of much of the clerical detail of coordinating `fork`, `exec`, `close` and `dup`. We will discuss them further in Chapter 9.

6.4 FIFOs or named pipes

Pipes are an elegant and powerful interprocess communication mechanism. However, they have several serious drawbacks.

Firstly, and most seriously, pipes can only be used to connect processes that share a common ancestry, such as a parent process and its child. This drawback becomes apparent when trying to develop a 'server' program that remains permanently in existence in order to provide a system-wide service. Examples include network control servers and printer spoolers. Ideally, client processes should be able to come into being, communicate with a unrelated server process via a pipe and then go away again. Unfortunately, this cannot be done using conventional pipes.

Secondly, pipes cannot be permanent. They have to be created every time they are needed and they are destroyed when the processes accessing them terminate.

To address these deficiencies, a variant of the pipe was introduced with the release of UNIX System III. This new(ish) interprocess communication mechanism is called the **FIFO** or **named pipe**. As far as `read` and `write` are concerned, FIFOs are identical to pipes, acting as one-way, first-in-first-out communications channels between processes. Indeed, FIFOs and pipes share a great deal of common code at kernel level. Unlike a pipe, however, a FIFO is a permanent fixture and is given a UNIX file name. A FIFO also has an owner, a size and associated access permissions. It can be opened, closed and deleted like any other UNIX file, but displays properties identical to pipes when read or written.

Let us take a look at the use of FIFOs at command level before examining the programming interface. The command `mknod` is used to create a FIFO:

```
$ /etc/mknod channel p
```

Here `channel` is the name of the FIFO (it could be replaced with any valid UNIX pathname). The second argument *p* tells `mknod` to create a FIFO. It is needed since `mknod` is also used to create the special files which represent devices.

A newly created FIFO can be identified with the `ls` command in the following way:

```
$ ls -l channel
prw-rw-r--    1 ben    usr         0 Aug  1 21:05 channel
```

The letter `p` in the first column of the listing indicates that channel is a file of type FIFO. Notice how `channel` has access permissions (read/write for the owner and the owner's group, read only for everyone else); an owner and a group owner (`ben`, `usr`); a size (0 bytes, i.e. currently empty) and a creation date.

This FIFO can be read and written using standard UNIX commands, for example:

```
$ cat < channel
```

If this command was executed just after *channel* had been created it would 'hang'. This is because, by default, a process opening a FIFO for reading will block until another process attempts to open the FIFO for writing. Similarly, a process attempting to open a FIFO for writing will block until a process attempts to open it for reading. This is entirely sensible, since it saves system resources and makes program coordination simpler. As a consequence, if we wanted to create a reader and a writer for our last example we would have to execute one of the processes in the background, for example:

```
$ cat < channel &
102
$ ls -l > channel; wait
total 17
prw-rw-r--    1 ben      usr            0 Aug  1 21:05 channel
-rw-rw-r--    1 ben      usr            0 Aug  1 21:06 f
-rw-rw-r--    1 ben      usr          937 Jul 21 22:30 fifos
-rw-rw-r--    1 ben      usr         7152 Jul 21 22:11 pipes.cont
$
```

Let us analyse this further. The listing of the directory is initially produced by `ls` and then written down the FIFO. The waiting `cat` command then reads data from the FIFO and displays it onto the screen. The process running `cat` now exits. This is because, when a FIFO is no longer open for writing, a read on it will return 0 just like a normal pipe, which cat takes to mean end of file. The wait command, by the way, causes the shell to wait until cat exits before redisplaying the prompt.

6.4.1 Programming with FIFOs

For the most part programming with FIFOs is identical to programming with ordinary pipes. The only significant difference is in initialization. Instead of using pipe, a FIFO is instead created with mknod, which we first met in Chapter 4. A value of octal 010000 must be added to the mode value to signify a FIFO. So, for example, the code fragment

```
if(mknod("fifo", 010600, 0) < 0)
        perror("mknod (fifo) call");
```

creates a FIFO called fifo which has permissions of 0600 and is therefore readable and writable by the FIFO owner. (Note that, rather like S_IFDIR, the header file stat.h defines the symbolic constant S_IFIFO to stand for 010000. Using this to create a FIFO will make your program both more readable and more reliable. Unfortunately, it is not defined in the *SVID*.)

Once created, a FIFO must be opened using open. So, for example, the call

```
#include <fcntl.h>
  .
  .
  .
fd = open("fifo", O_WRONLY);
```

opens a FIFO for writing. As we saw in the previous section, this call will block until another process opens the FIFO for reading (of course if the FIFO was already open for reading, our open call will return immediately).

Non-blocking open calls on a FIFO are possible. To achieve this the open call must be made with the O_NDELAY flag (which is defined in fcntl.h) bitwise ORed with one of O_RDONLY, O_WRONLY and O_RDWR. For example:

```
if((fd = open("fifo", O_RDONLY|O_NDELAY)) < 0)
        perror("open on fifo");
```

If no process has the FIFO open for writing, then this open will return −1 instead of blocking and errno will contain ENXIO. If, on the other hand, the open was successful, future read calls on the FIFO will also be non-blocking.

It is time for an example. We will introduce two programs that show how a FIFO can be used to implement a message system. They exploit the fact that read and write calls on a FIFO or any other sort of pipe are atomic. If fixed-size messages are passed through a FIFO, individual messages will remain intact when read, even when several processes are concurrently writing the pipe.

We will look first at sendmsg which sends individual messages to a FIFO named fifo. It is called as follows:

```
$ sendmsg "message text 1" "message text 2"
```

Notice how each message is enclosed in quotes and so counts as one long argument. If this isn't done, then each word will be treated as a separate message. The code for `sendmsg` follows:

```
/*sendmsg -- send messages via FIFO*/

#include <fcntl.h>
#include <stdio.h>
#include <errno.h>
#define MSGSIZ 63

extern int errno;
char *fifo = "fifo";

main(argc, argv)
int argc;
char *argv[];
{
     int fd, j, nwrite;
     char msgbuf[MSGSIZ+1];

     if(argc < 2){
          fprintf(stderr, "Usage:sendmsg msg ...\n");
          exit(1);
     }

     /*open fifo with O_NDELAY set*/
     if((fd = open(fifo, O_WRONLY|O_NDELAY)) < 0)
          fatal("fifo open failed");

     /*send messages*/
     for(j = 1; j < argc; j++){

          if(strlen(argv[j]) > MSGSIZ){
               fprintf(stderr, "message too long %s\n", argv[j]);
               continue;
          }

          strcpy(msgbuf, argv[j]);

          if((nwrite = write(fd, msgbuf, MSGSIZ+1)) <= 0){

               if(nwrite == 0)          /*full FIFO    */
                    errno = EAGAIN;     /*so fake error*/
               fatal("message write failed");
          }
     }
     exit(0);
}
```

Again we make use of our error routine `fatal`. Messages are sent as 64-character chunks, via a non-blocking `write` call. The actual message text is restricted to 63 characters to allow for a trailing null character. Notice how a return value of zero from `write`, indicating a full pipe, is treated; `errno` is forced to take the value `EAGAIN` before `fatal` is called.

The program that receives the messages by reading the FIFO is called `rcvmsg`. It does nothing useful, and is intended just to serve as a basic framework.

```
/*rcvmsg -- receive message via fifo*/

#include <fcntl.h>
#include <stdio.h>
#define MSGSIZ 63

char *fifo = "fifo";

main(argc, argv)
int argc;
char *argv[];
{
	int fd;
	char msgbuf[MSGSIZ+1];


	/*open fifo for reading and writing*/
	if((fd = open(fifo, O_RDWR)) < 0)
		fatal("fifo open failed");

	/*receive messages*/
	for(;;){

		if(read(fd, msgbuf, MSGSIZ+1) <0)
			fatal("message read failed");

		/*
		 *print out message, in real life
		 *something more interesting would
		 *be done
		 */

		printf("message received:%s\n", msgbuf);
	}
}
```

Notice how the FIFO is opened for reading and writing (via the `O_RDWR` flag). To understand why this is done, suppose the FIFO was opened with just `O_RDONLY`. The program would first block at the `open` call. As soon as an invocation of `sendmsg` opened the FIFO for writing, the `open` call would return; `rcvmsg` would then read through each message sent. However, when the FIFO was empty, and the `sendmsg` process had vanished, `read` would start to return 0 immediately it was called, because no process would have the FIFO open for writing. The program would therefore enter an unnecessary loop. Using `O_RDWR` makes sure that at least one process, i.e. the invocation of `rcvmsg` itself, has the FIFO open for writing. As a result, the `read` call will always block until data is actually written to the FIFO.

The following dialogue shows how these programs can be used. Since neither program creates the FIFO, the first step in the dialogue is to do just this using `mknod`. `rcvmsg` is then placed into the background to receive messages from different invocations of `sendmsg`.

```
$ mknod fifo p
$ rcvmsg&
40
$ sendmsg "message 1" "message 2"
message received:message 1
message received:message 2
$ sendmsg "message number 3"
message received:message number 3
```

Exercise 6.11 `sendmsg` and `rcvmsg` form the basis of a simple spooling system. The messages sent to `rcvmsg` could, for example, be the names of files which are to be processed in some way. The problem here is that the current directories of `sendmsg` and `rcvmsg` may be different and so relative pathnames will be misinterpreted. How could you solve this problem? Is use of a FIFO alone adequate for, say, a printer spooler on a large system?

Exercise 6.12 If `rcvmsg` was replaced by a true server program, we would normally want to make sure that only one copy of the server was running at any one time. There are several ways of doing this. Perhaps the most usual method involves the creation of a lock file. Consider the following routine:

```
#include <errno.h>
#include <fcntl.h>

extern int errno;
char *lck = "/tmp/lockfile";

makelock()
{
      int fd;
      if((fd = open(lck, O_RDWR|O_CREAT|O_EXCL, 0600)) < 0){
          if (errno == EEXIST)
              exit(1);     /*someone else has got in*/
          else
              exit(127);  /*unexpected error*/
      }
```

```
    /*lock created if we get here, so return*/
    close(fd);
    return(0);
}
```

This uses the fact that the `open` call will be done atomically. So, if several processes race to execute `makelock`, one will get there first, create the lock file, and so 'lock' out the rest. Add this routine to `sendmsg`. Make sure that, when killed with `SIGHUP` or `SIGTERM`, `sendmsg` removes the lock file before exiting. Why do you think we used `open` rather than `creat` in `makelock`?

Chapter 7 Interprocess Communications: 2

7.1 Introduction

The interprocess communication facilities we examined in Chapter 6 have been, for the most part, available in UNIX for many years. With System V.2, AT&T introduced some novel features in this area, and these have been incorporated in the AT&T *System V Interface Definition*.

The first and most straightforward topic is **record locking**. This is not really a form of direct process communication, more a method of process cooperation. (Indeed, we originally intended to discuss record locking in one of the chapters on the file structure. On reflection it fits far more easily here.) It allows a process to temporarily reserve part of a file for its own exclusive use, thus resolving some difficult problems in database management. Historically, 'standard' UNIX has been deficient in this area and many of the first commercial UNIX variants contained their own, *ad hoc* locking calls. This diversity of approaches has presented portability problems for software developers. However, because of the UNIX system's increasing commercial importance, the *SVID* now defines a variety of operations for record locking.

The other new interprocess communication mechanisms in System V are rather more exotic, and are regarded in the *SVID* as an extension to System V's basic facilities. They may not be found in all System V implementations. Generically, these new features are described as **IPC facilities** (where *IPC* stands for *interprocess communication*). This single descriptive term emphasizes similarities in structure and usage, although there are three distinct types of facility gathered under this heading, namely:

1. *Message passing* The message passing facility allows a process to send and receive messages; a message being in essence an arbitrary sequence of bytes or characters.
2. *Semaphores* Compared with message passing, semaphores provide a rather low-level means for process synchronization, not suited to the transmission of large amounts of information. They have their theoretical origin in work by E. W. Dijkstra (*Cooperating Sequential Processes*, Programming Languages, Academic Press, New York, 1968.)

3. *Shared memory* This final IPC facility allows two or more processes to share the data contained in specific memory segments. Usually, of course, the data area of a process is private to itself. It is probably the fastest of the IPC mechanisms, but needs some hardware support.

7.2 Record locking

7.2.1 Motivation

As a first step, it is worth pursuing a simple example to demonstrate why record locking is essential in some situations.

Our example concerns that well known corporation, *ACME Airlines*, who use a UNIX computer for their booking system. They have two booking offices, called A and B, each of which has its own terminal connected to the airline's computer. The booking clerks use a program called `acmebook` to access the bookings database, which is implemented as an ordinary UNIX file. This program allows the user to read and update the database. In particular, a booking clerk can decrement by one the number of free seats for a particular flight, signifying that a booking has been made.

Now suppose that on flight ACM501 to London just one free seat remains, and that Ms Jones enters office A at the same time as Mr Smith enters office B. Both ask for a seat on flight ACM501. The following series of events is then entirely possible:

1. The clerk at office A starts `acmebook`. Let's call the resultant process *PA*.
2. Immediately afterwards, the clerk at office B starts up another copy of `acmebook`. We shall call this process *PB*.
3. Process *PA* now reads the relevant part of the database using the `read` system call. It discovers that there is one seat available.
4. Process *PB* reads the database just after *PA*. It too discovers that there is one seat left on ACM501.
5. Process *PA* then sets the free seat count for the flight to zero by using the `write` system call to change the relevant part of the database. The clerk at office A gives a ticket to Ms Jones.
6. Immediately afterwards process *PB* also writes to the database, again inserting zero for the free seat count. This time however the value is erroneous; if anything it should be −1. The point to emphasize here is that although *PA* has already updated the database, *PB* has no way of knowing this and presses on as if a seat was still available. As a consequence Mr Smith also receives a ticket and the flight is overbooked.

The problem arises because a UNIX file may be accessed by any number of processes simultaneously. A logical operation which is made up of several calls to `lseek`, `read` and `write` can be performed by two or more processes concurrently and, as we saw in our simple example, this can have disastrous consequences.

One solution is to allow a process to lock the part of the file it is working on. The lock, which doesn't alter the file contents in any way, serves as an indication to other processes that the data in question is in use. It prevents another process from interfering during a series of discrete physical operations which form one logical action or transaction. This type of mechanism is often called **record locking**, where record just refers to an arbitrary subsection of a file. To make things absolutely secure, the locking operation itself must be atomic, so that it cannot overlap with a conflicting locking attempt in another process.

In order for locking to work, it must be performed in some centralized way. Perhaps the best way is to let the kernel take care of locking, although a user process acting as a database agent could, with care, serve the same purpose. Earlier AT&T versions of UNIX (earlier meaning before System V Version 2.00 and the *SVID*) lacked any type of kernel-based record locking. This was a reflection of UNIX's academic origins, since record locking is most often needed in commercial database software. Now, however, kernel-based record locking can be performed via two calls: `lockf` and our old friend `fcntl`.

`lockf` first appeared in commercial variants of UNIX (and was known in its earliest incarnations as `locking`). Because of its popularity, `lockf` was adopted by the Standards Committee of the UNIX user group /usr/group. Although independent, this group has influenced AT&T in the evolution of the current System V standard. The more general facilities provided by `fcntl` owe their origin to AT&T.

7.2.2 The `lockf` call

Usage

```
#include <unistd.h>

int filedes, purpose, status;
long recsize;
  .
  .
  .
status = lockf(filedes, purpose, recsize);
```

`lockf` is the simplest mechanism for record locking defined in the *SVID*. According to *Issue 2* of the *SVID*, the locking performed by `lockf` (and indeed `fcntl`) is *advisory* only. This means that, file permissions allowing, a process can write to a part of a file which is supposedly locked. This may seem to negate the idea of locking, but if two processes explicitly cooperate by using lockf or fcntl, the desired effect will be obtained. *Mandatory* locking, which would cause such a write to fail, will be added to the *SVID* in the future (and will be available in UNIX System V.3).

lockf's first argument filedes must be an open file descriptor; it identifies the file on which the lock is to be made, and must have been opened using O_WRONLY or O_RDWR.

The purpose argument decides what lockf will actually do. Its allowed values are defined in the file unistd.h (taken from the /usr/group standard) along the following lines:

```
#define F_ULOCK 0   /*Unlock a locked record          */
#define F_LOCK  1   /*lock a record for exclusive use*/
#define F_TLOCK 2   /*test for lock, lock if none     */
#define F_TEST  3   /*test for existing lock only     */
```

lockf's last parameter, recsize, gives the length of the section to be locked, unlocked or simply tested. The section starts at the current position of the file's read-write pointer. For this reason, a call to lockf will often be preceded by a call to lseek. If recsize is negative then the record is considered to extend backwards (a zero value for recsize has a special meaning, but we will discuss this later).

The F_LOCK request

If lockf is called with purpose set to F_LOCK, the system will attempt to lock the file section defined by the file's read-write pointer and recsize. For example,

```
lockf(fdes, F_LOCK, 512L);
```

will lock 512 bytes, starting from the current position of the read-write pointer. The locked section is regarded as being 'reserved' for the exclusive use of the process. The lock information itself is placed into a free slot in a system-maintained table of locks. To save space in this table, if the new lock overlaps locks previously applied by the process, then all relevant locks will be combined into a single entry. This also occurs for immediately adjacent locks (that old-fashioned word 'contiguous' would be better here).

If all or part of the specified section has already been locked by another process, the calling process will sleep until the whole section becomes available. Sleeping in this way can be interrupted by a signal; in particular alarm can be invoked to provide a timeout. If the sleeping process isn't interrupted, and the section does eventually become free, then the lock will be applied and lockf will return 0. If an error occurs, for example if lockf is passed a bad file descriptor or the system lock table is full, then −1 is returned.

The next example program, lockit, opens a file locktest (which must already exist) and locks the first ten bytes with lockf. It then forks; the child attempts to lock the first five bytes; meanwhile, the parent sleeps for five seconds, then exits. At this point, the system automatically releases the parent's lock.

```
/*lockit -- demonstration of lockf call*/

#include <fcntl.h>
#include <unistd.h>

main()
{
      int fd;

      /*open file*/
      fd = open("locktest", O_RDWR);

      /*lock first ten bytes*/
      lockf(fd, F_LOCK, 10L);
      printf("parent:locked record\n");

      if(fork() == 0){

            lockf(fd, F_LOCK, 5L);
            printf("child: locked\n");
            printf("child: exiting\n");
            exit(0);
      }


      sleep(5);

      /*now exit, which releases lock*/
      printf("parent:exiting\n");
      exit(0);

}
```

The actual output produced by lockit will look something like

```
parent:locked record
parent:exiting
child: locked
child: exiting
```

Notice the order in which the messages are displayed. It shows that the child process could not apply the desired lock until the parent had exited and released its lock, otherwise the "child: locked" message would appear second, not third. This example also shows that the lock made by the parent affected the child, even though the sections used by each were not identical. In other words, a lock attempt will fail even if the section only partially overlaps an already locked section. The program illustrates several other interesting points: first, lock information is not inherited across `fork` calls; the child and parent processes in our example are independent as far as locking goes. Second, a call to `lockf` does not alter the file's read-write pointer. Throughout the execution of both child and parent, this pointed to the beginning of the file. Third, all locks belonging to a process are removed automatically when the process dies.

The `F_ULOCK` option

`F_ULOCK` unlocks a section previously locked by the calling process. It will usually be used some while after a previous `F_LOCK` or `F_TLOCK` request. If there are any other processes waiting to lock the section which has been released, then one of these will be restarted.

If the section to be unlocked happens to lie in the middle of a larger locked section of the file, then the system will create two smaller locks that exclude the section to be unlocked. This means that an extra slot in the system lock table is taken up. As a consequence, an `F_ULOCK` request can fail, somewhat counter-intuitively, because the system lock table is full.

The *ACME Airlines* problem revisited

Taken together, the `F_LOCK` and `F_ULOCK` requests provide a solution to the contention problem we encountered in our *ACME Airlines* example. To ensure the integrity of the database, we simply need to bracket the critical section of code in the `acmebook` between an `F_LOCK` and an `F_ULOCK` request, as follows:

```
lock database section with F_LOCK

update database section

unlock database section with F_ULOCK
```

Providing no other program bypasses the locking mechanism, the `F_LOCK` request ensures the calling process has exclusive access to the crucial part of the database when it needs it. The closing `F_ULOCK` request makes the area again available for public use. Any competing copy of `acmebook` that attempts to access the relevant part of the database while it is locked will be put to sleep as soon as it makes its own `F_LOCK` request.

The actual code might look like:

```
/*skeleton of acmebook update routine*/

/*seek to start of record*/
lseek(fd, recstart, 0);
```

```
/*lock record, will sleep here if*/
/*record already locked         */
if(lockf(fd, F_LOCK, RECSIZE) < 0)
        fatal("lock failed");

/*code to examine and update bookings data*/
.
.
.
/*now free record for use by another process*/
lseek(fd, recstart, 0);
lockf(fd, F_ULOCK, RECSIZE);
```

The F_TEST request

F_TEST is used to detect if a section is already locked by another process. Again, the section is identified by the current position in the file and the value of the recsize parameter. If no lock exists, lockf returns 0. If a lock does exist, then lockf returns −1 and the external error variable errno will contain the error EACCES. For example,

```
#include <unistd.h>
#include <stdio.h>
#include <errno.h>

extern int errno;
 .
 .
 .

if(lockf(fd, F_TEST, 10L) == -1){
        if(errno == EACCES)
                fprintf(stderr, "record locked\n");
        else
                perror("unexpected lockf error");
}
```

Two words of warning: first, do *not* use constructions of the following kind:

```
/*See if record locked. If not write to it.*/

if(lockf(fd, F_TEST, somevalue) == 0)
      write(fd, buf, somevalue);        /*WRONG!!*/
```

This operation is not indivisible, and it would be possible for another process to apply a lock between the invocations of lockf and write. The only safe way to use locking to protect data is to make sure all processes explicitly lock a section before writing to it.

Second, it is planned to change lockf (and fcntl) so that EAGAIN is returned instead of EACCES when a section is already locked. This is more appropriate, since EAGAIN stands for 'Resource temporarily unavailable, try again later'. The *SVID* advises programmers to allow for both possibilities. For example,

```
.
.
.
if(lockf(fd, F_TEST, 10L) == -1){
    if(errno == EACCES || errno == EAGAIN)
        fprintf(stderr, "record locked\n");
    else
        perror("unexpected lockf error");
}
.
.
.
```

The F_TLOCK request

This request combines F_TEST and F_LOCK, and is useful when a program is required to take some other action, apart from sleeping, when it attempts to lock an already locked section of a file. If an F_TLOCK request is made on a section that is not already locked, a lock is applied as with F_LOCK. If however a lock already exists, lockf returns −1 and sets errno to EACCES (or EAGAIN in future versions of UNIX).

Exercise 7.1 Devise another solution to the *ACME Airlines* problem, where F_TLOCK is used instead of F_TEST, and the user is advised to try again if the relevant record is locked.

Effect of zero value for recsize parameter

If lockf's final parameter recsize is zero, the file section to be processed is assumed to extend from the current file offset until the largest possible file offset (which is implementation-dependent). This means that the file is locked up until the current end of file, and any possible future end of file. It illustrates that a lock may extend, or indeed exist entirely beyond, the current end of file.

The following code fragment is of particular interest:

```
lseek(fd, 0L, 0);
lockf(fd, F_LOCK, 0L);
```

This simple sequence will lock the *entire* file.

Deadlock

Let us assume that two processes, *PA* and *PB*, are working on the same file. Suppose that *PA* locks (with F_LOCK) section *SX* of the file and *PB* locks a completely separate section *SY*. Problems arise if *PA* then attempts to lock *SY* with an `F_LOCK` request and *PB* attempts to lock *SX*. If nothing was done, *PA* would sleep, waiting for *PB* to release *SY*, while *PB* would also sleep, waiting for *PA* to release *SX*. Barring some outside intervention, it would seem that the two processes are doomed to remain sleeping in this deadly embrace forever.

This sort of situation is described as deadlock for obvious reasons. Happily UNIX prevents it from occurring. If an `F_LOCK` request would cause deadlock in this way, the call fails, −1 is returned and `errno` is set to `EDEADLK`. (Rather peculiarly, `EDEADLK` can also mean that the system lock table is full.) On the negative side, `lockf` can only detect deadlock between two processes, and it is possible to devise a three-way deadlock. Complex applications which use locks should always incorporate a timeout to avoid this kind of thing.

The following example should clarify things. The program first locks bytes 0 to 9 of the file `locktest`. It does this with `vlockf` which is simply a rather verbose interface to `lockf`. The program then forks. The child, at points commented `/*B*/ and /*C*/`, immediately applies a lock to bytes 10 to 14 and attempts to apply a lock to bytes 0 to 9. Because the parent has already done the latter, the child will then sleep. Meanwhile the parent has executed a 10-second `sleep` call. Hopefully this is enough to allow the child to perform its two `lockf` calls. When the parent awakens, it attempts, at point `/*D*/`, to lock bytes 10 to 14, which of course have been locked previously by its child process. This is the point at which deadlock would occur and `lockf` should fail.

```
/*deadlock -- demonstrate deadlock error*/

#include <fcntl.h>
#include <unistd.h>

main()
{

    int fd;

    fd = open("locktest", O_RDWR);

    lseek(fd, 0L, 0);
    vlockf(fd, F_LOCK, 10L, "A");       /*A*/

    if(fork() == 0){ /*child*/

        lseek(fd, 10L, 0);
        vlockf(fd, F_LOCK, 5L, "B");  /*B*/

        lseek(fd, 0L, 0);
        vlockf(fd, F_LOCK, 10L, "C"); /*C*/
```

```
        }else{ /*parent*/

            printf("parent sleeping\n");
            sleep(10);

            lseek(fd, 10L, 0);
            vlockf(fd, F_LOCK, 5L, "D");  /*D*/
        }

}


vlockf(fdes, purpose, size, msg)
int fdes, purpose;
long size;
char *msg;
{

        if(lockf(fdes, purpose, size) != -1)
            printf("%s: lockf succeeded (proc %d)\n",
                        msg, getpid());
        else{
            perror(msg); exit(1);
        }
}
```

When run, this program produces output like:

```
A: lockf succeeded (proc 80)
parent sleeping
B: lockf succeeded (proc 81)
D: Deadlock avoided
C: lockf succeeded (proc 81)
```

Here `lockf` fails at point `/*D*/` and `perror` prints the corresponding system error message. Notice how, once the parent has exited and so has its locks released, the child is able to apply its second lock.

Exercise 7.2 Write routines which duplicate the actions of `read` and `write` but which fail if a lock on the file section exists. Adapt the `read` lookalike so that it locks the section it reads (where possible). Each lock should be removed at the next call to the `read` routine.

7.2.3 Record locking with `fcntl`

We have already met the file control call `fcntl`. Apart from its more usual functions, `fcntl` can be used to perform a more general form of record locking than `lockf`. It offers two types of lock:

Read locks A read lock simply prevents any process from applying the other type of `fcntl` lock, which is called a write lock. Several processes may read lock the same segment simultaneously. Read locks would, for example, be useful when a programmer wants to prevent data from being updated, but does not want it hidden from scrutiny by other users. (In the *SVID* the term **section** is used for the parts of a file locked by `lockf`, while **segment** is used for `fcntl`. Presumably the difference in terminology is intended to underline the differences between the two routines.)

Write locks A write lock stops any other process from applying a read or write lock to the file. In other words, only one write lock may exist for a given segment at a time. Write locks therefore correspond to the locks available via `lockf`. Write locks could be used, for example, to remove segments from the public gaze while an update is being performed.

Again we must stress that, according to *Issue 2* of the *SVID*, the locks available via `fcntl` are advisory only. Processes must therefore explicitly cooperate in order for `fcntl` locking to be effective.

As a record locking call, `fcntl` is used as follows.

Usage

```
#include <fcntl.h>

struct lock ldata;
int filedes, cmd, status;
  .
  .
  .
status = fcntl(filedes, cmd, &ldata);
```

As usual, the argument `filedes` must be a valid, open file descriptor. For read locks, `filedes` must have been opened using `O_RDONLY` or `O_RDWR`, so a file descriptor from `creat` won't do. For write locks, `filedes` must have been opened using `O_WRONLY` or `O_RDWR`.

As we saw in our previous encounters with `fcntl`, the `cmd` parameter specifies the required action, via values defined in `fcntl.h`. The following three values relate to record locking:

`F_GETLK` Get lock description based on data passed via the `ldata` argument. (The information returned describes the first lock that 'blocks' the lock described in `ldata`.)

`F_SETLK` Apply lock to file, return immediately if this is not possible. Also used to remove an active lock.

`F_SETLKW` Apply lock to file, sleep if lock blocked by lock owned by another process. As with `F_LOCK` and `lockf`, a process sleeping on a `fcntl` lock can be interrupted by a signal.

The structure `ldata` carries the lock description. Its template `flock` is defined in `fcntl.h` and includes the following members:

```
short l_type;      /*describes type of lock */
short l_whence;    /*offset type, like lseek*/
long  l_start;     /*offset in bytes        */
long  l_len;       /*segment size in bytes  */
short l_pid;       /*set by F_GETLK command */
```

The three members `l_whence`, `l_start` and `l_len` specify the file segment to be locked, tested or unlocked. `l_whence` is exactly like the third argument of `lseek`. It takes the values 0, 1 and 2 to indicate that the offset is to be taken from the file's beginning, the current position of the read-write pointer or the end of file. The member `l_start` gives the start position of the segment, relative to the point indicated by `l_whence`. `l_len` is the length of the segment in bytes; as with `lockf` a value of zero here denotes a segment from the specified start position to the largest possible offset.

`l_type` gives the type of lock to be applied. It can take one of three values, also defined in `fcntl.h`:

- `F_RDLCK` Lock to be applied is read lock.
- `F_WRLCK` Lock to be applied is write lock.
- `F_UNLCK` Lock on specified segment is to be removed.

`l_pid` is only relevant when the `fcntl` command selected is `F_GETLK`. If a lock exists which blocks the lock described by the other members of the structure, `l_pid` will be set to the process-id of the process that set it. The other members of the structure will also be reset by the system to give more information on the lock maintained by the other process.

Setting a lock with `fcntl`

We will now introduce a small example that shows how locks can be applied with `fcntl`. The example is based on fixed-length records, and a routine `setreclen` must be called to set the record length. After this, the function `reclock` can be called to lock record number `recno`, counting from 1.

```
/*setreclen, lockrec -- record locking routines*/

#include <fcntl.h>
#include <stdio.h>

/*will hold record length*/
static long reclen = -1l;

/*set record length*/
setreclen(len)
long len;
{
```

```
    reclen = len;
}

/*lock record number "recno"*/
reclock(fd, recno, type)
int fd;                    /*file descriptor*/
long recno;                /*record number  */
short type;                /*operation type */
{

       int retval;
       struct flock fl;

       if(reclen < 1){
           fprintf(stderr, "reclock: invalid reclen\n");
           return(-1);
       }
       switch(type){
          case F_RDLCK:
          case F_WRLCK:
          case F_UNLCK:
               fl.l_type   = type;
               fl.l_whence = 0;
               fl.l_start  = (recno - 1L)*reclen;
               fl.l_len    = reclen;
               if((retval = fcntl(fd, F_SETLK, &fl)) == -1)
                       perror("reclock");
               return(retval);
           default:
               fprintf(stderr, "reclock: invalid type arg\n");
               return(-1);
         }
}
```

These routines can be used as follows:

```
setreclen(RECLEN);

/*write-lock record*/
reclock(fd, 1l, F_WRLCK);
 .
 .
 .
/*unlock record*/
reclock(fd, 1l, F_UNLCK);
 .
 .
 .
```

Exercise 7.3 Design and implement a limited, record-orientated scheme of read and write locks using just `lockf`. (Hint: you can lock portions of the file near the maximum possible file offset, even when data doesn't exist there. A portion of the file in this region could be reserved, each byte representing a logical record. Locking here could then be used for flag purposes.)

Exercise 7.4 Devise your own locking method, one that does not use either `lockf` or `fcntl`. It is worth trying this exercise again after you have read the section on IPC facilities.

7.3 IPC facilities

7.3.1 Introduction and basic concepts

UNIX System V offers a variety of interprocess communication mechanisms which are new to UNIX and which are described as IPC facilities. These allow the UNIX programmer to use methods of communicating between processes which traditionally have not been possible under UNIX, although they can be found in certain other environments. The presence of the IPC facilities makes UNIX an extremely rich system in the process communication area, and allows a developer to use a variety of methodological approaches when programming a system made up of cooperating tasks. On the negative side, the interface to the IPC facilities does not fit the normal UNIX paradigm and the package seems to sit rather uncomfortably with the rest of the system. This is a shame because it may discourage use of what are powerful tools.

The IPC facilities fall into the following categories, roughly in order of usefulness:

1. Message passing.
2. Semaphores.
3. Shared memory.

These facilities are, under at least some implementations, an optional part of the operating system, and can be left out of the kernel altogether by the system administrator. So you should check before trying to use them.

IPC facility keys

The programming interface for all three IPC facilities has been made as similar as possible, reflecting a similarity of implementation within the kernel. The most important common feature is the IPC facility **key**. Keys are numbers used to identify an IPC object on a UNIX system in much the same way as a filename identifies a file. In other words, a key allows an IPC resource to be easily shared between several processes. The object identified can be a message queue, a set of semaphores or a shared memory segment. The actual data type of a key is determined by the implementation-dependent type `key_t`, which is defined in the system header file `types.h`; on an AT&T 3B2 computer running System V, `key_t` is equivalent to a `long` integer.

Of course keys aren't file names and carry less meaning. They should be chosen carefully to avoid clashes between programs, perhaps on the basis of 'project numbers' assigned to the different developments on a particular machine. (One well known database product uses a hexadecimal key value of 0xDB. A nice idea, but one that could occur to another developer.) Some versions of UNIX provide a simple library function that maps a file's path name into a key. The routine is called `ftok`, although it is perversely described under the heading *STDIPC* in some manuals. It is not part of the AT&T *SVID*.

Usage

```
#include <sys/types.h>
#include <sys/ipc.h>

key_t keyval, ftok();
char *path, id;
  .
  .
  .
keyval = ftok(path, id);
```

The routine returns a key number based on information associated with the file `path`. The parameter `id` is also taken into account and provides an extra level of uniqueness; in other words, the same `path` will produce different keys for different values of `id`. `ftok` is rather an awkward routine; for example, if a file is deleted, then replaced by one with the same name, the keys returned will differ. The routine fails, and so returns `(key_t) -1`, if the file `path` doesn't exist. `ftok` is probably most useful with applications where IPC functions are specifically used in the manipulation of named files, or when given the name of a file which is an essential, permanent and unchanging part of the application.

IPC `get` operations

A program uses a key to either create an IPC object or gain access to an existing one. Both options are called out by an IPC `get` operation. The result of a `get` operation is an integer IPC **facility identifier** which can be used in calls to other IPC routines. If we pursue the file analogy further, the `get` operation is like a call to either `creat` or `open`, while the IPC facility identifier acts rather like a file descriptor. Actually, unlike file descriptors, an IPC facility identifier once created is unique. Different processes will use the same value for the same IPC object.

As an example, the following statement uses the IPC call msgget to create a new message queue (don't worry about what a message queue actually is, we will discuss that later):

```
msg_qid =
    msgget( (key_t)0100, 0644|IPC_CREAT|IPC_EXCL);
```

Here, the first argument to msgget is the message queue key. If successful, the routine will return a non-negative value in msgq_id, which acts as the message queue identifier. The corresponding calls for semaphores and shared memory are semget and shmget, respectively.

Other IPC operations

There are two other types of operation that can be performed with IPC facilities. First, there are control operations which can be used to get status information, or set control values. The actual calls that perform these functions are msgctl, semctl, and shmctl. Second, there are more specific operations which perform the interesting work; these are grouped under the headings msgop, semop, and shmop in a manual organized in standard fashion, even though the calls themselves may be named differently. For example, under msgop there are two functions: msgsnd places a message onto a message queue and msgrcv reads a message from a message queue.

Status data structures

When an IPC object is created, the system also creates an **IPC facility status structure** which will contain any administrative information associated with the object. There is one type of status structure for messages, semaphores and shared memory. Each type necessarily contains information which relates only to the specific IPC facility. However, all three types of status structure contain a common permission structure. This permission structure, identified via the tag ipc_perm, includes the following members:

```
ushort cuid;        /*user-id of creator of IPC object*/
ushort cgid;        /*group-id of creator              */
ushort uid;         /*effective user-id                */
ushort gid;         /*effective group-id               */
ushort umode;       /*permissions                      */
```

This decides whether a user can 'read' an IPC object (that is obtain information on the object) or 'write' to it (which means manipulate it). The permissions are constructed in exactly the same way as with files. So the value 0644 for the umode member means that the owner can read and write the associated object, while other users can only read it. Note that it is the effective user- and group-ids (recorded in the members `uid` and `gid`) that determine access rights in conjunction with `umode`. It should also be clear that execute permission has no meaning here. As usual, superuser has carte blanche.

7.3.2 Message passing

We will start our detailed examination of the IPC facilities by looking at the message passing primitives.

In essence, a message is simply a sequence of characters or bytes (not necessarily null-terminated). Messages are passed between processes by means of **message queues,** which are created or accessed via the `msgget` primitive. Once a queue is established, a process may, given appropriate queue permissions, place a message onto it with `msgsnd`. Another process can then read this message with `msgrcv`, which also removes it from the queue. You might be able to see from this brief description that message passing in the IPC sense is similar to what can be achieved using `read` and `write` calls with pipes (as discussed in Section 6.4.1).

The initialization function `msgget` is called as follows.

Usage

```
#include <sys/types.h>
#include <sys/ipc.h>
#include <sys/msg.h>

int msg_qid, permflags;
key_t key;
  .
  .
  .
msg_qid = msgget(key, permflags);
```

Again, it is best to think of this call as paralleling the action of `open` or `creat`. As we saw in Section 7.3.1, the `key` parameter, essentially just a number, identifies the message queue to the system. If the call is successful, and a new queue is created or an existing one accessed, `msg_qid` will hold an integer **message queue identifier**.

The `permflags` parameter determines the exact action performed by `msgget`. Two constants are of relevance here, both defined in the file `ipc.h`; they can be used alone, or bitwise ORed together:

`IPC_CREAT` This tells `msgget` to create a message queue for the value `key` if one does not already exist. If we pursue our file metaphor, this flag causes `msgget` to act along the lines of a `creat` call, although the message queue won't be 'overwritten' if it already exists. If the IPC_CREAT flag isn't set, then a message queue identifier is only returned by msggest if the queue already exists.

IPC_EXCL If this and IPC_CREAT are both set, then the call is intended only to create a message queue. So, when a queue for key already exists, msgget will fail and return −1. The error variable errno then contains the value EEXIST.

When a message queue is created, the low-order nine bits of permflags are used to give the permissions for the message queue, rather like a file mode. These are stored in the ipc_perm structure which is created along with the queue itself.

We can now return to the example we met in Section 7.3.1:

```
msgq_id =
    msgget( (key_t)0100, 0644|IPC_CREAT|IPC_EXCL);
```

This call is intended to create (and only create) a message queue for the key value (key_t)100. If the call is successful, the queue will have permissions 0644. These are interpreted in the same way as file permissions, indicating that the creator of the queue can send or read messages to and from the queue, while members of the creator's group and all others can only read from it. If necessary, msgctl can be used later to alter the permissions and ownerships associated with the queue.

The msgop routines: msgsnd and msgrcv

Once a queue has been created, there are two msgop primitives which can be used to manipulate it. The first of these is msgsnd.

Usage

```
#include <sys/types.h>
#include <sys/ipc.h>
#include <sys/msg.h>


int msg_qid, size, flags, retval;
struct my_msg{
    long mtype;
    char mtext[SOMEVALUE];
}message;
 .
 .
 .
retval = msgsnd(msg_qid, &message, size, flags);
```

msgsnd is used to send a message to the queue denoted by msg_qid, the value of which will normally have been obtained from msgget.

The message itself is contained, unsurprisingly, in the structure `message`, which is declared with a user-supplied template (`my_msg` above). The form of this template is:

```
struct my_msg{
      long mtype;
      char mtext[SOMEVALUE];
};
```

The `mtype` member can be used by the programmer to categorize messages; each possible value representing a different potential category. Only positive values are meaningful here; negative and zero values won't work. `mtext` will hold the text of the message itself (the constant `SOMEVALUE` is entirely arbitrary). The length of the message to be actually sent is given by the `size` parameter to `msgsnd`, and this can range from zero to the smaller of `SOMEVALUE` or a system determined maximum.

The `flags` parameter for `msgsnd` can take just one meaningful value: `IPC_NOWAIT`. If `IPC_NOWAIT` is *not* set, the calling process will sleep if there are insufficient system resources to send the message. In practice, this will occur when the total length of messages on the queue exceeds either a per-queue or a system-wide maximum. If `IPC_NOWAIT` is set, the call will return immediately if the message can't be sent. Its return value will then be −1, and `errno` will be set to `EAGAIN`, meaning try again.

`msgsnd` can also fail because of the permissions associated with the message queue. If, for example, the user has neither the effective user-id nor the effective group-id associated with the queue, and the queue permissions are 0660, then a call to `msgsnd` for that queue will fail. `errno` will then contain `EACCES`.

The other routine that comes under the `msgop` heading is `msgrcv`.

Usage

```
#include <sys/types.h>
#include <sys/ipc.h>
#include <sys/msg.h>

int msg_qid, size, flags, retval;
struct my_msg{
      long mtype;
      char mtext[SOMEVALUE];
}message;
long msg_type;
  .
  .
  .
retval = msgrcv(msg_qid, &message, size, msg_type, flags);
```

`msgrcv` is used to read a message off the queue identified by `msg_qid`, providing the queue's permissions allow the process to do this. The act of reading a message causes it to be removed from the queue.

This time `message` is used to hold a received message, and the `size` parameter gives the maximum length that can be held within the structure. If the call is successful, then `retval` will contain the length of the received message.

The `msg_type` parameter decides exactly what message is actually received. It selects according to the value of a message's `mtype` field. If `msg_type` is zero, the first message on the queue, i.e. the earliest sent, is read. If `msg_type` has a non-zero, positive value then the first message with that value is read. For example, if the queue contains messages with `mtype` values of 999, 5 and 1, and `msgrcv` is called with `msg_type` set to 5, then the message of type 5 is read. Finally, if `msg_type` has a non-zero, *negative* value, the first message with the lowest `mtype` number that is less than or equal to `msg_type`'s absolute value is received. This is a cumbersome way of saying a simple thing; staying with our previous example where there are three messages with `mtypes` values of 999, 5, 1 on the queue, if the `msg_type` parameter is set to −999 (cast to `long` of course), and `msgrcv` is called three times, then the messages will be received in the order 1, 5 and 999.

The last parameter `flags` again contains control information. Two values, `IPC_NOWAIT` and `MSG_NOERROR`, can be set, alone or ORed together. `IPC_NOWAIT` means much as it did before; if it isn't set then the process will sleep if there isn't a suitable message on the queue, retuning when a message of the appropriate type arrives. If it is set, the call will return immediately, whatever the circumstances.

If `MSG_NOERROR` is set, a message will be truncated if it is longer than `size` bytes, otherwise the call to `msgrcv` would fail. There is unfortunately no way of knowing when truncation has occurred.

You may well have found this section heavy going; the formulation of the IPC facilities goes rather against the UNIX grain in its complexity and style. However, the message passing routines are in fact simple to use, with many potential applications. We hope the next example shows this to some extent.

A message passing example: a queue with priorities

In this section we will develop a straightforward message passing application. The aim is to implement a queuing system where each item queued can be given a priority. A server process will then take the items from the queue and in some unspecified way process them. The items queued could for example be file names, and the server process could copy the files to a line printer. It is similar to the FIFO example developed in Section 6.4.1.

Our starting point is a header file called `q.h`, which contains the following:

```
/*q.h -- header for message facility example*/

#include <sys/types.h>
#include <sys/ipc.h>
#include <sys/msg.h>
```

```
#include <errno.h>

extern int errno;

#define QKEY      (key_t)0105   /*identifying key for queue*/
#define QPERM     0660          /*permissions for queue    */
#define MAXOBN    50            /*maximum length obj. name */
#define MAXPRIOR  10            /*maximum priority level   */

struct q_entry {                /*struct we will use for messages*/
      long mtype;
      char mtext[MAXOBN+1];
};
```

The first part of this file just groups together `#include` statements and the `errno` definition. The `QKEY` definition gives the key value that will identify the message queue to the system. `QPERM` gives the permissions that will be associated with the queue. Since it is defined as 0660, the owner and members of the queue's group will be able to to read or write the message queue. As we shall see, `MAXOBN` and `MAXPRIOR` will impose limits on the messages that can be placed on the queue. The final part of the include file contains a structure template definition with tag `q_entry`. We will use structures of this type to hold the messages transmitted and received by our routines.

The first routine we shall investigate is called `enter`, which places a null-terminated object name onto the queue. It has the following form:

```
/*enter -- place an object into queue*/

#include "q.h"

static int s_qid = -1; /*message queue identifier*/

enter(objname, priority)

char *objname;       /*object name   */
int  priority;       /*priority level*/
{

    int len;
    char *strncpy();
    struct q_entry s_entry; /*structure to hold message*/

    /*validate name length,priority level*/

    if((len = strlen(objname)) > MAXOBN){
        warn("name too long" );
        return (-1);
    }
```

```
        if(priority > MAXPRIOR || priority < 0){
            warn("invalid priority level");
            return (-1);
        }

        /*initial message queue as necessary*/

        if(s_qid == -1 && (s_qid = init_queue()) == -1)
            return (-1);

        /*initialize s_entry*/
        s_entry.mtype = (long)priority;
        strncpy(s_entry.mtext, objname, MAXOBN);

        /*send message, waiting if necessary*/

        if(msgsnd(s_qid, &s_entry, len, 0) == -1){
            perror("msgsnd failed");
            return (-1);
        }else
            return (0);
    }
```

The first action of `enter` is to check the object name length and the priority level. Notice how the minimum value for `priority` is 1, since a zero value would cause `msgsnd` to fail. `enter` next checks to see if the current process has 'opened' the queue, indicated by a non-negative value for `s_qid`. If not, `init_queue` is called. We will see how this is implemented shortly.

If all is well, the routine constructs the message and attempts to send it with `msgsnd`. Notice how we use a `q_entry` structure called `s_entry` to hold the message. Also notice how the last parameter for `msgsnd` is zero. This means that the system will put the calling process to sleep if the queue is full (because `IPC_NOWAIT` is not set).

`enter` indicates problems by using `warn` or the library function `perror`. For the sake of simplicity, we will implement `warn` as follows:

```
#include <stdio.h>

warn(s)
char *s;
{
    fprintf(stderr, "warning:%s\n", s);
}
```

In a real-life system, it might well be better to have `warn` write to an error log file.

Returning to `init_queue`, the purpose of this function is clear. It initializes, if possible, the message queue identifier:

```
/*init_queue -- get queue identifier*/

#include "q.h"

init_queue()
{
    int queue_id;

    /*attempt to create message queue*/
    if((queue_id = msgget(QKEY, IPC_CREAT|QPERM)) == -1)
        perror("msgget failed");

    return (queue_id);
}
```

The next routine is used by the server process to handle items from the queue. We have given it the imaginative name `serve`. It is a reasonably straightforward inverse of `enter`.

```
/*server -- serve object with highest priority on queue*/

#include "q.h"

static int r_qid = -1;

serve()
{

    struct q_entry r_entry;
    int mlen;

    /*initialize queue as necessary*/
    if(r_qid == -1 && (r_qid = init_queue()) == -1)
        return (-1);


    /*get and process next message, waiting if necessary*/

    for(;;){


        if((mlen = msgrcv(r_qid, &r_entry, MAXOBN,
                    (long) -1*MAXPRIOR, MSG_NOERROR)) == -1){

            perror("msgrcv failed");
            return (-1);

        }else{
```

```
            /*make sure we've a string*/
            r_entry.mtext[mlen] = '\0';

            /*process object name*/
            proc_obj(&r_entry);
        }
    }
}
```

Notice how msgrcv is called. Because the negative value -1*MAXPRIOR is given as the type parameter, the system will first examine the queue for messages with mtype equal to 1, then equal to 2 and so on, up to and including MAXPRIOR. To put it another way, the messages with the lowest type numbers will have the highest priority. The routine proc_obj actually does the work. In the case of a printer system, it might copy a file to the printer device.

The following two simple programs demonstrate the interaction of these routines; etest places an item on the queue, while stest processes an item (actually it just prints the contents and type of the message).

The etest program

```
/*etest -- enter object names on queue*/

#include <stdio.h>
#include "q.h"

main(argc, argv)
int argc;
char *argv[];
{
    int priority;

    if(argc != 3){
        fprintf(stderr, "usage: %s objname priority\n", argv[0]);
        exit(1);
    }


    if((priority = atoi(argv[2])) <= 0 || priority > MAXPRIOR){
        warn("invalid priority");
        exit(2);
    }

    if(enter(argv[1], priority) < 0){
        warn("enter failure");
        exit(3);
    }

    exit(0);
}
```

The `stest` program

```
/*stest -- simple server for queue*/
#include <stdio.h>
#include "q.h"

main()
{
    int pid;

    switch(pid = fork()){
      case 0:        /*child*/
        /*break link with terminal*/
        setpgrp();
        serve();
        break;     /*actually, serve never exits*/
      case -1:
        warn("fork to start server failed");
        break;
      default:
        printf("server process pid is %d\n", pid);
    }
    exit( pid != -1 ? 0 : 1);
}

proc_obj(msg)
struct q_entry *msg;
{
    printf("\npriority: %ld name: %s\n", msg->mtype, msg->mtext);
}
```

Notice the way `stest` forks then breaks its relationship with its control terminal by calling `setpgrp`. This allows it to remain in the background even when the user logs out.

An example of the use of these two simple programs follows. Four messages are entered on the queue with `etest`, before the server `stest` is started. Notice the order in which the messages are finally printed:

```
$ etest objname1 3
$ etest objname2 4
$ etest objname3 1
$ etest objname4 9
$ stest
server process pid is 2545
$
priority: 1 name: objname3


priority: 3 name: objname1
```

```
priority: 4 name: objname2

priority: 9 name: objname4
```

Exercise 7.5 Adapt `enter` and `serve` so that control messages can be sent to the server. Reserve message type one for such messages (what should happen to priority values?). Implement the following options:

1. Halt server.
2. Flush all messages from queue.
3. Flush messages at a given priority level.

The `msgctl` system call

The `msgctl` routine serves three purposes: it allows a process to get status information about a message queue, to change some of the limits associated with a message queue, or to delete a queue from the system altogether.

Usage

```
#include <sys/types.h>
#include <sys/ipc.h>
#include <sys/msg.h>

int msg_qid, command, retval;
struct msqid_ds msq_stat;
  .
  .
  .
retval = msgctl(msg_qid, command, &msq_stat);
```

`msg_qid` is, of course, a valid message queue identifier. Skipping `command` for the moment, the third parameter `&msq_stat` is the address of an `msgid_ds` structure. This unattractively named template is defined in `msg.h` and includes the following members:

```
struct
  ipc_perm msg_perm;    /*ownership/perms*/

ushort     msg_qnum;    /*no. messages on queue   */
ushort     msg_qbytes;  /*max. no. bytes for queue*/
ushort     msg_lspid;   /*pid of last msgsnd      */
ushort     msg_lrpid;   /*pid of last msgrcv      */
time_t     msg_stime;   /*last msgsnd time        */
time_t     msg_rtime;   /*last msgrcv time        */
time_t     msg_ctime;   /*last change time        */
```

We have met `ipc_perm` structures before. They will hold the ownerships and access permissions associated with the message queue. The types `ushort` and `time_t` are system dependent and are defined in `types.h`. Typically, they will reduce to `unsigned short` and `long` respectively. The `time_t` variables will hold times as seconds elapsed since 00:00 GMT, 1st January, 1970. (The next example will show you how to convert such values into readable strings.)

The `command` parameter to `msgctl` tells the system what operation is to be performed. There are three options available here, all of which apply to all three IPC facilities. They are identified by constants defined in `ipc.h`.

`IPC_STAT` Tells system to place status information about the structure into `msq_stat`.

`IPC_SET` Used to set the values of control variables for the message queue, according to information held within `msq_stat`. Only the following items can be changed :

```
msq_stat.msg_perm.uid
msq_stat.msg_perm.gid
msq_stat.msg_perm.mode
msq_stat.msg_qbytes
```

An `IPC_SET` operation will succeed only if executed by superuser or the current owner of the queue as indicated by `msq_stat.msq_perm.uid`. In addition, only superuser can increase the `msg_qbytes` limit, which gives the maximum number of characters that may exist on the queue at any one time.

`IPC_RMID` This removes the message queue from the system. Again, this can be done only by superuser or the queue owner.

The following example program `show_msg` prints out some of the status information associated with a message queue. It is intended to be invoked as:

```
$ show_msg keyvalue
```

`show_msg` uses the `ctime` library routine to convert `time_t` values to readable form. (`ctime` and its companions will be discussed in Chapter 11.) The program text follows:

```
/*showmsg -- show message queue details*/

#include <sys/types.h>
#include <sys/ipc.h>
#include <sys/msg.h>
#include <stdio.h>

main(argc, argv)
int argc;
```

```
char *argv[];
{

    key_t mkey;
    int msq_id;
    struct msqid_ds msq_status;

    if(argc != 2){
        fprintf(stderr, "usage:showmsg keyval\n");
        exit(1);
    }

    /*get message queue identifier*/
    mkey = (key_t) atoi(argv[1]);
    if((msq_id = msgget( mkey, 0)) < 0){
        perror("msgget failed");
        exit(2);
    }

    /*get status information*/
    if(msgctl(msq_id, IPC_STAT, &msq_status) < 0){
        perror("msgctl failed");
        exit(3);
    }

    /*print out status information*/
    mqstat_print(mkey, msq_id, &msq_status);
    exit(0);
}

mqstat_print(mkey, mqid, mstat)
key_t mkey;
int mqid;
struct msqid_ds *mstat;
{
    /*ctime() is a standard library function*/
    char *ctime();

    printf("\nKey %d, msg_qid %d\n\n", mkey, mqid);

    printf("%d message(s) on queue\n\n", mstat->msg_qnum);

    printf("Last send by proc %d at %s\n",
        mstat->msg_lspid, ctime(&(mstat->msg_stime)));
    printf("Last recv by proc %d at %s\n",
        mstat->msg_lrpid, ctime(&(mstat->msg_rtime)));
}
```

Exercise 7.6 Adapt `show_msg` so that it prints out the ownerships and permissions associated with the message queue.

Exercise 7.7 Write a program `msg_chmod` that alters the permissions associated with a message queue. Model it on the `chmod` program. Again, the message queue should be identified via its key value.

7.3.3 Semaphores

The semaphore as a theoretical construct

The semaphore concept was first put forward by the Dutch theoretician, E. W. Dijkstra, as a solution to the problems of process synchronization. In these terms, a semaphore *sem* can be seen as an integer variable on which the following operations are allowed (note that the *p* and *v* mnemonics come from the Dutch terms for *wait* and *signal*, the latter not to be confused with the UNIX call `signal`):

```
p(sem)  or wait(sem)

        if(sem != 0)
              decrement sem by one
        else
              wait until sem becomes non-zero

v(sem) or  signal(sem)

        if( queue of waiting processes not empty)
              restart first process in wait queue
        else
              increment sem by one
```

The active part of both operations must be indivisible, which means that only one process can ever change *sem* at any one time.

Formally, the nice thing about semaphores is the fact that the statement:

```
(semaphore's initial value
 + number of v operations
 - number of completed p operations) >= 0
```

is always true. This is the **semaphore invariant**. Computer scientists love such invariant conditions since they make programs amenable to systematic, rigorous proofs.

Semaphores can be used in a variety of ways. Most simply, they can be used to ensure **mutual exclusion**, where only one process can execute a particular region of code at any one time. Consider the following program skeleton:

```
p(sem);

something interesting ...

v(sem);
```

Let us assume further that the initial value of *sem* is one. From the semaphore invariant, we can see that

```
(number of completed p operations -
 number of v operations) <= initial value of semaphore
```

or

```
(number of completed p operations -
 number of v operations) <= 1
```

In other words, only one process can execute the group of statements between these particular *p* and *v* operations at any one time. Such an area of program is often called a **critical section**.

The UNIX System V implementation of semaphores is based upon these ideas, although the actual facilities offered are rather more general (and possibly overly complex). The first routines we shall examine are `semget` and `semctl`:

Usage

```
#include <sys/types.h>
#include <sys/ipc.h>
#include <sys/sem.h>


key_t key;
int sem_id, nsems, permflags, command;
int retval, sem_num;
union semun {
   int val;
   struct semid_ds *stat;
   ushort *array;
} ctl_arg;

   .
   .
   .

sem_id = semget(key, nsems, permflags);

retval = semctl(sem_id, sem_num, command, ctl_arg);
```

The `semget` call is analogous to `msgget`. The extra parameter `nsems` gives the number of semaphores required in the semaphore set; this raises an important point – the UNIX semaphore operations are geared to work with sets of semaphores, not single objects. As we shall see, this complicates the interface to the remaining semaphore routines.

The return value from a successful `semget` call is a **semaphore set identifier**, which acts much like a message queue identifier. Following normal C usage, an index into a semaphore set can run from 0 to `nsems-1`. Associated with each semaphore in the set are the following values:

`semval` The semaphore value, always a positive integer. This must be set via the semaphore system calls, i.e. the semaphore is not directly accessible as a data object to a program.

`sempid` This is the pid of the process that last acted on the semaphore.

`semncnt` Number of processes that are 'waiting' for the semaphore to reach a value greater than its current value.

`semzcnt` Number of processes that are 'waiting' for the semaphore to reach the value zero.

As you can see from its definition, the `semctl` function is considerably more complicated than `msgctl`. `sem_id` must be a valid semaphore identifier. `command` has much the same meaning as in `msgctl`, giving the exact function required. These fall into three categories: standard IPC functions (such as `IPC_STAT`), functions which affect only a single semaphore, and functions which affect the whole semaphore set. All the available functions are shown in Table 7.1.

Table 7.1 `semctl` function codes.

Standard IPC functions (note that the `semid_ds` structure is defined in `sem.h`)	
`IPC_STAT`	Place status information into `ctl_arg.stat`
`IPC_SET`	Set ownership/permissions information from `ctl_arg.stat`
`IPC_RMID`	Remove semaphore set from system
Single semaphore operations (these apply to semaphore `sem_num`, values returned in `retval`)	
`GETVAL`	Return value of semaphore (i.e. `semval`)
`SETVAL`	Set value of semaphore to `ctl_arg.val`
`GETPID`	Return value of `sempid`
`GETNCNT`	Return `semncnt` (see above)
`GETZCNT`	Return `semzcnt` (see above)
All semaphore operations	
`GETALL`	Place all `semvals` into `ctl_arg.array`
`SETALL`	Set all `semvals` according to `ctl_arg.array`

The sem_num parameter is used with the second group of semctl options to identify a particular semaphore. The final parameter ctl_arg is a union with three members, each member corresponding to one of the three types of semctl function.

One important use of semctl is to set the initial values of semaphores, since semget doesn't allow a process to do this. This explains why we introduced semget and semctl together. The following example function can be used by a program to either create a single semaphore, or simply obtain the semaphore set identifier associated with it. If the semaphore is indeed created, it is assigned an initial value of one with semctl.

```
/*initsem -- semaphore initialization*/

#include "pv.h"

initsem(semkey)
key_t semkey;
{
    int status = 0, semid ;


    if((semid = semget(semkey, 1, SEMPERM|IPC_CREAT|IPC_EXCL)) == -1){
        if(errno == EEXIST)
            semid = semget(semkey, 1, 0);
    }else /*if created...*/
        status = semctl(semid, 0, SETVAL, 1);


    if(semid == -1 || status == -1){
        perror("initsem failed");
        return (-1);
    }else
        return semid; /*all okay*/
}
```

The include file pv.h contains the following:

```
/*semaphore example header file*/

#include <sys/types.h>
#include <sys/ipc.h>
#include <sys/sem.h>

#include <errno.h>

extern int errno;

#define SEMPERM 0600
#define TRUE     1
#define FALSE    0
```

We shall use `initsem` as part of an example in the next section.

Semaphore operations: the `semop` call

`semop` is the call that actually performs the fundamental semaphore operations. This time `semop` is actually the name of a function; not just a manual entry.

Usage

```
#include <sys/types.h>
#include <sys/ipc.h>
#include <sys/sem.h>

int retval, sem_id;
struct sembuf op_array[SOMEVALUE];
  .
  .
  .
retval = semop(sem_id, op_array, SOMEVALUE);
```

`sem_id` is the semaphore set identifier, which will probably have been obtained from a previous call to `semget`. `op_array` is an array of `sembuf` structures, the template `sembuf` being defined in `sem.h`. `SOMEVALUE` is a purely arbitrary integer constant. Each `sembuf` structure holds a specification of an operation to perform on a semaphore.

Again, the stress is on actions on sets of semaphores, the `semop` function allowing a group of operations to be performed atomically. This means that, if one of the operations can't be done, then none will be done. Unless otherwise specified, the process will then normally block until it can do all the operations at once.

Let's dissect the `sembuf` structure further. It includes the following members:

```
short sem_num;
short sem_op;
short sem_flg;
```

`sem_num` contains the index of a semaphore in the set. If, for example, the set contains only one member, then `sem_num` must be zero. `sem_op` contains a signed integer which is what really tells the `semop` function what to do. There are three cases.

Case 1 `sem_op` *value negative*
This is a generalized form of the semaphore `p()` command we discussed earlier. In pseudo-code, we can summarize the action of `semop` as follows (note that *ABS* is used to represent a variable's absolute value):

```
if( semval >= ABS(sem_op) ){

    set semval to semval-ABS(sem_op)
```

```
}else{

      if( (sem_flg&IPC_NOWAIT) )
              return -1 immediately
      else{
            wait until semval reaches or exceeds
            ABS(sem_op), then subtract
            ABS(sem_op) as above
      }
}
```

The basic idea is that the `semop` function first tests the value of the *semval* associated with semaphore `sem_num`. If the *semval* is large enough, it is decremented immediately. If not, the process normally waits until *semval* becomes large enough. However, if the `IPC_NOWAIT` flag is set in `sem_flg`, `sem_op` returns −1 immediately and places `EAGAIN` into `errno`.

Case 2: `sem_op` *value positive*
This matches the traditional `v()` operation. The value of `sem_op` is simply added to the corresponding *semval*. Other processes waiting on the new value of the semaphore will be woken up.

Case 3: `sem_op` *value zero*
In this case `sem_op` will wait until the semaphore value becomes zero, but *semval* is not altered. If `IPC_NOWAIT` is set in `sem_flg`, and *semval* isn't already zero, then `semop` returns an error immediately.

The `SEM_UNDO` flag

This is another flag that can be set in the `sem_flg` member of a `sembuf` structure. It tells the system to automatically 'undo' the operation when the process exits. To keep track of what could be a series of such operations, the system maintains an integer called the *semadj* value for the semaphore. It is important to understand that *semadj* values are allocated on a per-process basis, and so different processes will have different *semadj* values for the same semaphore. When a `semop` operation is applied, and `SEM_UNDO` is set, the value of `sem_num` is simply subtracted from the *semadj* value. Here, the sign of `sem_num` is significant; the *semadj* value decreases when `sem_num` is positive, and increases when `sem_num` is negative. When a process exits, the system adds all its *semadj* values to their matching semaphores, and so negates the effect of any `semop` calls. In general, `SEM_UNDO` should be used, unless the values set by a process can retain a meaning beyond the boundaries of that process's existence.

A semaphore example

We will now continue the example we started with the `initsem` routine. It centres around the two routines `p()` and `v()` which are implementations of the traditional semaphore operations. First, let's look at `p()`:

```
/*pc -- semaphore p operation*/

#include "pv.h"

p(semid)
int semid;
{

    struct sembuf  p_buf;

    p_buf.sem_num = 0;
    p_buf.sem_op  = -1;
    p_buf.sem_flg = SEM_UNDO;


    if(semop(semid, &p_buf, 1) == -1){
        perror("p(semid) failed");
        exit(1);
    }else
        return(0);
}
```

Notice how we use the `SEM_UNDO` flag. The code for `v()` follows:

```
/*v.c -- semaphore v operation*/

#include "pv.h"

v(semid)
int semid;
{

    struct sembuf v_buf;

    v_buf.sem_num = 0;
    v_buf.sem_op  = 1;
    v_buf.sem_flg = SEM_UNDO;

    if(semop(semid, &v_buf, 1) == -1){
        perror("v(semid) failed");
        exit(1);
    }else
        return(0);
}
```

We can demonstrate the use of these relatively simple routines to perform mutual exclusion. Consider the following program:

```
/*testsem -- test semaphore routines*/

#include "pv.h"
```

```
main()
{

    key_t semkey = 0x200;

    if(fork() == 0)
        handlesem(semkey);

    if(fork() == 0)
        handlesem(semkey);

    if(fork() == 0)
        handlesem(semkey);
}

handlesem(skey)
key_t skey;
{

    int semid, pid = getpid();

    if((semid = initsem(skey)) < 0)
        exit(1);

    printf("\nprocess %d before critical section\n", pid);

    p(semid);

    printf("process %d in critical section\n", pid);

    /*in real life do something interesting*/
    sleep(10);

    printf("process %d leaving critical section\n", pid);

    v(semid);

    printf("process %d exiting\n", pid);
    exit(0);
}
```

`testsem` spawns three child processes which use `p()` and `v()` to stop more than one of them performing a critical section at the same time. Running `testsem` on one machine produced the following results:

```
process 799 before critical section

process 800 before critical section
```

```
process 801 before critical section

process 799 in critical section
process 799 leaving critical section
process 799 exiting
process 801 in critical section
process 801 leaving critical section
process 801 exiting
process 800 in critical section
process 800 leaving critical section
process 800 exiting
```

7.3.4 Shared memory

The shared memory operations allow two or more processes to share a segment of physical memory (normally, of course, the data areas of any two programs are entirely separate). They provide the most efficient of all the IPC mechanisms. All shared memory operations require special hardware support. If that isn't present, then the shared memory operations will not be available. For this reason, you should only use shared memory when efficiency is very important, since you will be limiting the range of systems on which your application will run.

The `shmget` and `shmop` system calls

Shared memory segments are created with the `shmget` call.

Usage

```
#include <sys/types.h>
#include <sys/ipc.h>
#include <sys/shm.h>

key_t key;
int size, permflags, shm_id;
  .
  .
  .

shm_id = shmget(key, size, permflags);
```

This call closely corresponds to `msgget` and `semget`. The most interesting parameter is `size` which gives the required minimum size (in bytes) of the memory segment. `key` is the key value that identifies the segment. `permflags` gives the permissions for the memory segment and, as with `msgget` and `semget`, these can be ORed with `IPC_CREAT` and `IPC_EXCL`.

The memory segment created is part of *physical* memory, and not the process's *logical* data space. To use it, the process (and any cooperating process) must explicitly attach the memory segment to its logical data space using the `shmat` call, which is part of the `shmop` group (like `msgop` there is no actual `shmop` call).

Usage

```
#include <sys/types.h>
#include <sys/ipc.h>
#include <sys/shm.h>

int shm_id, shmflags;
char *memptr, *daddr, *shmat();
  .
  .
  .
memptr = shmat(shm_id, daddr, shmflags);
```

`shmat` associates the memory segment identified by `shm_id` (which will have come from a `shmget` call) with a valid address for the calling process. This is returned in `memptr` (in C, data addresses are usually represented by a pointer to `char` like `memptr`).

`daddr` gives the programmer some control over the address selected by the call. If it is zero, i.e. `(char *)0`, the segment is attached at the first available address as chosen by the system. This, of course, is the most straightforward case to program. If `daddr` is non-zero, the segment will be attached at, or near, the address held within it, the exact action depending on flags held in the `shmflags` argument. This presents many more difficulties than a zero value, since you will have to know about the layout of your program in memory.

`shmflag` is constructed from the two flags `SHM_RDONLY` and `SHM_RND` which are defined in `<sys/shm.h>`. `SHM_RDONLY` requests that the segment is attached for reading only. `SHM_RND` affects the way `shmat` treats a non-zero value for `daddr`. If it is set, the call will round `daddr` to a page boundary in memory. If not, `shmat` will use the exact value of `daddr`.

If an error occurs, `memptr` will contain the rather nasty value:

```
(char *)-1
```

There is one other `shmop` call, named `shmdt`. It is the inverse of `shmat` and detaches a shared memory segment from the process's logical address space (meaning that the process can no longer use it!). It is called, straightforwardly,

```
retval = shmdt(memptr);
```

`retval` is an integer and is 0 on success, −1 on error.

The `shmctl` system call

Usage

```
#include <sys/types.h>
#include <sys/ipc.h>
#include <sys/shm.h>

int shm_id, retval, command;
struct shmid_ds shm_stat;
.
.
.
retval = shmctl(shm_id, command, &shm_stat);
```

This exactly parallels `msgctl`, and `command` can take the values `IPC_STAT`, `IPC_SET` and `IPC_RMID`. We will use it, with `command` set to `IPC_RMID`, in the next example.

A shared memory example: `shmcopy`

In this section we will construct a simple example program `shmcopy` to demonstrate a practical use of shared memory. `shmcopy` just copies its standard input to its standard output, but gets round the UNIX property that all `read` and `write` calls block until they complete. Each invocation of `shmcopy` results in two processes, a reader and a writer, that share two buffers implemented as shared memory segments. While the reader process reads data into the first buffer, the writer will write the contents of the second buffer, and vice versa. Since reading and writing are being performed simultaneously, data throughput should be increased. This approach is used, for example, in programs that need to drive tape streamers at speed.

To coordinate the two processes, and so prevent the writer writing a buffer before the reader has filled it, we will use two binary semaphores. Almost all shared memory programs will need to use semaphores in one form or another for synchronization, the shared memory facilities providing no synchronization features of their own.

`shmcopy` uses the following header file `share_ex.h`:

```
/*header file for shared memory example*/

#include <stdio.h>
#include <signal.h>
#include <sys/types.h>
#include <sys/ipc.h>
#include <sys/shm.h>
#include <sys/sem.h>

#define SHMKEY1   (key_t)0x10    /*shared mem key*/
#define SHMKEY2   (key_t)0x15    /*shared mem key*/
```

```
#define SEMKEY    (key_t)0x20    /*semaphore  key*/

/*buffer size for reads and writes*/
#define SIZ       5*BUFSIZ

/*will hold data and read count*/
struct databuf {
        int d_nread;
        char d_buf[SIZ];
};
```

Remember that BUFSIZ is defined in stdio.h, and gives the system's disk blocking factor. The template databuf shows the structure we will impose on each shared memory segment. In particular, the member d_nread will enable the reader process to pass the number of characters read to the writer via the memory segments.

The next file contains routines for initializing the two shared memory segments and semaphore set. It also contains the routine remove which deletes the various IPC objects at the end of program execution. Notice in particular the way shmat is called to attach the shared memory segments to the process's address space.

```
/*initialization routines*/

#include "share_ex.h"

#define IFLAGS (IPC_CREAT|IPC_EXCL)
#define ERR  ((struct databuf *) -1)

static int shmid1, shmid2, semid;

getseg(p1, p2)      /*create + attach shared memory segments*/
struct databuf **p1, **p2;
{
     char *shmat();

     /*create shared memory segments*/
     if((shmid1 = shmget(SHMKEY1, sizeof(struct databuf), 0600|IFLAGS
          )) < 0)fatal("shmget");
     if((shmid2 = shmget(SHMKEY2, sizeof(struct databuf), 0600|IFLAGS
          )) < 0)fatal("shmget");

     /*attach shared memory segments*/
     if((*p1 = (struct databuf *) shmat(shmid1, 0, 0)) == ERR)
          fatal("shmat");
     if((*p2 = (struct databuf *) shmat(shmid2, 0, 0)) == ERR)
          fatal("shmat");
}
```

```
int getsem()        /*get semaphore set*/
{
     /*create two semaphore set*/
     if((semid = semget(SEMKEY, 2, 0600|IFLAGS)) < 0)
          fatal("semget");

     /*set initial values*/
     if(semctl(semid, 0, SETVAL, 0) < 0)
          fatal("semctl");
     if(semctl(semid, 1, SETVAL, 0) < 0)
          fatal("semctl");
     return(semid);
}

/*remove shared memory identifiers + sem set id*/
remove()
{
     if(shmctl(shmid1, IPC_RMID, (struct shmid_ds *)0) < 0)
          fatal("shmctl");
     if(shmctl(shmid2, IPC_RMID, (struct shmid_ds *)0) < 0)
          fatal("shmctl");
     if(semctl(semid,  IPC_RMID, (struct semid_ds *)0) < 0)
          fatal("semctl");
}
```

Errors in these routines are handled with `fatal`, which we have used in previous examples. It simply calls `perror`, then `exit`.

The `main` function for `shmcopy` follows. It is very simple, just calling the initialization routines, then creating the reading (parent) and writing (child) processes. Notice how it is the writing process that calls `remove` when the program finishes.

```
/*shmcopy -- main function*/

#include "share_ex.h"

main()
{
     int semid, pid;
     struct databuf *buf1, *buf2;

     /*initialize semaphore set*/
     semid = getsem();

     /*create and attach shared memory segments*/
     getseg(&buf1, &buf2);

     switch((pid = fork())){
        case -1:
          fatal("fork");
```

```
            case 0: /*child*/
              writer(semid, buf1, buf2);
              remove();
              break;

            default: /*parent*/
              reader(semid, buf1, buf2);
              break;
        }

        exit(0);
}
```

`main` creates the IPC objects before the `fork`. Note that the addresses that identify the shared memory segments (held `buf1` and `buf2`) will be meaningful in both processes.

`reader`, which takes its input from standard input, i.e. file descriptor 0, is the first interesting routine. It is passed the semaphore set identifier in `semid`, and the addresses of the two shared memory segments in `buf1` and `buf2`.

```
/*reader -- handle reading of file*/

#include "share_ex.h"

/*these define p() and v() for two semaphores*/
struct sembuf p1 = {0, -1, 0}, p2 = {1, -1, 0};
struct sembuf v1 = {0,  1, 0}, v2 = {1,  1, 0};

reader(semid, buf1, buf2)       /*read from std. input*/
int semid;                      /*sem set id          */
struct databuf  *buf1, *buf2;   /*shared memory segs  */
{
        for(;;){

              /*read into buffer buf1*/
              buf1->d_nread = read(0, buf1->d_buf, SIZ);

              /*synchronization point*/
              semop(semid, &v1, 1);
              semop(semid, &p2, 1);

              /*test here to avoid writer sleeping*/
              if(buf1->d_nread <= 0)
                    return;

              buf2->d_nread = read(0, buf2->d_buf, SIZ);

              semop(semid, &v1, 1);
              semop(semid, &p2, 1);
```

```
            if(buf2->d_nread <= 0)
                return;
        }
    }
```

The `sembuf` structures here just define *p()* and *v()* operations for a two semaphore set. However, this time they aren't used for locking a critical section of code. Instead they are used to synchronize the reader and writer. `reader` uses `v2` to signal that a read has been completed, and waits, by calling `semop` with `p1`, for the writer to signal that a write has been completed. This will become clearer when we describe the `writer` routine. Other techniques are possible, involving either four binary semaphores, or semaphores that can take more than two values.

The final routine called by `shmcopy` is `writer`:

```
/*writer -- handle writing*/
#include "share_ex.h"

extern struct sembuf p1, p2;  /*defined in reader.c*/
extern struct sembuf v1, v2;  /*defined in reader.c*/

writer(semid, buf1, buf2)   /*write to std output*/
int semid;
struct databuf *buf1, *buf2;
{
    for(;;){

        semop(semid, &p1, 1);
        semop(semid, &v2, 1);

        if(buf1->d_nread <= 0)
            return;

        write(1, buf1->d_buf, buf1->d_nread);


        semop(semid, &p1, 1);
        semop(semid, &v2, 1);

        if(buf2->d_nread <= 0)
            return;

        write(1, buf2->d_buf, buf2->d_nread);
    }
}
```

Again notice the use of the semaphore set to coordinate `reader` and `writer`. This time `writer` uses `v2` to signal and waits on `p1`. It is also important to note that the values for `buf1->d_nread` and `buf2->d_nread` are set by the reading process.

When compiled, `shmcopy` can be used with a command such as:

```
$ shmcp < big > /tmp/big
```

Exercise 7.8 Improve the error handling and reporting of `shmcopy` (especially for calls to `read` and `write`). Make `shmcopy` accept file names as arguments in a `cat`-like manner. What are the consequences of interrupting `shmcopy`? Can you improve things?

Exercise 7.9 Devise a message passing system that uses shared memory. Benchmark and compare with the IPC message passing routines.

7.3.5 The `ipcs` and `ipcrm` commands

There are two shell level commands provided for use with IPC facilities. The first is `ipcs` which prints out information on the current status of IPC facilities. A simple example is

```
$ ipcs


IPC status from /dev/kmem as of Wed Feb 26 18:31:31 1986
T     ID     KEY          MODE        OWNER    GROUP
Message Queues:
Shared Memory:
Semaphores:
s     10 0x00000200 --ra-------     keith    users
```

The other command is `ipcrm` which is used to remove IPC facilities from the system (providing the user is the owner of the facility, or superuser). For example,

```
$ ipcrm -s 0
```

removes the semaphore associated with identifier 0, and

```
$ ipcrm -S 200
```

removes the semaphore associated with key value 200.

For more details of the options available, see your system manual.

Chapter 8 The Terminal

8.1 Introduction

Whenever a program and a user interact via a terminal, there is a lot more going on than might at first meet the eye. For example, if a program writes a string to a terminal device, that string is first processed by a section of the kernel called the **terminal device driver**. Depending on the value of certain state flags held by the system, the string might simply be passed on verbatim, or altered in some way by the driver. One common alteration is the replacement of `line-feed` or `newline` by the two-character sequence `carriage-return`, `newline`. This ensures that each line always begins on the left-hand side of the terminal screen.

Similarly, the terminal driver will, in normal circumstances, allow the user to edit mistakes in an input line with the current `erase` and `kill` characters. The `erase` character will delete the last character typed, while the `kill` character will erase up to the beginning of the line. Only when the user is happy with the line, and presses the `RETURN` key (called `ENTER` on some systems) will the terminal driver pass it to the program.

This is not the end of the story. For example, once an output string reaches the terminal, the terminal hardware may either display the string directly or interpret it as an **escape-sequence** sent for screen control. The final result might therefore be an English message, or a cleared screen.

Figure 8.1 shows the various components of a link between computer and terminal more clearly. It consists of four nodes:

- *The program (A)* This generates output character sequences and interprets input character sequences. It might interact with the terminal using system calls such as `read` or `write`, a higher-level library such as *Standard I/O*, or a special library package designed for screen control. Ultimately of course, all I/O will be via `read` and `write`, since higher-level libraries must eventually call these fundamental primitives.
- *The terminal device driver (B)* This is a piece of software built into the kernel itself. A major part of the driver is written to interface to the specific hardware that allows the computer to communicate with its terminals. Indeed some systems may require drivers to deal with more

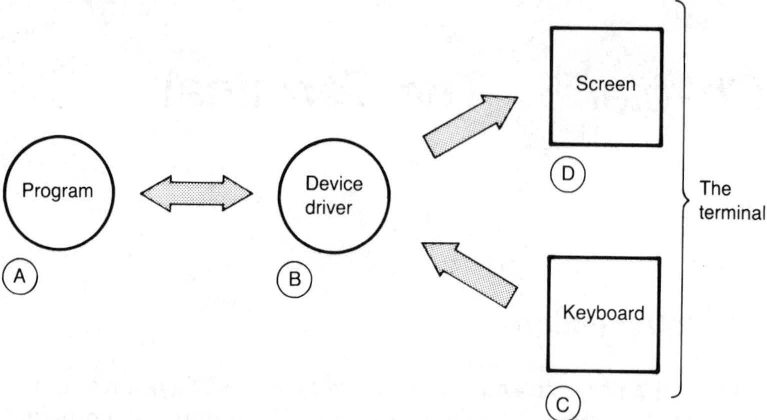

Figure 8.1 The link between a UNIX system and a terminal.

than one type of hardware. Built on this low-level layer are facilities which ensure the basic features the terminal driver supports are general, whatever the hardware.

The terminal device driver's main function is to transfer data from the program to the peripheral device, and vice versa. Aside from just this fundamental transmission function, the terminal driver may perform a degree of logical processing of input and output data, mapping one sequence of characters to another. It can also provide a variety of functions to aid the end user, such as input line editing. The exact processing and mappings performed depend upon state flags held by the system for each terminal port. These can be set by the programmer using the `ioctl` system call.

- *Keyboard and screen (C and D)* These two nodes represent the terminal itself and emphasize its dual nature. Node (C) stands for the terminal keyboard and acts as a source of input. Node (D) represents the terminal's screen and acts as a sink for output. However, a program can gain access to a terminal both as an input source and an output sink via just one terminal name, and ultimately a single file descriptor. To make this possible, the terminal driver maintains an input and an output queue of characters for each terminal.

So far, we have assumed that the peripheral device connected to a terminal line is a standard VDU. However, the peripheral device could equally well be a serial line-printer, a plotter, an entry point to a network, or even another computer. Nevertheless, whatever the nature of the peripheral device, it can act both as a source and a sink for input and output streams of characters, respectively.

This chapter will concentrate on nodes (A) and (B) in the diagram. In other words, we will examine the interaction between the program and the terminal device driver at system call level. We will not consider the entirely separate issue of screen handling in this chapter, since the terminal driver plays no part in constructing the appropriate escape sequences for screen control. Instead we will delay this topic until Chapter 10, where we consider the `curses` library.

Before proceeding we should add two caveats. First, we will only consider **asynchronous** terminals, which are the terminals most often found under UNIX. The **synchronous** terminal interfaces found on mainframes are rare in UNIX environments (although they are becoming more common as UNIX moves onto 'big iron'). They present their own special problems which we will not consider. Second, terminal handling under UNIX and UNIX derivatives is an area notorious for inconsistencies. There are major differences between 'standard' versions of UNIX, such as Version 7, System III and System V. Other variants, such as Xenix and Berkeley UNIX, have their own idiosyncrasies. As usual we will stick to Issue 2 of the AT&T *System V Interface Definition*.

8.2 The UNIX terminal

As you might expect from Chapter 4, terminals are identified by special files (and, because of the nature of terminals, they are treated as character devices). As a consequence terminals, or more precisely terminal ports, can be accessed via filenames in the `dev` directory. Typical terminal names include:

```
/dev/console
/dev/tty01
/dev/tty02
/dev/tty03
 ...
```

tty is a synonym for terminal much used in UNIX.

Because of the generality of the UNIX file concept, terminals can be accessed using the standard system call primitives such as `write` and `read`. File permissions retain their usual meanings, and so control access by users to terminals on the system. To ensure that this arrangement behaves sensibly, the system changes the ownership of a terminal when a user logs in, all users owning the terminals they are working on.

A process will not normally need to open explicitly a terminal file to interact with its user. This is because its standard input and standard output, unless redirected, will be connected to the user's terminal. So, assuming standard output isn't assigned to a file, the following statement results in data being written to the terminal screen:

```
#define FD_STDOUT 1
   .
   .
   .
write(FD_STDOUT, mybuffer, somesize);
```

Login terminals are actually first opened during system startup, under the control of the process supervisor program `init`. The terminal file descriptors are passed down to `init`'s children, and ultimately each user's shell process will inherit three file descriptors connected to the user's terminal. These are, of course, the shell's standard input, standard output and standard error. They in turn are passed to any programs started from within the shell.

8.2.1 Control terminals

In normal circumstances, the terminal associated with a process through its standard file descriptors is the **control terminal** for that process and its process group. A control terminal is an important process attribute that determines the handling of interrupts generated at the keyboard. For example, if a user hits the current interrupt key for a terminal then all processes that recognize the terminal as their control terminal will receive the signal `SIGINT`. Control terminals, like other process attributes, are inherited across `fork` calls. (More specifically, a terminal becomes a control terminal for a process group when the process group leader opens it, providing the terminal isn't already associated with a process group and the process group leader hasn't already acquired a control terminal. As a corollary, a process can break its relationship with its control terminal by changing its process group with `setpgrp`. We saw this, rather prematurely, in Chapter 5. You should now also be able to gain an insight into how `init` arranges things.)

In cases when a process must gain access to its control terminal, whatever the state of its standard file descriptors, the file name

```
/dev/tty
```

can be used. It is always interpreted as meaning the process's current control terminal. Consequently, the terminal this file identifies varies from process to process.

8.2.2 Data transmission

The fundamental task of the terminal device driver is to transmit characters between program and the terminal device. This, in fact, is a complicated requirement, since the user may type characters at any time, even while output is occurring. To understand the situation, go back to Figure 8.1 and imagine data passing along the paths (C) to (B) and (B) to (D) simultaneously. Remember that the program represented at node (A) in the diagram can only issue a single `read` or `write` request at any one time.

To manage two simultaneous streams of characters, while only one is being processed by a user program, the device driver stores both input and output data in internal buffers. Input data is passed to the user program when it issues a `read` request. Input characters can be lost when either the buffers maintained by the kernel become completely full, or the number of characters associated with the terminal exceeds a system-specific maximum. A typical figure for this limit is 256, generous enough to make loss of data rare in normal use. However, there is no way of determining when data has been lost; the system simply throws the extra characters away unannounced.

The situation with output is somewhat simpler. Each `write` to a terminal places characters into an output queue. If this queue ever becomes full, a successive `write` will 'block' (that is, hang) until the output queue drains to a suitable level.

8.2.3 Echoing and type-ahead

Because terminals are used for interaction between human beings and computer programs, the UNIX terminal driver provides a large number of additional facilities to make things easier for mortals.

Perhaps the most basic of these additional facilities is character echoing. After all, it helps to see an 'A' appear on the screen when you type 'A' on the keyboard. Terminals attached to UNIX systems normally work in **full-duplex** mode, which means that character echoing is the responsibility of the UNIX system, not the terminal. Consequently, a character when typed is first transmitted by the terminal to the UNIX system. When it is received, the terminal driver immediately places a copy into the output queue for that terminal. It is then 'echoed' on the terminal screen. Returning again to Figure 8.1, it means that a character is sent first along the path (C) to (B), then immediately echoed along the path (B) to (D). All this may occur before the program (A) is ready to read the character. It leads to the interesting phenomenon of input echoing in the middle of output when a user types at the same time a program is writing to the screen. In other systems, the echoing of input may be suppressed until the program is ready to read it.

8.2.4 Canonical mode, line editing and special characters

A terminal can be set to a variety of modes according to the type of program attached to it. A screen editor will want maximum control and so will place the terminal into a 'raw' state, where the terminal driver simply passes characters to the program as they arrive, without any processing.

However, UNIX would not be the programming environment it is if all programs had to deal with the minutiae of terminal control. So the UNIX driver provides a mode of operation specifically tailored to simple, line-oriented, interactive use. This is described as **canonical mode**, and is used by the shell, the `ed` editor and similar programs.

In canonical mode, the terminal driver performs special actions when certain keys are pressed. Many of these actions are concerned with line-editing. As a corollary, input is only made available to a program in the form of complete lines when the terminal is in its canonical state (more of this later).

The most familiar editing key provided in canonical mode is the `erase` character. Pressing this causes the previous character on a line to be rubbed out. For example, the command line:

```
$ whp<erase>o
```

followed by newline will result in the terminal driver sending the string `who` to the shell. If the terminal is correctly set, the '`p`' should also be physically erased from the screen.

The `erase` character can be set by the user to any ASCII value. The most common character used for this purpose nowadays is probably ASCII `backspace`, although the system default is, for historical reasons, the hash (#) character.

The simplest way to change things at shell level is to use the `stty` command. For example:

```
$ stty erase  "^h"
```

sets the erase character to `CTRL-H`, which is another name for backspace. Note that you can usually type the string '`^h`', rather than the `CTRL-H` character itself.

What follows is a systematic description of the other characters that have special meanings to the shell in canonical mode, as defined in the *SVID*. Unless otherwise stated, their exact values can be set by the user or system administrator.

`kill` This results in all characters up to the beginning of the line being erased. So the input sequence:

```
$ echo<kill>who
```

followed by a newline results in the command `who` being executed. The default value for `kill` is '`@`'. Common alternatives include `CTRL-X` and `CTRL-U`. The `kill` character can be reset with the shell command:

```
$ stty kill <new_char>
```

`intr` The `interrupt` character. If the user types this, the signal `SIGINT` is sent to the program reading from the terminal, and all other processes that recognize the terminal as their control terminal. A program like the shell is sensible enough to trap the signal, since the default action on receipt of `SIGINT` is program termination. The default value for the `intr` character under UNIX System V is ASCII `delete`, sometimes referred to as `DEL`. A common alternative is `CTRL-C`. To change the current value of `intr` at shell level use

```
$ stty intr <new_char>
```

Refer back to Chapter 6 for more details of signal processing.

`quit` This character, if typed by the user, causes the signal `SIGQUIT` to be sent to the process group associated with the terminal. Again, the shell will trap the signal leaving the user program to take appropriate action. As we saw in Chapter 6, the normal consequence is a core dump, where the contents of the program's memory space are written to disk and program execution is ungracefully terminated with the message `Quit - core dumped`. The normal `quit` character is ASCII `FS`, or `CTRL-\`. It can be changed with

```
$ stty quit <new_char>
```

`eof` This is the character used to mark the end of an input stream from the terminal (to do so, it must be typed on a new line by itself). It is, for example, the character used to force logout. Its standard initial setting is ASCII `eot`, otherwise known as `CTRL-D`. Popular alternatives include `CTRL-Z`. It can be changed with:

```
$ stty eof <new_char>
```

`nl` This is the normal line delimiter. It always has the value ASCII `line-feed`, which is the C `newline` character. It cannot be set or changed by the user. On terminals which send `carriage-return` instead of `line-feed`, the terminal driver can be set to map carriage-returns into line-feeds.

`eol` This is an additional line delimiter which acts like `nl`. It is not normally used and has a default value of ASCII `NUL`.

`stop` This always has the value `CTRL-S` (ASCII `DC3`) and cannot be altered by the user, at least in standard System V.2. It is used to temporarily suspend the output being written to the terminal. It is particularly useful when using a VDU terminal, since it can be used to suspend output before it vanishes for ever off the top of the terminal screen.

`start` This always has the value `CTRL-Q` (ASCII `DC1`). Again, it cannot be altered by the user. It is used to restart output which has been halted by a previous CTRL-S. If no CTRL-S has been typed, then CTRL-Q is ignored. (In some implementations of System V, there is also a swtch character (default CTRL-Z) used by a special job control facility called shl. This lies outside the *SVID*.)

The erase, kill and eof characters may be 'escaped' by immediately preceding them with a backslash (\) character. When this is done the function associated with the escaped character in question is not performed and it is sent to the reading program. For example, the line

```
aa\<erase>b<erase>c
```

results in *aa*\<erase>*c* being sent to the program currently reading from the terminal.

8.3 The program's view

So far, we have studied the facilities offered by the terminal driver in terms of the user interface. Now, we will consider things from the viewpoint of a program using the terminal.

8.3.1 The open system call

open can be used to open a terminal line in much the same way as an ordinary disk file. For example,

```
fd = open( "/dev/tty0a", O_RDWR);
```

However, an attempt to open a terminal will not return until a connection has been established. For terminals with modem control this means that the open will not return until the modem control signals are correctly set up and 'carrier-detect' is valid, which can take time or fail to happen at all.

The following routine uses alarm (introduced in Chapter 6) to force a timeout if open fails to return after a reasonable period:

```
/*ttyopen  -- open with timeout*/

#include <stdio.h>
#include <signal.h>

#define  TIMEOUT 10
#define  FALSE    0
#define  TRUE     1

static int   timeout = FALSE;
static char *termname;
```

```
static int settimeout()
{
        fprintf(stderr, "timeout on opening %s\n", termname);
        timeout = TRUE;
}

ttyopen(filename, flags)
char *filename;
int flags;
{

        int (* sigfn)(), fd = -1;


        termname = filename;

        /*set timeout flag*/
        timeout = FALSE;

        /*set SIGALRM action*/
        sigfn = signal(SIGALRM, settimeout);

        alarm(TIMEOUT);

        fd = open(filename, flags);

        /*reset things*/
        alarm(0);
        signal(SIGALRM, sigfn);

        return (timeout ? -1: fd);
}
```

8.3.2 The `read` system call

Out of all the file access primitives, it is the `read` system call that is most affected when used with a terminal special file, rather than an ordinary disk file. This is particularly so when the terminal is in canonical mode, the mode intended for normal interactive use. In this state, the line becomes the fundamental unit of input. Consequently, characters cannot be read from a line by a program until the user types the `RETURN` or `ENTER` key, which is interpreted by the system as meaning newline. Equally importantly, a call to `read` will always return after a newline, even if the number of characters on the line is less than the number of characters requested in the `read` call. If just a `RETURN` is typed and an empty line is sent to the system, the corresponding `read` call will return a value of 1, since the newline is itself made available to the program. A return value of zero can still therefore be used to detect end of file.

We first saw this kind of interaction between `read` and the terminal driver in the `io` example way back in Chapter 2. However, the topic really deserves a fuller explanation, so consider the statement

```
nread  = read(0, buffer, 256);
```

If the process's standard input is being taken from an ordinary file, the interpretation of this call is straightforward; while more than 256 characters remained in the file, the call to `read` would return exactly 256 characters in `buffer`. Since the relationship between `read` and a terminal is a little more complicated, we will use Figure 8.2, which shows a brief interaction between program and user, to make things clearer. The diagram illustrates a possible sequence of actions when the `read` call above is applied to a terminal. At each step there are two boxes shown. The top box shows the current state of the input line as the terminal driver sees things; the lower, labelled *read buffer*, shows the data currently available to be read by a program. We should stress that the diagram shows a logical

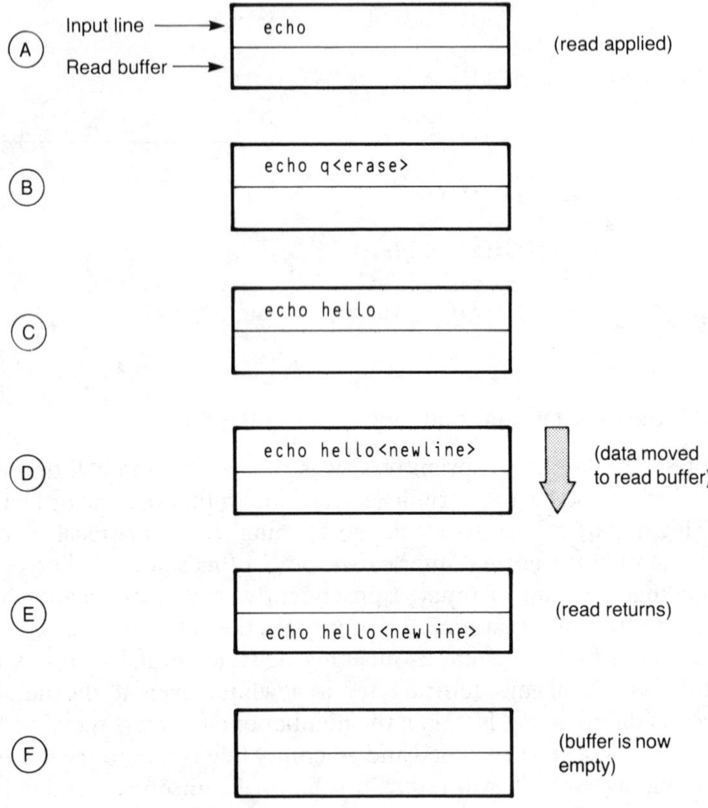

Figure 8.2 Stages in reading from a terminal in canonical mode.

picture only, taken from the viewpoint of a user process. However, the most common implementation of the terminal driver also uses a two-buffer or queue arrangement which is not much more complicated than the scheme presented in the diagram.

Step A represents the situation when the program makes the `read` call. The user has at this point already typed the string *echo*, but since no newline has yet been entered, there is no data in the read buffer, and the execution of the process is suspended.

At step B, the user has typed *q*, then changed his or her mind, and pressed the current erase key to remove the character from the input line. This part of the diagram emphasizes how editing can be performed on the input line without involving the program which is performing the `read`.

At step C, the input line is complete except for the final newline. The part of the diagram marked as step D shows the instant at which newline is entered, and the terminal driver transfers the input line, including the terminating newline, into the read buffer. This leads to step E, where the entire input line has suddenly become available for reading. Within the process that made the `read` call, the call returns, giving a value of 11 for `nread`. Step F shows the situation just after the call has been satisfied in this way; both the input line and read buffer are temporarily empty.

The next example reinforces the above discussion. It centres on the entirely trivial program `read_demo`, which has just one distinguishing feature: the small size of the buffer it uses to take bites at standard input.

```
/*read_demo -- read/ terminal driver interaction*/

#define SMALLSZ 10

main(argc, argv)
int argc;
char **argv;
{

    int nread;
    char smallbuf[SMALLSZ+1];

    while((nread = read(0, smallbuf, SMALLSZ)) > 0){
      smallbuf[nread] = '\0';
      printf("nread:%d %s\n", nread, smallbuf);
    }
}
```

If this program is presented with the following keyboard input:

```
1
1234
This is a much longer line.
<EOF>
```

the following dialogue would be produced:

```
1
nread:2 1

1234
nread:5 1234

This is a much longer line.
nread:10 This is a
nread:10 much longe
nread:8 r line.
```

Notice how the longest line requires several consecutive reads to absorb it. Also note that figures for `nread` include the trailing newline at the end of each line. Again, we have not explicitly shown these for clarity.

What happens if the terminal is not in canonical mode? In this case, a program must set additional state variables associated with the terminal in order to fully control input. This is done via the `ioctl` system call which we shall discuss in detail later.

Exercise 8.1 Try the `read_demo` example with the same input redirected from a file.

8.3.3 The `write` system call

This is, as far as terminal interaction goes, a much simpler beast. The only limitation is that a `write` will block if the output queue for the terminal is full. Program execution will resume only when the number of characters in the queue drains below some threshold level.

8.3.4 `ttyname` and `isatty`

We will now introduce two useful utilities which we can make use of in later examples. `ttyname` returns the name of a terminal device associated with an open terminal file descriptor, while `isatty` returns 1 (that is, *true* in C terms) if a file descriptor describes a terminal device, 0 (*false*) otherwise.

Usage

```
int filedes, bool;
char *name, *ttyname();
 .
 .
 .
name = ttyname(filedes);

bool = isatty(filedes);
```

In both cases `filedes` is the open file descriptor. If `filedes` does not represent a terminal, `ttyname` returns `NULL`. The return value from `ttyname` otherwise points to a static data area which is overwritten by each call to `ttyname`.

The following example routine `what_tty` prints out the terminal associated with a file descriptor, if possible:

```
/*what_tty -- print tt§y name*/


what_tty(fd)
int fd;
{
    if(isatty(fd))
       printf("fd %d =>> %s\n", fd, ttyname(fd));
    else
       printf("fd %d =>> not a terminal!\n", fd);
}
```

Exercise 8.2 Adapt the `ttyopen` routine from the last section so that it will only return a file descriptor for a terminal special file, not a disk file or any other file type. Use `isatty` to perform the checking. Are there other ways to achieve this?

8.3.5 Changing terminal characteristics: `termio` structures

At shell level, the user can invoke the `stty` command to alter the characteristics of a terminal line. A program can do much the same thing by using `termio` structures in conjunction with the system call `ioctl` (the name stands for I/O control). These taken together provide a general programming interface to all UNIX asynchronous communication ports, whatever the nature of the underlying hardware. This assumes of course that the system conforms to the *SVID*.

An occurrence of a `termio` structure can be thought of as representing a possible state for a terminal, corresponding to state flags held by the system for each terminal device. `termio` structures can be used in conjunction with the `ioctl` system call as follows:

```
#include <termio.h>

int ttyfd;
struct termio tsaved;
      .
      .
      .

ioctl(ttyfd, TCGETA, &tsaved);
```

This particular `ioctl` call saves the present state of the terminal associated with `ttyfd` in the `termio` structure `tsaved`. `ttyfd` must be a file descriptor that describes a terminal. `TCGETA` is a constant defined in the standard include file `termio.h`. Similarly,

```
#include <termio.h>

int ttyfd;
struct termio tnew;
      .
      .
      .

ioctl(ttyfd, TCSETA, &tnew);
```

will set the terminal represented by `ttyfd` into a new state.

The structure template for `termio` structures is found in the include file `termio.h` and has the following form:

```
#define      NCC     8

struct termio {
 unsigned short      c_iflag;      /*input modes*/
 unsigned short      c_oflag;      /*output modes*/
 unsigned short      c_cflag;      /*control modes*/
 unsigned short      c_lflag;      /*line disc. modes*/
 char                c_line;       /*line discipline*/
 unsigned char       c_cc[NCC];    /*control chars*/
};
```

We can dismiss the `c_line` member more or less at once. It was introduced to allow system developers to introduce special line disciplines or protocols of their own. (The term **protocol** is used a great deal in discussing data communications. In essence a protocol is simply a set of rules for transmitting and receiving information.) `c_line` has rarely been exploited, and the following discussion assumes that the default value of 0 is in use.

The `c_cc` array

The line-editing characters we examined in Section 8.2.4 are actually contained in the array `c_cc`. Their relative positions are given by constants also defined in `termio.h`. Those of interest to us are shown in Table 8.1.

The following program fragment shows how to alter the value of the `quit` character for the terminal associated with standard input (file descriptor 0):

```
struct termio tdes;

/*get initial terminal characteristics*/
ioctl(0, TCGETA, &tdes);
```

```
tdes.c_cc[VQUIT] = 031; /*CTRL-Y*/

/*reset terminal*/
ioctl(0, TCSETA, &tdes);
```

This example serves to illustrate the safest approach to changing the state of a terminal. First, get the terminal's current state. Second, alter only those parameters you are interested in, without touching anything else. Third, change the terminal state with the modified `termio` structure. As we shall see, it is also worth saving the original values to reset the terminal before exiting.

Table 8.1 Control character codes.

Constant	*Value*	*Meaning*
`VINTR`	0	Interrupt key
`VQUIT`	1	Quit key
`VERASE`	2	Erase character
`VKILL`	3	Kill (line erase) character
`VEOF`	4	End of file character
`VEOL`	5	Optional end of line marker

The `c_cflag` field

The `c_cflag` field defines the hardware control of the terminal. Normally, a process should leave the `c_cflag` field for its control terminal well alone. It becomes useful in applications such as communications packages, or when a program opens an extra terminal line such as a printer port. Values for `c_cflag` are constructed by ORing constants defined in `termio.h`. In general, each constant represents a single bit within the flag field which can be set on or off. There are a large number of such constants which we will not discuss in full (consult your local manual for complete details). However, the following series of examples gives an idea of the options available. The first sets the terminal speed to 9600 baud. Both `CBAUD` and `B9600` are defined in `termio.h`.

```
/*first turn off current baud rate */
/*this masks off all baud rate bits*/
tdes.c_cflag &=~CBAUD;

/*now set new rate*/
tdes.c_cflag |= B9600;
```

Of course, this will have no effect until `ioctl` is called, as follows:

```
ioctl(somefd, TCSETA, &tdes);
```

The next example enables parity generation and detection:

```
tdes.c_cflag |= (PARENB|PARODD);
ioctl(somefd, TCSETA, &tdes);
```

Here, it is the `PARENB` flag that enables parity checking. The `PARODD` flag indicates that the parity desired is odd. If `PARODD` is turned off with `PARENB` set, then even parity is assumed.

The term **parity** describes the use of check bits in data transmission. There is one such check bit per character, which is possible because the ASCII character set takes up only seven bits out of the eight used to hold a byte on most machines. The value of the check bit can be used to make the total number of bits set per byte either odd or even. Alternatively, the programmer can choose to ignore parity altogether.

The `c_iflag` field

The `c_iflag` field within a `termio` structure describes basic terminal input control. Again we will not examine all the possible settings, but will study a selection of those that are used most often in practice.

Three of the flags associated with this field are concerned with the treatment of carriage return. These can be useful with terminals that send a sequence involving carriage return to mark end of line. (UNIX of course expects ASCII line-feed or newline as its end of line character.) The flags in question are:

`INLCR`	Map, i.e. translate, newline to carriage-return.
`IGNCR`	Ignore carriage-return.
`ICRNL`	Map carriage-return to newline.

Three other `c_iflag` fields are concerned with flow control:

`IXON`	Allow start/stop control over output.
`IXANY`	Allow any character to restart output.
`IXOFF`	Allow start/stop control over input.

The `IXON` flag gives the user control over output. If set, then the user can stop output with `CTRL-S`. `CTRL-Q` will restart the output. If `IXANY` is also set, any character can be pressed to restart suspended output, although `CTRL-S` must always be used to halt it. If the `IXOFF` flag is set, the system itself will transmit a stop character (`CTRL-S` as usual) to the terminal when its input buffer is nearly full. `CTRL-Q` will be sent to restart input once the system is ready to accept data again.

The `c_oflag` field

The `c_oflag` field specifies the system's treatment of output. The most important flag here is `OPOST`. If this is not set, then output characters are transmitted without alteration. If it is, characters are post-processed as indicated by the remaining flags set within `c_oflag`. Some of these are concerned about the processing of carriage-return in output to the terminal:

`ONLCR`	Map newline to carriage-return – newline.
`OCRNL`	Map carriage-return to newline.
`ONOCR`	No carriage-return output at column 0.
`ONLRET`	Newline to perform carriage-return function.

If `ONLCR` is set, newlines are mapped to the sequence `carriage-return, newline`. This ensures that each line begins on the left-hand side of the screen. Conversely, if `OCRNL` is set, then carriage-returns are translated into newlines. The flag `ONLRET` tells the terminal driver that newlines themselves will perform the carriage-return function for the type of terminal being used. If `ONOCR` is set then no carriage-return will be sent if a line of zero length is output.

Almost all the other flags for the `c_oflags` member are concerned with delays in transmission associated with specific characters such as newline, tab, form-feed, etc. These delays allow for mechanical or screen movements which take up a finite time. Again see your local manual for details.

The `c_lflags` field

Perhaps the most interesting member of the `termio` structure for the programmer is the `c_lflags` member. It is used by the current line discipline to control terminal functions. As we mentioned previously, you will almost certainly need only to deal with the default line discipline, indicated by a value of zero for the `c_line` member. In this case, `c_lflags` controls the standard end user line-editing and interrupt facilities. The available flags are:

`ICANON`	Canonical, line-oriented input.
`ISIG`	Enable interrupt processing.
`XCASE`	Controls upper/lower-case mappings.
`ECHO`	Enable basic echoing of input.
`ECHOE`	Echo erase as backspace-space-backspace.
`ECHOK`	Echo newline after kill.
`ECHONL`	Echo newline.
`NOFLSH`	Disable flush after interrupt.

If `ICANON` is set, then canonical processing is performed. As we saw above, this enables use of the line-editing characters and the assembly of input in lines before they can be read. If `ICANON` is not set, the terminal is in a 'raw' mode usually associated with screen-oriented software and communications packages. Calls to `read` will now be satisfied directly from the input queue. In other words, the basic unit of input becomes the single character rather than the logical line. Programs can choose to read data a character at a time (useful for screen editors), or in large blocks of fixed size (useful for communications software). However, the programmer must now specify two additional parameters in order to fully control the behaviour of `read`. These are `MIN`, the minimum number of characters to be received before a `read` returns, and `TIME`, a timeout period for a `read`. Both parameters are stored in the `c_cc` array. This is an important topic, which we study in full detail in the next section. For now, just note that the following example shows how to turn the `ICANON` flag off:

```
#include <termio.h>

struct termio tdes;
 .
 .
 .
tdes.c_lflag &= ~ICANON;

ioctl(0, TCSETA, &tdes);
```

If the `ISIG` flag is set, the processing of the interrupt keys `INTR` and `QUIT` is enabled. Normally, of course, this allows a user to abort a running program. If `ISIG` isn't set, no checking is done and the `intr` and `quit` characters are passed without alteration to the reading program.

The `XCASE` flag, when combined with `ICANON`, enables the terminal driver to work with terminals that have restricted character sets, especially those that send upper-case characters only. Hopefully, you will never need to use this flag, which is mainly of historical interest.

If `ECHO` is set, then you will not be surprised to learn that characters will be echoed as they are typed. Turning this flag off is useful for password-checking routines, programs that use keys for special functions such as cursor movement and the like.

The rest of the echo control flags only have meaning when the terminal is being used in canonical mode.

If `ECHOE` is set, and `ECHO` is on, then the `erase` character will be echoed as the sequence `backspace-space-backspace`. This physically rubs out the last character on a terminal with a screen, giving the user positive feedback that the character has actually been erased. If `ECHOE` is set when `ECHO` is not, `erase` is instead echoed as `space-backspace`, and so rubs out the character under the cursor on a CRT/VDU-type terminal.

If `ECHOK` is set, a newline will be output when the kill character is hit. Again this makes plain to the user what is happening.

If `ECHONL` is set, newline will always be echoed even if other echoing is turned off; a useful feature with terminals that do their own, local echoing (in what is often referred to as **half-duplex** mode).

The last flag in this group, `NOFLSH`, suppresses the normal flushing of both input and output queues when the `intr` or `quit` keys are pressed.

Exercise 8.3 Write a program `ttystate` that prints out the current state of the terminal associated with standard input (if any). Output should be in terms of the names of preprocessor constants introduced in this section (for example `ICANON` and `ECHOE`). Use your system's UNIX manual to obtain a full list of the available names.

Exercise 8.4 Write a program `ttyset` that takes the output of `ttystate` and sets the terminal associated with its standard output to the state described. Are `ttystate` and `ttyset` in any way useful, singularly or as a pair?

8.3.6 The `MIN` and `TIME` parameters

The `MIN` and `TIME` parameters have meaning only when the `ICANON` flag is turned off. They are intended to fine-tune a program's control over data input, which is another way of saying the `read` statement. `MIN` gives the minimum number of characters that the terminal driver must receive before a call to read from the terminal returns. `TIME` specifies a timeout value that allows an additional degree of control. The actual timeout period is measured in tenths of a second.

The `MIN` and `TIME` values are held in the `c_cc` array of the `termio` structure that describes the terminal state. Their position in the array is defined by the constants `VMIN` and `VTIME` from `termio.h`. The following program fragment shows how to set them:

```
#include <termio.h>

struct termio tdes;
int ttyfd;

/*get current state*/
ioctl(ttyfd, TCGETA, &tdes);

tdes.c_lflag     &= ~ICANON; /*turn off canonical mode*/
tdes.c_cc[VMIN]  =  64;      /*in characters*/
tdes.c_cc[VTIME] =  2;       /*tenths of a second*/
```

`VMIN` and `VTIME` have the same values as `VEOF` and `VEOL`. This means that `MIN` and `TIME` occupy the same storage positions as the `eof` and `eol` characters. The moral here is that, when switching from canonical to non-canonical mode, be sure to give `MIN` and `TIME` values. Otherwise strange behaviour may result. (In particular, if `CTRL-D` is your `eof` character, you may find your program reading input in blocks of four characters. Why?) A similar argument applies in the reverse direction.

There are four possible `MIN` and `TIME` combinations.

Case 1: `MIN` *and* `TIME` *are both zero*
Here, a `read` will always return immediately. If characters are present within the input queue for that terminal (remember input may arrive at any time) they will be placed in the program buffer. So, if a program puts its control terminal into a 'raw' state with `ICANON` off, and `MIN` and `TIME` both equal to zero, the statement

```
nread = read(0, buffer, SOMESZ);
```

can return any number of characters from zero up to `SOMESZ` depending on how many characters are waiting in the queue when the call is made.

Case 2: `MIN` *greater than zero,* `TIME` *zero*
The timer plays no role here. A call to `read` will be satisfied only when there are `MIN` characters waiting to be read. This occurs even if the `read` call requested less than `MIN` characters.

The most trivial setting in this category has `MIN` equal to one, with `TIME` zero. This causes `read` to return each time the system receives a character on the terminal line. This may be useful when simply reading from a terminal keyboard, although keys which send multiple character sequences present a problem.

Case 3: `MIN` *zero,* `TIME` *greater than zero*
In this case, `MIN` plays no role. The timer is started as soon as the `read` call is made. The `read` returns as soon as the first character is received. If the timer expires (when `TIME` tenths of a second elapse) the `read` returns zero characters.

Case 4: both `MIN` *and* `TIME` *greater than zero*
This is perhaps the most useful and flexible case. The timer is now activated when the first character is received, rather than when the `read` call is made (in the words of the *SVID* it acts as an **interchange timer**). If `MIN` characters are received before the timeout period elapses, the `read` call returns. If the timeout point is reached, just the characters currently in the input queue will be returned to the user program. This mode of operation is useful when input arrives in bursts sent over a short period of time. It simplifies programming and also reduces the number of system calls that might otherwise need to be made. It would be useful, for example, in dealing with function keys that send a series of characters when pressed.

8.3.7 The `ioctl` system call

`ioctl` is a general-purpose call for controlling the devices associated with character special files, and can take a variety of argument types. We have already introduced the most basic functions of `ioctl` for standard UNIX terminals. In this section we will discuss all the `ioctl` calls that can be used with the standard terminal interface.

The terminal `ioctl` calls divide into two sub-types: **primary calls** and **additional calls**. Primary calls have the following usage.

Usage

```
#include <termio.h>

struct termio targ;
int ttyfd, cmd, retval;
 .
 .
 .

retval = ioctl(ttyfd, cmd, &targ);
```

`ttyfd` must be an open file descriptor for a terminal line. `targ` is a structure of type `termio`; it will hold a terminal state. The parameter `cmd` decides the action of `ioctl`. It can take the following values, which are defined in `termio.h`:

- `TCGETA` This instructs `ioctl` to copy the current terminal state parameters into `targ`.
- `TCSETA` The inverse of `TCGETA`, this command value will set the terminal parameters to the same values as held in `targ`. The effect is instantaneous, which can cause problems if the terminal driver is simultaneously writing to the terminal and you alter the `c_oflags` field. Imagine what could happen if you turned `OPOST` off for example.
- `TCSETAW` This performs the same function as `TCSETA`. However, it waits for the current output queue to empty before setting the new parameters. Consequently, this value should be used when altering parameters concerned with output to the terminal.
- `TCSETAF` Another version of `TCSETA`, this waits for the output queue to empty, then flushes the input queue, before setting the terminal parameters to the values held in `targ`.

The only thing worth saying about the return value `retval` from `ioctl` is that it is −1 on error. This applies to both primary and additional calls.

The additional `ioctl` calls provide the programmer with some degree of control over the input and output queues maintained by the terminal driver. They have the following usage.

Usage

```
#include <termio.h>

int ttyfd, cmd, arg, retval;
 .
```

```
.
.
retval = ioctl(ttyfd, cmd, arg);
```

Here, ttyfd and cmd retain their previous meanings. arg is now an integer that will carry additional information. The values for cmd available with this type of ioctl call are:

TCFLSH If arg is zero, the input queue is flushed. In other words all characters in the input queue are discarded. If arg is 1, the output queue is flushed. If arg is 2, both input and output queues are flushed.

TCXONC This provides start/stop control over the terminal driver. When arg is zero, output is suspended. It can be restarted by making a new call with the value of arg set to 1.

TCBRK This is used to send a break, which corresponds to zero bits for a quarter of a second. This is done only after the output queue has emptied.

The following two subroutines make use of primary ioctl calls. tsave saves the current parameters associated with the process's control terminal, and tback restores the last set of saved parameters. A Boolean variable saved is used to stop tback setting a terminal state when tsave hasn't been used.

```
#include <stdio.h>
#include <termio.h>

#define SUCCESS  0
#define ERROR    (-1)

/*tsaved will hold terminal parameters*/
static struct termio tsaved;

/*TRUE if parameters saved*/
static int saved = 0;

tsave() /*save terminal state*/
{
        if( !isatty(0) )
                return (ERROR);

        if(ioctl(0, TCGETA, &tsaved) >= 0){
                saved = 1;
                return (SUCCESS);
        }else
                return (ERROR);

}
```

```
tback() /*restore terminal state*/
{
        if( !isatty(0) || !saved)
                return (ERROR);

        return ioctl(0, TCSETAW, &tsaved);
}
```

These two routines can be used to bracket a section of code that temporarily alters the terminal state, as follows:

```
#include <stdio.h>

char *failed="couldn't save terminal parameters\n";

main()
{

        if(tsave() < 0){
                fprintf(stderr, failed);
                exit(1);
        }

        /*do the interesting part*/

        tback();
        exit(0);
}
```

8.3.8 The hangup signal

In Chapter 6 we saw that the hangup signal `SIGHUP` is sent to the members of a process group when the process leader exits (providing it has a control terminal). It also has another use, intended for environments where the connection between computer and terminal can be broken and the carrier signal associated with the terminal line can 'drop'. This can occur, for example, when terminals are connected over phone lines, or with certain local area networks. In such circumstances, the terminal driver should send `SIGHUP` to all processes that recognize the terminal as their control terminal. Unless trapped, this signal will cause program termination. (Unlike `SIGINT`, `SIGHUP` will normally halt a shell. In effect, a user is automatically logged out when his or her connection to the system is broken – a nice security feature.)

Normally a programmer should leave `SIGHUP` alone – it serves a good purpose. However, you might want to trap it in order to perform some clean-up operations:

```
#include <signal.h>

int hup_action();
   .
   .
   .

signal(SIGHUP, hup_action);
```

This approach is used in some editors which save your edited file and send you mail before exiting. If `SIGHUP` is ignored altogether (using `SIG_IGN` as the second argument to `signal`), and the terminal is hung up, future `read` calls on the terminal will return 0 to simulate end of file.

8.4 The `connect` example

In this section we will introduce a largish, and we hope useful, example program. `connect` is a communications program that has two modes of operation. In the first, it allows the user to 'connect' to one UNIX machine from another. In the second, it allows the user to transfer text files between the two machines. It parallels the standard UNIX communication program `cu`, and provides you with the framework to build your own data transfer utility.

The relationship between user, program and the two machines is shown in Figure 8.3. The machine on the left-hand part of this diagram is the **local machine**. This is the machine that the user first logs onto to run the `connect` program. There are two terminal ports of interest to us on this machine: `ttya` and `ttyb`. (Of course, the choice of names here is entirely arbitrary.)

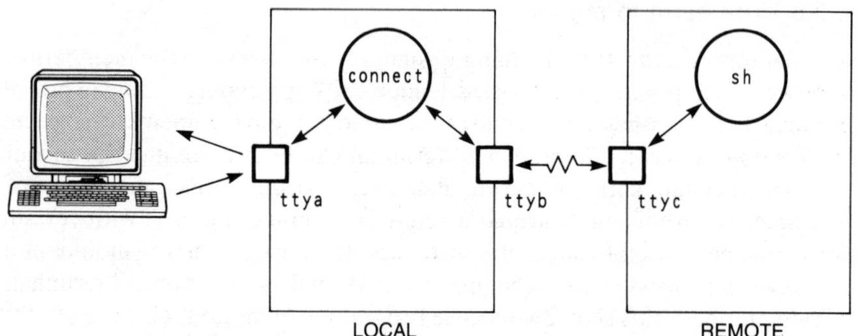

Figure 8.3 Machine relationship for `connect` example.

The terminal connected to terminal port `ttya` is the line through which the user first logs in. It will be the control terminal for the `connect` program.

The port ttyb provides the link to the other UNIX machine, which is described in the diagram as the **remote machine**. This port must be specially reserved for communications use. In particular, the system must not regard ttyb as a login port, otherwise the system would spawn a getty process (getty is the program that controls user logins, initially at least) and user programs would not have complete control over input and output through the port.

ttyb is connected to port ttyc on the remote machine. ttyc is a straightforward login port like ttya on the local machine. In fact, the remote machine treats port ttyc as if it was attached to a terminal rather than another machine. When a process running on the local machine writes to ttyb, the output string is passed to ttyc where it is regarded as input to the remote machine. In this way, a local process could login to the remote machine by sending a username, then a password. After that, it could send commands to be executed by the local shell.

For the purposes of our discussion, we will assume that the connection between ttyb and ttyc is, or appears to be, a simple cable. In reality, the connection might involve a modem and phone link, or a local area network. These bring their own complications which, for the sake of clarity, we shall ignore.

Our first task is to allow the user to login to the remote machine exactly as if his or her terminal were connected directly to it. All connect needs to do is pass data unchanged from ttya to ttyb, and vice versa. The only problem is how to deal with the fact that the user can type input, and the remote system deliver output simultaneously. The solution is both simple and elegant. Each invocation of connect will result in two independent processes. The first will pass characters from ttya to ttyb, from where they are passed to ttyc on the remote machine. The second receives characters from the remote machine as they arrive at ttyb and passes them to ttya. We are in effect letting the terminal driver deal with the problem of managing two independent streams of data.

The first file of the program we shall examine is the header connect.h. This file includes in turn the system header files we shall be using, such as termio.h. There are also several constants defined. Of these, the string STARTCOM will be used to form the command that will initiate a transfer from the local to the remote machine.

```
/*header file for connect program*/

#include <stdio.h>
#include <fcntl.h>
#include <termio.h>
#include <signal.h>
#include <setjmp.h>
```

```
#define ERROR       (-1)
#define SUCCESS      0
#define TRUE         1
#define FALSE        0

#define SENDFILE     1
#define EXIT         2
#define MAXTIME      30          /*1/10ths sec*/

#define STARTCOM\
 "mesg n; stty -opost; cat - > %s; stty opost; mesg y"

#define CTRLD       004          /*Control-D*/
#define CTRLP       020          /*Control-P*/
#define CTRLY       031          /*Control-Y*/
```

The first function we will look at is `main` itself. You should be able to see from it that the `connect` program is intended to be invoked as follows:

```
$ connect term-name speed
```

For example:

```
$ connect /dev/ttya 9600
```

The purpose of the `main` function is to validate the command line arguments and open the terminal line. Aside from standard system calls and library routines, the functions it calls are: `getspeed`, `ttyopen`, `cfatal` and `connect`. The `getspeed` function converts the second command line argument into a form suitable for `ioctl`. `ttyopen` is the terminal opening function we introduced earlier. (Those of you who intend to try this example for yourselves might like to alter `ttyopen` so that it uses the manifest constants from `connect.h`, rather than define them itself.) The `cfatal` function prints an error message, then causes the program to exit. `connect` is the final function invoked by `main`. It does the essential work, spawning the two child processes and handling file transfer.

```
/*main body of "connect" program*/

#include "connect.h"

main(argc, argv)
int argc; char *argv[];
{

    int speed = 0;    /*will hold speed for outward tty*/
    int linefd;       /*file descriptor for outward tty*/

    /*check command line*/
    if(argc < 2 || argc > 3)
```

```
        cfatal("usage: connect ttyname [speed]\n");

    /*get speed of outward line*/
    if(argc ==  3 && (speed = getspeed(argv[2])) == ERROR)
        cfatal("Invalid speed specified");

    /*open outward terminal line*/
    if( (linefd = ttyopen(argv[1], O_RDWR)) == ERROR)
        cfatal("Could not open outward line");

    /*check line is terminal*/
    if(!isatty(linefd))
        cfatal("device given is not a terminal");

    /*check std input/output attached to terminal*/
    if(!isatty(0) || !isatty(1))
        cfatal("Std. input/output not attached to terminal");

    /*call main routine*/
    connect(linefd, speed);

    close(linefd);
    exit(0);
}
```

`getspeed` is an extremely simple function; it converts its single string argument into one of the baud rate codes from `termio.h`. The value `ERROR` is returned if the input string isn't recognized.

```
/*get terminal speed from string*/

#include "connect.h"

getspeed(s)
char *s;
{
    int speed;

    switch(atoi(s)){
        case 300:  speed = B300;  break;
        case 1200: speed = B1200; break;
        case 2400: speed = B2400; break;
        case 4800: speed = B4800; break;
        case 9600: speed = B9600; break;
        default:   speed = ERROR;
    }

    return speed;
}
```

The cfatal routine is one of two that print error messages on standard error. The other is cwarn. The distinguishing feature of cfatal is that it stops program execution. Both cwarn and cfatal are contained in the same source file as follows:

```
/*cfatal and cwarn functions*/

#include "connect.h"


/*printf error message and die*/

cfatal(s)
char *s;
{
   cwarn(s);
   exit(1);
}

/*cwarn -- print message on standard error*/

cwarn(string)
char *string;
{

   if(isatty( fileno(stderr) ))
      fprintf(stderr, "\r%s\r\n",  string);
   else
      fprintf(stderr, "%s\n",   string);
}
```

The cwarn function extracts the file descriptor associated with the Standard I/O structure stderr by using the library function fileno. It then checks this with isatty to see whether standard error is connected to a terminal. If so, it inserts a carriage-return into the output sequence; this ensures that the error message always starts on the left-hand side of the screen, whatever the terminal state.

The connect function performs the real purpose of this example. It takes two parameters: the open file descriptor which came from ttyopen and the speed parameter which came from getspeed. Its job is to create two processes, one (the parent) to pass characters to the remote system, one (the child) to receive characters from the remote system. It also initiates a file transfer to the remote system when required. In pseudo-code, the action of the connect function can be represented as:

```
ignore standard signals

save initial states of control
terminal and outward terminal line

display "connecting" message

do{

    set terminal states to
    "raw" mode

    fork

    if (fork successful){

        if(parent  process)
              status = result of "to" function
        else
              call "from" function /*never returns*/

        kill child process

        if(status equals SENDFILE)
              call "sendfile" function


     }

}while(status not equal to EXIT)

restore terminal states and signal settings
```

The important points to understand here are as follows. First, the `from` routine executed by the child never exits. Hence the `kill` statement is only ever executed by the parent. Second, the `status` variable returned by `to` corresponds to a special command typed by the user. `SENDFILE` and `EXIT` are, of course, defined in `connect.h`.

The actual source code for `connect` follows:

```
/*connect function provides async. tty emulation*/

#include "connect.h"

connect(lfd, speed)
int lfd, speed;
{

   struct termio linesave, ctrlsave;
   int (*sigintr)(), (*sigquit)();
```

```
    int pid, status;

    /*ignore standard signals*/
    sigintr = signal(SIGINT,  SIG_IGN);
    sigquit = signal(SIGQUIT, SIG_IGN);

    /*save initial terminal-line states*/
    ioctl(0,   TCGETA, &ctrlsave);
    ioctl(lfd, TCGETA, &linesave);

    cwarn("Connecting");

    do{

       /*set terminal states to "raw" mode*/
       tty_raw(0, 0, 1, 0);
       tty_raw(lfd, speed, 1, 0);

       if((pid = fork()) != ERROR){
          if(pid > 0)
             status = to(lfd); /*to remote*/
          else
             from(lfd); /*from remote, never returns*/
       }else{
             cwarn("could not fork");
             break;
       }


       kill(pid, SIGTERM);
       wait((int *)0);

       if(status == SENDFILE)
           sendfile(lfd, &ctrlsave);

    }while(status != EXIT);


    /*restore terminal states*/
    ioctl(0,   TCSETAW, &ctrlsave);
    ioctl(lfd, TCSETAW, &linesave);

    /*restore signal handling*/
    signal(SIGINT,  sigintr);
    signal(SIGQUIT, sigquit);
}
```

The function `tty_raw` is called by `connect` to set both terminals on the local machine into a more or less ‘raw’ state; all logical processing is turned off, including echoing since the remote system will take care of that. In effect, the terminal driver makes both terminal ports transparent, simply passing data on as it receives it. Flow control is turned on, however, to make sure that data isn't lost unnecessarily. tty_raw is implemented as follows:

```
/*terminal handling routines*/

#include "connect.h"

/*set to "raw" mode*/
tty_raw(fd, speed, min, time)
int fd, speed, min, time;
{
    struct termio tdescrip;

    if(!isatty(fd)){
        cwarn("invalid terminal file descriptor in tty_raw");
        return ERROR;
    }

    /*get current state of terminal*/
    if(ioctl(fd, TCGETA, &tdescrip) == ERROR)
        return ERROR;

    /*change required characteristics*/
    tdescrip.c_iflag = (IXON|IXOFF);
    tdescrip.c_oflag = 0;
    tdescrip.c_lflag = 0;

    if(speed != 0){
        tdescrip.c_cflag &=~CBAUD;
        tdescrip.c_cflag |= speed;
    }

    tdescrip.c_cc[VMIN]  = min;
    tdescrip.c_cc[VTIME] = time;

    return ioctl(fd, TCSETAW, &tdescrip);
}
```

Notice the way ioctl is first used to get the current terminal state, which is then altered. The new state is applied with a second call to ioctl. The connect function actually calls tty_raw with a value of 1 for min, and zero for time. This allows the program to grab each character as it arrives, with no timeout.

If connect forks successfully, the nascent child process executes the from routine. This is simplicity itself, just taking characters from the remote machine and writing them to the control terminal. Looking back at Figure 8.3, characters are generated at terminal port ttyc, and passed to the local system via the line between `ttyc` and `ttyb`. The `from` function reads each character as it reaches `ttyb`. Characters are then written back to the process's controlling terminal `ttya`. Again note that `from` never exits.

```
/*echo back characters from outward line*/

#include "connect.h"

from(lfd)
int lfd;
{
   unsigned char c;

   for(;;){
      read(lfd, &c, 1);
      write(1, &c, 1);
   }
}
```

The `to` function executed by the parent is just a little more complicated; it reads characters from the keyboard one at a time, and if either `CTRL-Y` or `CTRL-P` is typed, then `SENDFILE` or `EXIT` is returned, respectively. Otherwise, each character is simply passed on to the remote system via a write to `ttyb` (identified by the file descriptor contained in the parameter `lfd`).

```
/*to -- handles input to outward terminal*/

#include "connect.h"

int to(lfd)
int lfd;
{
   unsigned char c;

   for(;;){

      read(0, &c, 1);
      if(c == CTRLY)
         return EXIT;
      else if (c == CTRLP)
         return SENDFILE;
      else
         write(lfd, &c, 1);
   }
}
```

The routines we have examined so far are the heart of the `connect` program, and fulfil our first functional requirement, allowing a user to login to a remote system. All that remains is to introduce the routines that perform the file transfer. The first of these is `sendfile`, which is invoked directly by the `connect` function itself. Together with its companion functions `intr` and `sendeot`, which must inhabit the same source file, `sendfile` looks like:

```
/*sendfile -- control function for file transfer*/

#include "connect.h"


static jmp_buf env;             /*used by intr()*/
static int slfd;                /*save lfd in this*/
static int in_xfer = FALSE;

sendfile(lfd, ctrl_term )
int lfd;
struct termio *ctrl_term;
{
   char name[256];
   int fd, intr(), intrflg;
   char remcom[256];

   /*save lfd for intr()*/
   slfd =    lfd;
   in_xfer = FALSE;

   /*restore original state ctrl terminal*/
   ioctl(0, TCSETAW, ctrl_term);

   /*set appropriate state for outward line*/
   tty_raw(lfd, 0, 0, MAXTIME);

   /*allow user to interrupt file transfer*/
   if((intrflg = setjmp(env)) != 0)
      return;

   signal(SIGINT, intr);
   signal(SIGQUIT, intr);

   /*get local file name*/
   printf("\nLocal file name >");
   scanf("%s", name);


   if((fd = open(name, O_RDONLY)) < 0){
      cwarn("couldn't open file");
      return;
   }
```

```
    /*send start command*/
    sprintf(remcom, STARTCOM, name);

    if( sendcommand(lfd, remcom) == SUCCESS){

        /*set flag for sendeot()*/
        in_xfer = TRUE;

        /*wait for stty to run*/
        sleep(3);

        /*do file transfer*/
        xfer(lfd, fd);
    }

    signal(SIGINT, SIG_IGN);
    signal(SIGQUIT, SIG_IGN);

    if(in_xfer)
        sendeot();

    close(fd);

}


/*handle interrupt during file transfer*/

intr()
{
    char nl = '\n';

    signal(SIGINT, SIG_IGN);
    signal(SIGQUIT, SIG_IGN);
    cwarn("Interrupted");

    if(in_xfer){
        /*make sure we're on new line*/
        write(slfd, &nl, 1);
        sendeot();
    }

    longjmp(env, 1);
}


sendeot()
{
```

```
    char eot = CTRLD;

    write(slfd, &eot, 1);
    printf("\r\nSent EOT\r\n");
}
```

As you can see, sendfile first performs some initialization, the most interesting part of which is the call to tty_raw with a timeout period of MAXTIME tenths of a second. sendfile then prompts for a local file name. At this point we use two routines from the Standard I/O library: scanf to read the filename from standard output and sprintf to form a command string. sprintf is very much like printf, but writes its output to a string (in this case remcom), rather than a file. (See Chapter 9 for a longer look at these and other Standard I/O functions.) The command is then sent to the remote machine by the function sendcommand, which also echoes the response to the user:

```
/*send command to remote*/

#include "connect.h"

sendcommand(line, string)
int line;
char *string;
{
    char cin = '\0',nl = '\n';

    write(line, string, strlen(string));
    write(line, &nl, 1);

    do{
        if(read(line, &cin, 1) == 1){
                write(1, &cin, 1);
        }else{
                cwarn("lost command echo");
                return ERROR;
        }

    }while(cin != '\n'); /*assumes NL echoed as CR-NL*/

    return SUCCESS;
}
```

Notice that sendcommand assumes that output lines from the remote system are terminated by carriage-return, newline.

The actual command sent will look something like:

```
mesg n; stty -opost; cat - > file; stty opost; mesg y
```

The first use of *mesg* suppresses messages being written by the remote system to `ttyc`. The *stty -opost* unsets the `OPOST` flag associated with `ttyc`, suppressing post-processing of output. This means that for each character sent to the remote system, only one will be echoed. In particular, `newline` will be read and echoed as just `newline`, not the pair `carriage-return, newline`. Just why this is necessary we will discover shortly. The *cat* part of the command does the essential work. It causes any output after this command line to be redirected to the named file. To put it another way, our program will transfer a file by writing it to the standard input of `cat` on the remote system. The rest of the command line is concerned with resetting things after `cat` has exited.

The routine that actually transfers the file byte by byte is `xfer`, which is implemented as follows:

```
/*xfer -- transfers data*/

#include "connect.h"

xfer(lfd, fd)
int lfd, fd;
{
   int nread, j ;
   char buf[BUFSIZ], cin;
   long nsent = 0l;


   while( (nread = read(fd, buf, BUFSIZ)) > 0){

      /*send data and wait for echo*/
      for(j = 0;j < nread; j++){

            write(lfd, &buf[j], 1);

            if(read(lfd, &cin, 1) != 1)
               cwarn("lost data (no echo)");

      }

      printf("\rsent %ld blocks", ++nsent);
      fflush(stdout); /*flushes messages*/

   }

}
```

Data is read from the input file in chunks of `BUFSIZ` bytes (the definition for which comes from `stdio.h`). `xfer` then writes out each character to the remote system. To pace the speed of the file transfer, and lessen the chance of data being lost, `xfer` waits for the remote machine to echo back each character before writing the next, perhaps the most natural of several ways of controlling the transfer speed. This was the reason for setting the remote terminal mode with *stty -opost*, ensuring that each character set results in just one being echoed. To provide some positive feedback, a message is written after each block has been transmitted.

An example dialogue

All that remains is to give an example dialogue. We will start just after our hypothetical user has logged onto the local machine. The `connect` program is invoked at shell level as follows:

```
$ connect /dev/tty6 9600
```

Once loaded and started by the system, `connect` displays the message: `Connecting`. What happens next depends partly on the exact nature of the link between the two machines and whether `connect` has been used before. Hopefully, a carriage-return or two should get the remote machine's login prompt. So the initial part of the dialogue might look something like:

```
$ connect /dev/tty6 96000

Connecting

login:keith
Password:<password>

This is the remote machine's login banner

$
```

The user has now logged onto the remote system. A file transfer can now be initiated with `CTRL-P`. The `connect` program's `sendfile` routine will then prompt for the local file name.

```
Local file name > localfile
```

Once return is typed, the remote system will echo the command sent by connect:

```
mesg n; stty -opost; cat - > localfile; stty opost; mesg y
```

and the file transfer proper will commence. As `connect` copies data to the remote system, it will print messages of the form `sent n blocks`. Each new message should overwrite the previous one on the screen. The final message, printed on a new line, is: `sent EOT` signifying the terminating end of text character has been sent. After that, the user can end the session by typing `CTRL-D` to logout from the remote, followed by `CTRL-Y` to terminate the `connect` program itself.

The whole dialogue might look like:

```
$ connect /dev/tty6 96000

Connecting

login:keith
Password:<password>

This is the remote machine's login banner

$
<CTRL-P>

Local file name >localfile


mesg n; stty -opost; cat - > localfile; stty opost; mesg y

sent 3 blocks
sent EOT
$ <CTRL-D>

login:<CTRL-Y>
```

Exercise 8.5 The version of `connect` shown here can only deal with text files with any certainty. If, for example, the file to be transferred contained the remote machine's `kill` or `intr` characters, the effect would be fairly dramatic. Can `connect` be adapted to allow binary data to be transferred? Hint: investigate the `stty` command more fully.

Exercise 8.6 Build in facilities that give the user more control over the characteristics of the outward port, e.g. flow control. What is the best way to alter or extend the user interface to deal with this? What facilities might be useful? Devise a method of allowing the user to execute a command on the local machine while connected to the remote. What problems are associated with this?

Exercise 8.7 Implement transfers in the other direction, i.e. from the remote to the local machine. How can reliability be maximized, if at all?

Exercise 8.8 A much more major project would be to add a file transfer protocol to `connect`. This would require a program on the remote to take care of that end of the protocol. Attempt this exercise only if you have the appropriate experience or confidence. Adapt the resulting package so that the remote end can be 'bootstrapped' without media transfer between the local and remote machines. (Hint: use a two-stage procedure involving the crude transfer method we introduced above.)

8.5 The past

That completes our look at the UNIX System V.2 terminal interface, but before moving on to some of the library functions provided by UNIX we would like make a couple of important points. The first is historical. The terminal interface discussed in this chapter first appeared in System III. Before that (for example in Version 7 of UNIX), the `termio` structure did not exist. Instead, terminal states were described by a somewhat simpler structure called `sgttyb`. With this structure type, the function of the `ioctl` call was more limited. Terminal parameters were obtained with a system call called `gtty` and set by one called `stty`.

The `sgttyb` structure and its associated calls can still be found, in a partial and undocumented form, on some more modern UNIX systems (although you should never use them). Some of the applications software you may meet may use these obsolete features, or at least have a structure influenced by them (the `curses` screen library falls into this latter category). In addition, some UNIX variants, notably Berkeley UNIX, have a terminal interface which has evolved from the `sgttyb` structure.

8.6 And the future

More important than a backward glance at `sgttyb` structures is the major innovation in the V.3 release of UNIX from AT&T.

This innovation centres on the idea of **streams**, a concept originated by Dennis Ritchie and described in a paper that appeared in the October 1984 edition of the *Bell Laboratories Technical Journal*. Streams represent a major structural change in the character I/O system. The motivation for such a change is twofold. First, the current developments in networking require better ways of building communication protocols. Second, the way the kernel traditionally handles terminal I/O is costly for some communication problems. This is because characters are treated internally on an individual basis. *Ad hoc* solutions to these problems have been implemented, but in no general, uniform manner.

The concept that Ritchie presents in his paper is both simple and elegant. In essence a stream is a linear sequence of processing modules, which can usefully be compared to a shell pipe line. However, unlike a pipe line, data is passed between modules in both directions. One end of each stream is bound to a user process, while the module at the other end is the device driver for the stream. The module closest to the user process forms the programmer's interface to the stream. The user process's calls to `write` are converted into messages which are sent down the stream and its `read` calls take data from the nearest stream module. To ensure homogeneity, control information is also passed in the form of inter-module messages.

When a stream is first opened (via a call to `open`), the two end modules are automatically connected together. This is the most primitive form of stream and presents the programmer with a very 'raw' interface. Additional modules can be inserted in a stream via calls to an extended version of `ioctl` (the fact that terminals are first opened in a very raw state results in a few changes being necessary to user level code).

In a stream version of UNIX, the terminal driver sits as such an additional module between the two end modules. If the actual device was an entry point to a network rather than a simple terminal, then another module might be introduced to handle the network protocol. If only file transfer was required, then the terminal driver could be discarded and just the protocol handler inserted into the stream. This illustrates the modularity and flexibility of the stream concept.

The structure of the modules that can be coupled to form a stream reflects the elegance of the overall design. Each module consists of two objects called **queues**, one for each direction, up and down the stream. In the scheme presented by Ritchie, each queue includes an actual character queue and related control information, a `put` procedure to place information on the queue and a `service` procedure to handle queued data. The `put` procedure is the point of access for other modules that might be connected to the module.

It would be premature of us to describe streams in more detail. However, they do seem to present the system programmer with a exciting prospect, especially if he or she is interested in the increasingly important area of data communications.

Chapter 9 The Standard I/O Library

9.1 Introduction

In the final chapters of the book we will turn our attention away from the system call interface and examine some of the standard subroutine libraries provided by UNIX (and, with varying degrees of completeness, by a host of C compiler systems in other environments).

We will start by studying the extremely important *Standard I/O Library* which was originally developed by Dennis Ritchie, and forms a major part of the C library provided with all UNIX systems. We briefly introduced Standard I/O in Chapter 2, and you have already met a few of its constituent routines, for example: `getchar` and `printf`.

The main aim behind the Standard I/O Library is the provision of efficient, extensive and portable file access facilities. The routines that make up the library achieve efficiency by providing an automatic buffering mechanism, invisible to the user, which minimizes both the number of actual file accesses and the number of low-level system calls made. The library is extensive because it offers many more facilities, such as formatted output and data conversion, than the file access primitives `read` and `write`. Standard I/O routines are portable because they are not tied to any specific features of the UNIX system and indeed have become part of the UNIX-independent ANSI standard for the C Language. Any C compiler worth its salt will offer access to a full implementation of the Standard I/O Library, whatever the host operating system.

In what follows, we will describe the UNIX implementation of the library, its major features and above all its usefulness for the systems programmer and software developer.

9.2 Streams and `FILE` structures

Standard I/O routines access files through entities called **streams** (not to be confused with the stream concept introduced at the end of Chapter 8, which is concerned with the kernel-level implementation of the character I/O system: an unfortunate clash of terminology). In essence a stream is simply the flow of data between a program and an open file. Aside from being highly evocative, this new piece of terminology emphasizes that Standard I/O acts on objects very different from the file descriptors used by the file access primitives we met in Chapter 2.

Within a program, a stream is identified by a pointer to a structure of type `FILE`. When a call to most Standard I/O routines is made, one of the parameters passed is a pointer to a `FILE` structure which indicates which input or output stream is to be used. A pointer to a `FILE` structure can therefore be compared to the integer file descriptors used with `read`, `write`, etc.

The definition of `FILE` is found in the standard header file: `stdio.h`. It must be stressed that a programmer will only very rarely be concerned with the actual implementation of the `FILE` type – indeed, its definition varies from system to system. However, for clarity, we will describe the definition of `FILE` from the `stdio.h` file on an AT&T 3B2 computer, which runs UNIX System V.2. It looks like this:

```
typedef struct _iobuf{
        int _cnt;
        unsigned char *_ptr;
        unsigned char *_base;
        char  _flag;
        char  _file;
} FILE;
```

The `_file` member is declared as `char`, but is in fact treated as a 'small', one-byte integer. It will hold a file descriptor when the stream identified by a `FILE` structure is associated with a file. This is a suitably explicit demonstration of the fact that Standard I/O ultimately uses the file access primitives `open`, `read`, `write`, `close`, etc. There is rarely any reason for a programmer to access this file descriptor directly. It is there for internal use by the Standard I/O Library.

The member `_flag` contains control information for the stream. It will, for example, allow the Standard I/O Library to tell whether the stream has been opened for writing, reading or both.

The structure members `_ptr`, `_cnt` and `_base` describe a character buffer that is associated with all open streams. `_base` points to the start of the buffer. `_ptr` points to the next character in the buffer available for processing, and the integer `_cnt` records how many characters are left in the buffer after the position indicated by `_ptr`. The size of the buffer will be `BUFSIZ` bytes. `BUFSIZ` is itself defined in `stdio.h` and, as we saw in Chapter 2, it gives the disk blocking factor for the host environment. Typical values include 512 and 1024.

All data read or written to a stream passes through its character buffer. For example, an output routine from the Standard I/O Library will fill the buffer character by character, adjusting `_ptr` and `_cnt` accordingly. If the buffer becomes full, an internal Standard I/O routine will write its contents to the file indicated by `_file`, using the `write` system call. This is invisible to the user program.

Similarly, an input routine will pull data out of the buffer associated with the stream. If the buffer is emptied, another buffer-full will be read from the file, using the `read` system call. Again, this remains invisible to the user program.

The Standard I/O Library's buffering mechanism ensures that data is always read or written to and from an external file in standard-size chunks. As a result, the numbers of file accesses and internal system calls are kept to an optimum level. However, since this buffering is performed internally by the Standard I/O routines themselves, a programmer can use routines from the library that logically read or write any number of bytes, even just one at a time. A program can therefore be written to reflect the structure of the problem, and efficiency matters largely left to the library. For this reason, Standard I/O is the preferred file access method for simple applications.

9.3 Opening and closing streams: `fopen` and `fclose`

Usage

```
#include <stdio.h>

FILE *stream;
char *filename, *type;
int retval;
  .
  .
  .

stream = fopen(filename, type);

retval = fclose(stream);
```

`fopen` and `fclose` are the Standard I/O Library's equivalents of `open` and `close`. The `fopen` routine opens the file identified by `filename` and associates a stream with it. If successful, `fopen` returns a pointer to a `FILE` structure to identify the open stream (the `FILE` structure actually pointed to is a member of an internally maintained table). `fclose` closes the file and associated stream identified by `stream`, and if the stream is an output stream, flushes any data remaining in the stream's buffers.

If `fopen` fails then it will return the constant `NULL`, which stands for a null pointer and is defined in `stdio.h`. Under these circumstances, the external integer `errno` will, as for `open`, contain a code indicating the cause of the error.

The second parameter to `fopen` points to a string which determines the mode of access. It can take the following basic values:

r Open filename for reading only. (If the file does not exist the call will fail and fopen will return NULL.)

w Create or truncate filename, and open it for writing only.

a Open filename for writing only, any data written will be automatically appended to the end of the file. If the file does not exist then create it for writing.

A file can also be opened for update, which in this context means a program can both read and write to the file. In other words, a program can mix input and output operations for the same file, without reopening it. However, this is more restrictive than the read/write mode supported by read and write, due to the Standard I/O Library's buffering mechanism. In particular, output cannot be followed by input unless an intervening call to one of the two Standard I/O routines fseek or rewind is made. These routines adjust the stream's read/write pointer and are discussed below. Similarly, input cannot be followed by output without a call first to fseek or rewind, or an input routine which positions the program at end of file.

Update mode is indicated by an additional '+' symbol on the type argument passed to open. All three of the strings we met above can be modified in this way:

r+ Open filename for update. Again, fopen will fail if the file doesn't exist.

w+ Create or truncate filename, and open it for update.

a+ Open for update. Data will be appended to file end as it is written. If the file does not exist then it will be created for writing.

When fopen creates a file it will usually give it permissions with value 0666. This enables all users to read and write the file. These default permissions can be changed by setting the process's umask value to a non-zero value. (We introduced the umask system call in Chapter 3.)

The following skeleton program demonstrates the use of fopen and its relationship to fclose. It will cause the file indata to be opened for reading providing it exists, and the file outdata to be either truncated or created. fatal is the error routine we introduced in previous chapters. It will simply pass its string argument to perror, then call exit to terminate execution.

```
#include <stdio.h>

char inname[]  = "indata";
char outname[] = "outdata";

main()
{
        FILE *inf, *outf;
```

```
        if( (inf = fopen(inname, "r")) == NULL)
                fatal("Could not open input file");

        if( (outf = fopen(outname, "w")) == NULL)
                fatal("Could not open output file");

        /*Do something interesting ......*/

        fclose(inf);
        fclose(outf);

        exit(0);
}
```

Actually, neither `fclose` call is needed in this particular context. The file descriptors associated with `inf` and `outf` will be automatically closed when the process exits, and `exit` will automatically 'flush' the data remaining in the buffer associated with `outf`, writing it to the file `outdata`.

A routine closely allied to `fclose` is `fflush`:

Usage

```
#include <stdio.h>

FILE *stream;
int retval;
  .
  .
  .
retval = fflush(stream);
```

This causes the output buffer associated with a stream to be flushed; in other words data in the buffer is written to the file immediately, regardless of whether the file buffer is full or not. It ensures that the external file matches the process's view of reality. (Remember, as far as the program is concerned, the data within the buffer has already been written to the file. The buffering mechanism is transparent.)

`stream` remains open after the call to `fflush`. Like `fclose`, `fflush` will return the constant `EOF` on error, zero on success. (`EOF` is defined in `stdio.h`. It actually stands for end of file, but is used for indicating errors as well.)

9.4 Single-character I/O: `getc` and `putc`

Usage

```
#include <stdio.h>

FILE *inf, *outf;
int c;
```

```
.
.
.

c = getc(inf);

putc(c, outf);
```

The simplest input and output routines provided by the Standard I/O Library are getc and putc. The routine getc returns the next character (more properly speaking the next *byte*) from the input stream inf. putc places a character, here denoted by c, onto the output stream outf.

For both routines the character c is defined, perhaps counter-intuitively, as int rather than char. This enables getc to return the constant EOF, which is defined in stdio.h to be −1, and therefore lies outside the possible range of values for an unsigned char variable. EOF is used by getc to indicate either that it has reached end of file or that an error has occurred. putc can also return EOF, if an error occurs.

The following example is a new version of the copyfile routine we introduced in Chapter 2; instead of using read and write, we have used getc and putc:

```
#include <stdio.h>

/*copy file f1 to f2 using Standard I/O*/

copyfile(f1, f2)
char *f1, *f2;
{

        FILE *inf, *outf;
        int c;

        if( (inf = fopen(f1, "r")) == NULL )
                return (-1);

        if( (outf = fopen(f2, "w")) == NULL){
                fclose(inf);
                return (-2);
        }

        while( ( c = getc(inf) ) != EOF)
                putc(c, outf);

        fclose(inf);
        fclose(outf);
        return (0);
}
```

The basic form of the inner `while` loop is probably the closest thing the C language has to a cliché. Again note how the variable `c` is defined as `int` rather than `char`.

Before moving on, a word of warning: `getc` and `putc` are not functions. They are macros defined in `stdio.h` which are expanded in line. For example, the definition of `getc` on a 3B2 running System V is:

```
( --(p)->_cnt < 0 ? _filbuf(p) : (int) *(p)->_ptr++)
```

This seemingly complex expression simply means: *decrement the* `_cnt` *member of the* `FILE` *structure. If it is greater than or equal to zero, pull the next character from the buffer. Otherwise call* `_filbuf` *to refill the buffer.*

Because they are macros, `getc` and `putc` will not behave sensibly if they are given arguments with side-effects. In particular, the expressions `getc(*f++)` and `putc(c, *f++)` will not produce the right results. Of course, the macro implementation ensures efficiency by eliminating unnecessary function calls. However, purists will be glad to know that `fgetc` and `fputc` are true functions, which do the same as their (almost) namesakes. They are rarely used, but are useful if function names need to be passed as parameters to other functions.

Exercise 9.1 In Exercises 2.3 and 2.4 we described a program called `count` which displayed the number of characters, words and lines in an input file. (Remember that a word is defined as either a single non-alphanumeric character or any contiguous sequence of alphanumeric characters.) Rewrite `count` using `getc`.

Exercise 9.2 Using `getc`, write a program which records the distribution of characters in a file, i.e. a program which records the number of times each separate character appears in the file. One way of doing this would be to declare an array of `long` integers to act as counts, then use the integer value of each input character as an index into the array. In this case, make sure your program behaves sensibly, even if the `char` type is by default `signed` on your machine (which means input bytes could take negative integer values). Using `printf` and `putc`, make your program display a simple histogram of the distribution it finds.

9.5 Pushing back characters onto a stream: `ungetc`

Usage

```
#include <stdio.h>

FILE *stream;
int c, retval;
  .
  .
  .
retval = ungetc(c, stream);
```

ungetc inserts the character c back onto the input stream stream. This is a logical operation only. The input file itself will not be altered. If ungetc is successful, the character contained in c will be the next character read by getc. Only one character of pushback is guaranteed. If the attempt to insert c fails, ungetc returns EOF. An attempt to push back EOF itself will always fail. This isn't usually a problem, however, since calling getc successively after end of file has been reached will result in EOF being returned on each occasion.

Typically, ungetc is used to restore a stream to its original state after one character too many has been read to test a condition. The following routine getword exploits this simple technique to return a string which contains either a contiguous sequence of alphanumeric characters or a single non-alphanumeric character. End of file is denoted by NULL. The routine getword takes a FILE pointer as argument. It uses two test macros from the standard header file ctype.h. The first is isspace which determines whether a character is a white-space character, such as space itself, tab or newline. The second is isalnum which tests whether a character is alphanumeric, i.e. a number or a letter.

```
#include <stdio.h>

/*for isspace and isalnum definitions*/
#include <ctype.h>

#define MAXTOK 256

static char inbuf[MAXTOK+1];

char *getword(inf)
FILE *inf;
{
        int c, count = 0;

        /*strip white space*/
        do{
             c = getc(inf);
        }while( isspace(c) );

        if( c == EOF)
             return (NULL);

        if( !isalnum(c) ) /*is character non-alphanumeric*/
             inbuf[count++] = c;
        else{

             /*assemble "word"*/

             do{
```

```
                    if( count < MAXTOK)
                        inbuf[count++] = c;

                    c = getc(inf);

                }while( isalnum(c) );
                ungetc(c, inf);  /*push back character*/
            }

            inbuf[count] = '\0'; /*make sure string returned*/
            return (inbuf);
}
```

If presented with the following input:

```
This is
the
  input data!!!
```

`getword` would return the following sequence of strings:

```
This
is
the
input
data
!
!
!
```

Exercise 9.3 Make `getword` understand numbers which might include a leading minus or plus sign and a decimal point.

9.6 Standard input, standard output and standard error

The Standard I/O Library offers three streams connected to standard input, standard output and standard error. (As we warned some way back, don't be confused by the terminology. The *Standard I/O Library* and *standard input* are two entirely different things.) These standard streams do not need to be opened, and are identified by the following `FILE` pointers:

`stdin` Corresponds to standard input.

`stdout` Corresponds to standard output.

`stderr` Corresponds to standard error.

The following statement will get the next character from `stdin`, which like file descriptor 0 defaults to the terminal keyboard:

```
inchar = getc(stdin);
```

Because `stdin` and `stdout` are used so much, two abbreviated forms of `getc` and `putc` are provided, namely `getchar` and `putchar`. `getchar` returns the next character from `stdin`, and `putchar` places a character onto `stdout`. Neither function takes a `FILE` pointer as argument.

The following program `io2` uses `getchar` and `putchar` to copy its standard input to its standard output:

```
/*io2 -- copy stdin to stdout*/

#include <stdio.h>

main()
{
        int c;

        while((c = getchar() ) != EOF)
                putchar(c);
}
```

When compiled, `io2` behaves exactly like the earlier `io` example from Chapter 2.

Like `getc` and `putc`, `getchar` and `putchar` are defined as macros. In fact, `getchar()` will usually expand to `getc(stdin)` and `putchar(c)` will similarly expand to `putc(c, stdout)`.

The stream `stderr` is intended for error messages. Because of this special function, output to `stderr` is normally unbuffered. In other words, a character sent to `stderr` will immediately be written to the file or device currently attached to standard error. If you are fond of embedding temporary trace statements in your code for test purposes, then it is advisable to write to `stderr`. Output to `stdout` is buffered and may be displayed one or two steps behind reality. (Alternatively, `fflush(stdout)` can be used to flush all messages held in the `stdout` buffer.)

Exercise 9.4 Using the standard time command, compare the performance of `io2` with the program `io` developed in Chapter 2. Adapt the original version of `io` so that it uses `read` and `write` to input, then output, a single character at a time. How do the performances of this and `io2` compare? Give reasons for any differences.

Exercise 9.5 Rewrite `io2` so that it more closely resembles the `cat` command. In particular, make it print out the contents of any files named in its command line arguments. Its input should default to `stdin` when no arguments are given.

9.7 Standard I/O status routines

A number of simple routines are provided for enquiring about the status of a stream. In particular, they allow a program to determine whether a Standard I/O input routine such as `getc` has returned `EOF` because end of file really has been reached, or because an error has occurred. The available routines are listed in the following usage description:

Usage

```
#include <stdio.h>

int retval, fd;
FILE *stream;
 .
 .
 .
retval = ferror(stream);

retval = feof(stream);

clearerr(stream);

fd = fileno(stream);
```

`ferror` is a Boolean function that returns non-zero, i.e. *true* as far as a C program is concerned, if an error has occurred on `stream` due to a previous input or output request. The error could have arisen due to a call to a file access primitive (`read`, `write`, etc.) failing within a Standard I/O routine. Conversely, if `ferror` returns zero (corresponding to *false*), no error has occurred. `ferror` can be used as follows:

```
if(ferror(stream)){
     /*handle error*/
     ...
}else{
     /*non-error branch*/
     ...
}
```

`feof` is a Boolean function that returns non-zero when an end of file condition has previously occurred on `stream`. A return value of zero indicates simply that `EOF` has not been reached.

`clearerr` is used to reset both the error and end of file indicators to zero on `stream`. This ensures that future calls to `ferror` and `feof` for that stream will return 0 unless some other exception has occurred in the mean time. For obvious reasons, `clearerr` is not a routine to be used lightly.

`fileno` is odd man out, since it is not concerned with error handling. It returns the integer file descriptor embedded in the `FILE` structure pointed to by `stream`. This is useful when you need to pass a file descriptor, instead of a `FILE` pointer, to a routine. However, do not use `fileno` to mix calls to the file access primitives and Standard I/O routines. Chaos will be the almost inevitable result.

The following example, `egetc`, uses `ferror` to distinguish between an error and genuine end of file when a Standard I/O routine returns `EOF`:

```
/*egetc - getc with error checking*/

#include <stdio.h>

int egetc(stream)
FILE *stream;
{

        int c;

        c = getc(stream);

        if( c == EOF){
            if(ferror(stream)){
                fprintf(stderr, "fatal error: input error\n");
                exit(1);
            } else
                fprintf(stderr, "warning: EOF\n");
        }

        return (c);
}
```

Note that all the functions described in this section are actually implemented as macros, and the usual caveats apply.

9.8 Input and output by line

Closely allied to the single-character I/O routines are a number of simple routines for reading and writing lines of data (a line being simply a sequence of characters terminated by a `newline`). These routines are suitable for interactive programs which read from the keyboard and write to the terminal screen. The basic line input routines are `gets` and `fgets`.

Usage

```
#include <stdio.h>

char *buf, *retstring;
FILE *inf;
```

```
int nsize;
  .
  .
  .

retstring = gets(buf);

retstring = fgets(buf, nsize, inf);
```

`gets` reads a sequence of characters from the standard input stream `stdin`, placing each character into a buffer pointed to by `buf`. Characters are read until a `newline` or end of file is encountered. The `newline` character is then discarded and a null character is placed into `buf` to give a well formed string. If successful, `gets` will return a pointer to `buf`. If an error occurs, or end of file is encountered and no characters have been read, `NULL` is returned instead.

`fgets` is a generalized version of `gets`. It reads characters from the stream `inf` into the buffer `buf` until `nsize - 1` characters have been read, or a `newline` or end of file has been encountered. With `fgets`, `newline` characters are not discarded and are placed at the end of the buffer (this helps the calling function determine the condition that caused `fgets` to return). Like `gets`, `fgets` returns a pointer to `buf` if successful or `NULL` otherwise.

`gets` is rather a primitive routine. Because it doesn't know the length of the buffer passed to it, an unexpectedly long line can cause a gross internal error. `fgets` (in conjunction with `stdin`) should be used instead.

The following routine, `yesno`, uses `fgets` in this manner to get a yes or no response from the user; it also calls `isspace` to skip white space in the answer:

```
/*yesno -- get yes or no response from user*/

#include <stdio.h>
#include <ctype.h>

#define YES     1
#define NO      0
#define ANSWSZ 80

static char pdefault[]="Type 'y' for YES, 'n' for NO";
static char error[]   ="Unexpected response";

int yesno(prompt)
char *prompt;
{

     char buf[ANSWSZ], *p_use, *p;
```

```
        /*if prompt not NULL use it. Otherwise use pdefault*/
        p_use = (prompt != NULL) ? prompt : pdefault;

        /*loop until correct response*/

        for(;;){

             /*print prompt*/
             printf("%s > ", p_use);

             if( fgets(buf, ANSWSZ, stdin) == NULL)
                    return EOF;

             /*strip leading white space*/
             for(p = buf; isspace(*p); p++)
                    ;

             switch(*p){
                case 'Y':
                case 'y':
                    return(YES);
                case 'N':
                case 'n':
                    return(NO);
                default:
                    printf("\n%s\n", error);
             }
        }
}
```

The inverse routines for gets and fgets are puts and fputs, respectively.

Usage

```
#include <stdio.h>

char *string;
FILE *outf;
int retval;
  .
  .
  .
retval = puts(string);

retval = fputs(string, outf);
```

puts writes the characters in string to the standard output stream stdout, excluding the terminating null character. fputs writes string to the output stream denoted by `outf`. To ensure compatibility with older versions of the system, `puts` appends a newline character while `fputs` does not. Both functions return `EOF` on error.

The following call to `puts` causes the message `Hello, world` to be printed on standard output. A `newline` is automatically added:

```
puts("Hello, world");
```

9.9 Binary input and output: `fread` and `fwrite`

Usage

```
#include <stdio.h>

char *buffer;
int size, nitems, result;
FILE *inf, *outf;
  .
  .
  .
result = fread(buffer, size, nitems, inf);

result = fwrite(buffer, size, nitems, outf);
```

These two highly useful routines are provided for binary input and output. `fread` reads `nitems` objects of data from the input stream corresponding to `inf`. The bytes read will be placed in the character array `buffer`. Each object read is represented as a sequence of bytes which is `size` in length. The return value in `result` gives the number of objects successfully read.

`fwrite` is the exact inverse of `fread`. It will write the data contained in `buffer` to the output stream denoted by `outf`. This buffer is considered as consisting of `nitems` objects which are `size` bytes long. The return value gives the number of records actually written.

These routines are typically used to transfer the contents of arbitrary C data structures to and from binary files. In such circumstances, the argument `buffer` is cast into a character pointer. The `size` parameter is then replaced by a call to `sizeof`, which gives the byte size of the structure.

The next example indicates how this works. It centres on a structure template `dict_elem`. An occurrence of this structure can be used to represent part of a record within a simple database system. To use database terminology, a `dict_elem` structure is intended to describe a database **field** or **attribute**. We have placed the definition of `dict_elem` in a header file called `dict.h`, which looks like:

```
/*dict.h -- header for data dictionary routines*/

#include <stdio.h>
```

```
/*dict_elem -- data dictionary element  */
/*describes a field in a database record*/

struct dict_elem{
    char d_name[15];          /*name of dictionary member*/
    int  d_start;             /*starting position in record*/
    int  d_length;            /*length of field*/
    int  d_type;              /*denotes type of data*/
};

#define ERROR      (-1)
#define SUCCESS     0
```

Without going into too much detail about the meaning of the structure, we will introduce two routines `writedict` and `readdict` which write and read an array of `dict_elem` structures respectively. The files these two routines create can be thought of as simple **data dictionaries** for records within the database system.

`writedict` takes two parameters, a name for the output file and the address of an array of `dict_elem` structures. This list is assumed to terminate at the first structure in the array in which the `d_type` member is equal to zero:

```
#include "dict.h"

writedict(dictname, elist)
char *dictname;
struct dict_elem elist[];
{

    register int j;
    FILE *outf;

    /*open output file*/
    if( (outf = fopen(dictname,  "w")) == NULL)
        return ERROR;

    /*calculate length of array*/
    for(j = 0; elist[j].d_type != 0; j++)
            ;


    /*write out list of dict_elem structures*/
    if(fwrite((char *)elist, sizeof(struct dict_elem), j, outf) < j){
            fclose(outf);
            return ERROR;
    }

    fclose(outf);
    return SUCCESS;
}
```

Notice how the address of the array `elist` is cast into a character pointer with `(char *)`. The use of `sizeof(struct dict_elem)` is another important aspect used to tell `fwrite` how big the `dict_elem` structure is in bytes.

The `readdict` routine uses `fread` to recover a list of structures from a file. It takes three parameters: `indictname`, which points to the name of the dictionary file, `inlist` which points to an array of `dict_elem` structures into which the list held on disk will be led, and `maxlength` which indicates the length of this array.

```
struct dict_elem *readdict(indictname, inlist, maxlength)
char *indictname;
struct dict_elem inlist[];
int maxlength;
{
	register int i;
	FILE *inf;

	/*open input file*/
	if((inf = fopen(indictname, "r")) == NULL)
	   return NULL;

	/*read in dict_elem structures from file*/
	for(i = 0; i < maxlength -1; i++)
	   if(fread( (char *)&inlist[i], sizeof(struct dict_elem),
	       1, inf) < 1) break;

	fclose(inf);

	/*mark end of list*/
	inlist[i].d_type = 0;

	/*return beginning of inlist*/
	return inlist;
}
```

Again, note the use of a cast and `sizeof`.

We should add an important caveat to this discussion. The binary data written to a file with `fwrite` reflects the internal storage of data within the system's memory. Since this is machine-dependent, due to issues such as byte ordering and padding, data written on one machine may not be readable on another, unless considerable care is taken to put the information into a machine-independent format.

One final point: we could have used `read` and `write` directly to achieve much the same result. For example:

```
write(fd, (char *)ptr, sizeof(struct dict_elem));
```

The main advantage of the Standard I/O version is again efficiency. Data will ultimately be read and written in large blocks, whatever the size of the `dict_elem` structure.

Exercise 9.6 The present versions of `writedict` and `readdict` manipulate dictionary files that can really describe only one record type. Adapt them so that information on several record types can be held in the same file. In other words, allow a dictionary file to contain several independent, named lists of `dict_elem` structures. (Hint: include a 'header' structure at the top of the file that contains information on the numbers of record and field types.)

9.10 Random file access: `fseek`, `rewind`, `ftell`

The Standard I/O Library provides routines for random access which allow the programmer to reposition a file pointer in a stream, or find out its current position. These routines are: `fseek`, `rewind` and `ftell`. They can be used only on files which support random access (which excludes terminals for example).

Usage

```
#include <stdio.h>

FILE *stream;
long offset, position;
int direction, result;
  .
  .
  .

result = fseek(stream, offset, direction);

rewind(stream);

position = ftell(stream);
```

`fseek` parallels its low-level counterpart `lseek` and sets the file pointer within the file associated with `stream`. It therefore redefines the position of the next input or output operation. The parameter `direction` determines the starting point from which the new position in the file is to be calculated. If it is given the value zero, the start of file is used; if it is 1, the current position is used; if it is 2 the end of file is used. `offset` gives the number of bytes to be added to this starting position. As with `lseek`, this value can be any valid long integer, including negative ones. Under normal circumstances `fseek` returns zero. A non-zero value indicates error.

`rewind(stream)` is a simple shorthand for

```
fseek(stream, 0L, 0).
```

In other words, it resets the read-write pointer to the beginning of the file. No value is returned (indeed, `rewind` is properly defined as a `void` function).

`ftell` returns the program's current position within the stream. This is given in terms of the number of bytes from the start of the file, counting from zero.

9.11 Formatted output: the `printf` family

Usage

```
#include <stdio.h>

char *fmt, *string;
FILE *outf;
int retval;

/*NB parameters arg1 ..  have arbitrary type*/
  .
  .
  .
retval = printf(fmt, arg1, arg2 ... argn);

retval = fprintf(outf, fmt, arg1, arg2 ... argn);

retval = sprintf(string, fmt, arg1, arg2 ... argn);
```

These routines each take a format string `fmt` and a variable number of arguments of arbitrary type (denoted here by `arg1`, `arg2`, etc.) to produce an output string. This string will contain the information held in the parameters `arg1` to `argn` using the format specified in `fmt`. With `printf` this string is then copied onto the `stdout` stream. With `fprintf` it is copied to the stream identified by `outf`. As for `sprintf`, it is not really an output function at all. The 'output' string created by `sprintf` is instead copied into the character array pointed to by the pointer `string`. For programming convenience, `sprintf` will also automatically add a terminating null character.

The format string argument `fmt` is a similar construct to the formats found in the FORTRAN language. It contains a mixture of ordinary characters, which are copied verbatim, and a series of **conversion specifications**. These are sub-strings which always begin with the percent sign '`%`' (if you need to print out the percent sign itself, you must represent it by two percent signs '`%%`').

There should be one such conversion specification for each of the arguments `arg1`, `arg2`, etc. Each conversion specification tells `printf` and its relatives the type of the corresponding argument, and how it is to be mapped to an output sequence of ASCII characters.

Before discussing the general form of these specifications, the following example demonstrates the use of a `printf` format for two simple cases. In the first there are no arguments apart from the `fmt` string itself. In the second there is one additional argument: the integer `iarg`.

```
int iarg = 34;
 .
 .
 .
printf("Hello, world!\n");
printf("The variable iarg has the value %d\n", iarg);
```

Because there are no arguments for conversion in the first call, there are no conversion specifications embedded in the format string. The statement therefore simply results in the message

```
Hello, world!
```

being displayed on standard output, followed by a newline (remember, the symbol `\n` within a string is interpreted by C as standing for `newline`). In the second `printf` statement, there is one additional argument `iarg` and therefore one conversion specification within the format string, namely `%d`. This tells `printf` that the additional argument is an integer which is to be printed in decimal form (hence the use of the letter `d`). The output from this statement will therefore be

```
The variable iarg has the value 34
```

The various forms of conversion specification possible include:

Integer conversions

`%d` As we have seen, this is the standard conversion code for a signed integer. If the value is negative, a minus sign will be automatically added.

`%u` Argument is an `unsigned int`, to be printed in decimal form.

`%o` Argument is an integer, to be printed in unsigned octal form.

`%x` Argument is an integer, to be printed in unsigned hexadecimal form. The characters `a`, `b`, `c`, `d`, `e`, `f` will be used for the additional hexadecimal digits. If the specification `%X` is given instead, then `A`, `B`, `C`, `D`, `E`, `F` will be substituted.

`%ld` Argument is a `long`, signed integer, to be printed in decimal form. The programmer can also use `%lo`, `%lu`, `%lx`, and `%lX`.

Floating-point conversion

`%f` Argument is of type `float` or `double`, to be printed in standard decimal form.

`%e` Argument is of type `float` or `double`, to be printed in exponential form, which is conventional in scientific applications. The letter `e` will be used to introduce the exponent. If the specification `%E` is given, upper case `E` will be used instead.

`%g` This is a mixture of the `%e` and `%f` specifications. It indicates that the argument it matches is either `float` or `double`. Floating-point or exponential notation (as for `%e`) will be used according to the size of the number. If `%G` is given instead, then the `%E` style will be used when appropriate.

String and character control

`%c` Argument is of type `char`, to be output exactly as it is, even if it is a 'non-printing' character. The numeric value held in a character can be displayed using an integer conversion code. This is useful if the character has no meaningful representation on your terminal.

`%s` The corresponding argument is taken to be a string (that is, a character pointer). The contents of this string will be transferred verbatim to the output stream. The string must, of course, be null-terminated.

The next example routine `warnuser` demonstrates use of the `%c` and `%s` conversions. It uses `fprintf` to print a warning message on standard error via the stream `stderr`. If `stderr` corresponds to a terminal, the routine also attempts to ring the bell three times by sending `CTRL-G` (ASCII `BEL`, which has value 0x07 in hexadecimal). The routine makes use of `isatty` which determines whether a file descriptor corresponds to a terminal, and `fileno` which returns the file descriptor associated with a stream. `isatty` is a standard UNIX function we introduced in Chapter 8, while `fileno` is a part of the Standard I/O Library itself, described in Section 9.7.

```
/*warnuser -- ring bell, print message*/

#include <stdio.h>

/*this works for most common terminals*/
char bel = 0x07;

warnuser(string)
char *string;
{

        /*is it a terminal??*/
        if(isatty(fileno(stderr)))
                fprintf(stderr, "%c%c%c", bel, bel, bel);

        fprintf(stderr, "Warning:%s\n", string);
}
```

Specifying width and precision

Conversion specifications can also include information about the minimum character **width** of a field in which an argument is printed, and the **precision** for that field. In the case of an integer argument, precision is taken to mean the minimum number of digits to appear. In the case of a `float` or `double` argument, the precision gives the number of digits to appear after the decimal point. With a string argument, it gives the maximum number of characters that can be taken from the string.

The width and precision information in a conversion specification appear immediately after the percent sign, separated by a decimal point. For example,

```
%10.5d
```

means: *print the corresponding* `int` *argument in a field 10 characters wide; if the argument has less than five digits, pad it with leading zeros*. The specification

```
%.5f
```

means: *print the corresponding* `float` *or* `double` *argument with five decimal places*. This particular example emphasizes that the precision part can occur on its own. Similarly, just the width can be given. So the specification

```
%10s
```

means: *print the corresponding string in a field which is a minimum of 10 characters in length*.

All the above examples will produce output which is right-justified within the character field specified. To ensure output is left-justified, a minus sign must appear immediately after the percent symbol. So, the conversion specification

```
%-30s
```

means that the corresponding string argument will be printed on the left-hand side of a field of at least 30 characters across.

On occasion, the width part of a conversion specification cannot be calculated until the program is actually running. To get around this, the width specification can be replaced with an asterisk (*). `printf` will then expect the asterisk to be matched by an integer giving the desired field width. So:

```
int width, iarg;
  .
  .
  .
printf("%*d", width, iarg);
```

will cause the integer `iarg` to be printed in a field `width` characters wide. (Note: this mechanism isn't available on all variants of UNIX.)

An economy pack example

The number of permutations of different formats is obviously immense, so to save space we have crammed several examples in the next, entirely unrealistic, example program. The function `atan` is the standard arctangent function from the UNIX maths library. (For this reason, if you try this example you must give the flag *-lm*, or similar, to `cc` in order to load the maths library during linking.)

```
/*cram -- economy pack printf demonstration*/

#include <stdio.h>

main()
{

	static char weekday[]  = "Sunday";
	static char month[]    = "September";
	static char string[] = "Hello, world";

	int i = 11058;
	int day = 15, hour = 16, minute = 25;

	extern double atan();

	/*print a date*/
	printf("Date is %s, %d %s, %d:%.2d\n",
	         weekday, day, month, hour, minute);

	/*print newline again*/
	putchar('\n');

	/*show width, precision interaction for string*/
	printf(">>%s<<\n", string);
	printf(">>%30s<<\n", string);
	printf(">>%-30s<<\n", string);
	printf(">>%30.5s<<\n", string);
	printf(">>%-30.5s<<\n", string);

	putchar('\n');

	/*print i in variety of styles*/
	printf("%d, %u, %o, %x, %X\n", i, i, i, i, i);

	/*print pi to 5 decimal places*/
	printf("PI is %.5f\n", 4*atan(1.0));

}
```

This produces the following output:

```
Date is Sunday, 15 September, 16:25

>>Hello, world<<
>>                  Hello, world<<
>>Hello, world            <<
>>                        Hello<<
>>Hello                   <<

11058, 11058, 25462, 2b32, 2B32
PI is 3.14159
```

Special symbols

Output conversion specifications can be complicated still further by some additional symbols. One such is hash or sharp, i.e. `#`. It must occur immediately before the width part of a specification. For unsigned integer conversions involving the `o`, `x`, and `X` conversion codes, it causes one of `0`, `0x` or `0X` to be automatically prepended to the output number as appropriate. So, the code fragment

```
int arg ;
arg = 0xFF;
printf("In octal, %#o\n", arg);
```

produces the output:

```
In octal, 0377
```

With floating point conversions, a `#` will force a decimal point to be printed, even with zero precision.

The plus sign (`+`) can also be introduced in conversion specifications to force a `+` symbol to be printed when the number is positive. (This only has meaning for signed integers or floating-point numbers.) It occupies rather a peculiar place in the conversion specification, coming immediately after the minus sign that indicates left-justification, or the percent symbol if no minus sign is present. The three lines of code

```
float farg;
farg = 57.88;
printf("Value of farg is %-+10.2f\n");
```

produce

```
Value of farg is +57.88
```

Notice the combination of the minus and plus symbols. The `+` symbol could also be replaced with a space. In this case, `printf` would print out a space where a plus sign would appear. This enables negative and positive numbers to be properly aligned.

The `sprintf` routine

Before moving on, there is one point to make about `sprintf`. It is simply this: don't think of `sprintf` as an output routine. It provides, in fact, the most flexible string manipulation and general conversion facilities in the C libraries. The following code fragment indicates how it might be used:

```
/*genkey -- generate key for use in database*/
/*          key will always be 20 chars long*/

#include <stdio.h>

char *genkey(buf, suppcode, orderno)

char *buf;          /*will hold generated key*/
char *suppcode;     /*supplier code*/
long orderno;       /*order number*/
{
        /*is suppcode valid?*/
        if(strlen(suppcode) != 10)
                return (NULL);

        sprintf(buf, "%s_%.9ld", suppcode, orderno);

        return (buf);
}
```

The following call to `genkey`:

```
printf("%s\n", genkey(buf, "abcedfghij", 12));
```

will produce this string:

```
abcedfghij_000000012
```

9.12 Formatted input: the `scanf` family

Usage

```
#include <stdio.h>

char *fmt, *string;
FILE *inf;
int retval;

/*NB: ptr1 .. ptrn are all pointers.
 *The type of the variable they point
 *to is arbitrary.
 */
 .
 .
 .
```

```
retval = scanf(fmt, ptr1, ptr2, ... ptrn);

retval = fscanf(inf, fmt, ptr1, ptr2 ... ptrn);

retval = sscanf(string, fmt, ptr1, ptr2 .. ptrn);
```

These routines are the inverses of the routines in the `printf` family. They all accept input from a stream (or string in the case of `sscanf`), decode this according to format information carried in the string `fmt`, and place the resulting data into the variables indicated by the pointers `ptr1` to `ptrn`. The file pointer for the stream is advanced by the number of characters processed.

`scanf` will always read from `stdin`, the stream associated with standard input. The routine `fscanf` reads from the stream `inf`. The routine `sscanf` is the black sheep of the family and decodes a string pointed to by `string`, rather than accept input from a stream. Because it acts on a string held in memory, `sscanf` is particularly useful when an input string has to be read more than once.

The format string `fmt` is similar in structure to the format strings used by `printf`. For example, the following statement reads the next integer on standard input:

```
int inarg;

scanf("%d", &inarg);
```

The most important thing to note here is that `scanf` is given the address of `intarg`. This is because C is only able to pass parameters *by value*, and never *by reference*. Therefore if we want `scanf` to alter a variable that lives in the calling routine, we must pass it a pointer which contains the address in memory of the variable. It is all too easy to forget the ampersand, and this can cause a memory fault. Enthusiastic novices should also resist the temptation to over-compensate by placing ampersands before existing pointers or addresses, such as the name of character arrays.

In general a `scanf` format string can contain:

1. *White-space characters*, i.e. blanks, tabs, newlines and form feeds. Usually, this matches all white space from the current position in the input stream, up until the first non-white-space character.
2. *Ordinary, non-white-space characters*. These must match exactly the corresponding characters in the input stream.
3. *Conversion specifications*. As we mentioned earlier, these are in general very similar to the specifications used with `printf`.

The next example shows use of `scanf` with several variables of different type:

```
/*demo program for scanf*/

#include <stdio.h>

main()
{
    int i1, i2;
    float flt;
    char str1[10], str2[10];

    scanf("%2d%2d %f %s %s", &i1, &i2, &flt, str1, str2);
      .
      .
      .
}
```

The first two conversion specifications within the format string tell `scanf` to look for two integers (in decimal format). Because a field width of two is given in each case, the first integer will be assumed to be held in the next two characters read, while the second will lie in the two positions after that (in general, a field width denotes the maximum number of characters that a value can occupy). The `%f` specification denotes a variable of type float. `%s` indicates that a string, delimited by white-space characters, is expected. So, if this program was to be presented with the input sequence

```
1112 34.07
keith ben
```

the result would be as follows:

`i1` would be set to `11`

`i2` would be set to `12`

`flt` would be set to `34.07`

The string `str1` would contain `"keith"`

The string `str2` would contain `"ben"`

Both strings would be null-terminated. Note that `str1` and `str2` must have been defined large enough to hold the expected input strings and the terminating null. It is not good enough to pass a non-initialized character pointer to `scanf`.

With the conversion specification `%s`, the string in question is expected to be delimited by white-space characters. To read white-space and other characters the `%c` conversion code should be used. For example, the statement

```
scanf("%10c", s1);
```

will read in the next 10 characters from the input stream, whatever they are, and place them into the character array `s1`. Because the `c` conversion code matches white space, the specification `%1s` should be used to get the next non-space character. For example,

```
/*read in 2 chars, starting at 1st non-space char*/
scanf("%1s%1c", &c1, &c2);
```

Another way of specifying string data, and one that has no equivalent in the format strings used with `printf`, is the **scan-set**. This is a sequence of characters placed between square brackets: `[` and `]`. The input field is taken to be the longest sequence of characters that matches characters in the scan-set (and in this case white space isn't skipped unless it is part of the scan-set). For example, the statement,

```
scanf("%[ab12]%s", str1, str2);
```

will, when presented with the input string,

```
2bbaa1other
```

place `2bbaa1` into the string `str1` and `other` into the string `str2`.

There are several useful conventions used in the construction of scan-sets, conventions that should be familiar to users of `grep` and `ed`. For example, a range of characters is denoted by a substring like `first-last`. So, `[a-d]` is equivalent to `[abcd]`. If the dash (-) is to appear as part of the scan-set itself, it must be the first or last character. Similarly, if the right square bracket `]` is to appear, then it must be first character after the opening `[`. If the circumflex (^) appears as the first character in the scan-set, then the scan-set is redefined as all the characters *not* in the present scan-set.

For assignments to `long` integers and floating-point variables of type `double`, an `l` (ell) must follow the percent symbol in the corresponding conversion specification. This enables `scanf` to determine the size of the parameter it is dealing with. The following program fragment shows how to read variables of both types from the input stream:

```
long l;
double d;

scanf("%ld %lf", &l, &d);
```

One other situation that will often occur is when the input stream contains more data than the programmer is interested in. To deal with this, a conversion specification can contain an asterisk (`*`) immediately after the leading percent symbol. This indicates **assignment suppression**. In effect, an input field which matches the specification is ignored. The call

```
scanf("%d %*s %*d %s", &ivar, string);
```

with the input line

```
131 cat 132 mat
```

will cause `scanf` to assign `131` to `ivar`, skip the next two fields, then place `mat` into `string`.

Finally, what of the return value for members of the `scanf` family? They will normally return the number of successfully matched and assigned items. This return value can be zero when an early conflict occurs between a format string and the actual input. If the input runs out before a successful match or a conversion conflict, then `EOF` is returned.

Exercise 9.7 Write a program that takes its arguments, which should be decimal integers, and displays them in hexadecimal and octal form.

Exercise 9.8 Write `savematrix`, which should save an integer matrix of arbitrary dimensions in a file in readable form, and `readmatrix` which recovers a matrix from file. Use only `fprintf` and `fscanf` to do the work. Ensure that the amount of white space (blanks, tabs, etc.) within the file is kept to a minimum. Hint: use the variable width symbol (*) when writing the file.

9.13 Running programs with the Standard I/O Library

The Standard I/O Library provides a small number of routines for running one program from another. The most basic of these is a routine we have met before: `system`.

Usage

```
#include <stdio.h>

int retval;
char *comstring;
 .
 .
 .
retval = system(comstring);
```

`system` runs the command contained in `comstring`. It does this by first creating a child process. This in its turn calls `exec` to run the standard UNIX shell (`/bin/sh`) with `comstring` as input. (Actually, the *SVID* just refers to a command interpreter, but this must behave like the usual UNIX shell.) The `system` routine in the first process invokes `wait` to ensure that it only continues execution after the command has finished. The eventual return value `retval` gives the exit status of the shell, from which the success or failure of the command can be determined. If either of the calls to `fork` or `exec` fails, then `retval` will contain -1.

Because the shell is invoked as intermediary, `comstring` can be any command that could be typed at a terminal. This enables the programmer to take advantage of facilities such as file name expansion, I/O redirection and so on. The following statement uses `system` to create a subdirectory with the `mkdir` program:

```
if( (retval = system("mkdir workdir")) != 0)
    fprintf(stderr, "system returned %d\n", retval);
```

Some points of detail. Firstly, `system` in the calling process will ignore the signals `SIGINT` and `SIGQUIT`. This allows the user to safely interrupt a command without disturbing the parent process. Secondly, the command run by `system` will inherit some open file descriptors from the calling process. In particular, the command will take its standard input from the same source as the parent process. If this is a file, then it can pose problems when `system` is used to run an interactive program, since the program will take its input from the file. The following program fragment shows one possible solution to this problem. In it, `fcntl` is used to ensure that standard input, identified by file descriptor 0, corresponds to the processes controlling terminal `/dev/tty`. The example calls the `fatal` subroutine we introduced earlier.

```
#include <stdio.h>
#include <fcntl.h>
        .
        .
        .
    int newfd, oldfd;
        .
        .
        .
    /*dup. current file descriptor for std input*/
    if( (oldfd = fcntl(0, F_DUPFD, 0)) == -1)
        fatal("fcntl failed");

    /*open controlling terminal*/
    if( (newfd = open("/dev/tty", O_RDONLY)) == -1)
        fatal("open failed");

    /*close standard input*/
    close(0);

    /*create a new standard input*/
    if( fcntl(newfd, F_DUPFD, 0) != 0)
        fatal("fcntl problem");

    close(newfd);

    /*start up interactive editor*/
    if(system("ed newfile") == -1)
        fatal("system failed");
```

```
    /*restore old standard input*/
    close(0);
    if( fcntl(oldfd, F_DUPFD, 0) != 0)
        fatal("fcntl problem");
    close(oldfd);
     .
     .
     .
```

system has one major disadvantage. It does not allow a program to directly access the output generated by the command it runs. To do this, the programmer can make use of two more routines from the Standard I/O Library: popen and pclose.

Usage

```
#include <stdio.h>

FILE *strm, *popen();
char *comstring, *typestring;
int retval;
 .
 .
 .
strm = popen(comstring, type);

retval = pclose(strm);
```

Like system, the popen routine creates a child shell process to run the command pointed to by comstring. Unlike system, it also creates a pipe between the calling process and the command. It then associates the pipe with a stream, which is returned into strm. If type is "w", the program is able to write to the standard input of the command via the stream. If type is "r" instead, the program will be able to read the command's standard output. In this way popen provides a simple, clean method of communicating with another program.

pclose should always be used to close a stream that has been opened by popen. It will wait for the command to terminate, then return its exit status in retval.

The following example routine, getlist, uses popen and the ls command to obtain a directory listing. Each file name is then placed into a two-dimensional character array, the address of which has been passed to getlist as a parameter. The advantage of this routine is that it provides a way of interrogating UNIX directories that is independent of the layout of the directory.

```
/*getlist -- routine for getting filenames from directory*/

#include <stdio.h>
```

```
#define MAXLEN   14 /*maximum filename length*/
#define MAXCMD   100 /*maximum length of command*/
#define ERROR    (-1)
#define SUCCESS  0


getlist(namepart, dirnames, maxnames)

char *namepart;               /*additional part of ls command*/
char dirnames[][MAXLEN+1]; /*will hold file names*/
int maxnames;                 /*max. no. file names*/
{
     char *strcpy(), *strncat(), *fgets();
     char cmd[ MAXCMD+1 ], inline[ MAXLEN+2];
     int i;
     FILE *lsf, *popen();

     /*first form command*/
     strcpy(cmd, "ls ");

     /*add additional part of command*/
     if(namepart != NULL)
          strncat(cmd, namepart, MAXCMD - strlen(cmd));


     if((lsf = popen(cmd, "r")) == NULL)  /*start up command*/
               return (ERROR);

     for(i = 0; i < maxnames; i++){

          if(fgets(inline, MAXLEN+2, lsf) == NULL)
                         break;

          /*remove newline*/
          if(inline[ strlen(inline)-1 ] == '\n')
               inline[ strlen(inline)-1 ] = '\0';

          strcpy(&dirnames[i][0], inline);
     }

     if(i < maxnames )
               dirnames[i][0] = '\0';

     pclose(lsf);
     return (SUCCESS);
}
```

`getlist` can be used with a call such as

```
getlist("*.c", namebuf, 100);
```

This will place the names of C programs in the current directory into `namebuf`.

The next example solves a common problem for the administrators of UNIX systems: how to quickly 'unfreeze' a terminal which has been jammed, for example, by an untested screen-oriented program. `unfreeze` takes a terminal name and a list of programs as its arguments. It then runs the process status command `ps` via `popen` to obtain the list of processes associated with the terminal. It searches this list for any processes running one of the named programs. For all processes that fulfil this criterion, `unfreeze` asks the user whether or not it should be killed.

`ps` is a highly system-dependent program. This is because it has to examine the kernel directly (via a special file that represents memory) to get hold of the system's process table. On the machine we used for this example, the `ps` command which displays the processes associated with a particular terminal has the general form:

```
$ ps -t ttyname
```

where *ttyname* is the name of a terminal special file in the `/dev` directory, such as `tty01`, `console`, etc. Again referring just to the machine on which we developed the example, this type of `ps` command produces output like:

```
PID TTY TIME COMMAND
 29 co  0:04 sh
 39 co  0:49 vi
 42 co  0:00 sh
 43 co  0:01 ps
```

Column 1 contains the process-id. Column 2 contains the name of the terminal in question, here `co` stands for **console**. Column 3 gives the cumulative execution time for the process. Lastly, column 4 gives the name of the program which is running. Notice the first line which acts as a column header. It will have to be discarded by `unfreeze`, the source for which follows:

```
/*unfreeze -- unfreeze a terminal*/

#include <stdio.h>
#include <signal.h>

#define LINESZ  50
#define SUCCESS  0
#define ERROR  (-1)

main(argc, argv)
int argc;
char *argv[];
{
```

```
    /*the init'n of these depends on your system*/
    static char pspart[]      = "ps -t ";
    static char fmt[]         = "%d %*s %*s %s";

    char comline[LINESZ], inbuf[LINESZ], header[LINESZ];
    char name[LINESZ];
    FILE *f, *popen();
    int killflag = 0, pid, j;

    if(argc <= 2){
        fprintf(stderr, "usage: %s tty program ...\n", argv[0]);
            exit(1);
    }

    /*assemble command line*/
    strcpy(comline, pspart);
    strcat(comline, argv[1]);

    /*start ps command*/
    if((f = popen(comline, "r")) == NULL){
        fprintf(stderr, "%s:could not run ps program\n", argv[0]);
        exit(2);
    }

    /*get and ignore first line from ps*/
    if( fgets(header, LINESZ, f) == NULL){
        fprintf(stderr, "%s:no output from ps?\n", argv[0]);
        exit(3);
    }

    /*look for programs to kill*/
    while(fgets(inbuf, LINESZ, f) != NULL ){

        if( sscanf(inbuf, fmt, &pid, name) < 2)
                break;

        for(j = 2; j < argc; j++){
                if(strcmp(name, argv[j]) == 0){
                        if(dokill(pid, inbuf, header) == SUCCESS){
                            killflag++;
                        }
                }
        }
    }

    /*this is a warning, not an error*/
    if(!killflag)
        fprintf(stderr, "%s: no program killed on %s\n", argv[0],
        argv[1]);

    exit(0);
}
```

The dokill routine called by unfreeze is implemented as shown below. Notice the use of scanf to read the first non-space character (we could have instead used the yesno function introduced in Section 9.8).

```
/*confirm then kill*/
dokill(procid, line, hd)
int procid;
char *line, *hd;
{
        char c;

        printf("\nProcess running named program found :\n");
        printf("\t%s\t%s\n", hd, line);
        printf("Type 'y' to kill process %d\n", procid);
        printf("\nAnswer > ");

        /*get next non-white space character*/
        scanf("%1s", &c);


        if(c == 'y' || c == 'Y'){
                kill(procid, SIGKILL);
                return (SUCCESS);
        }else
                return (ERROR);
}
```

Exercise 9.9 Write your own version of getcwd, the routine that returns a string containing the name of the current working directory. Call your version wdir. Hint: use the standard command pwd.

Exercise 9.10 Write a program called arrived that uses the who program in conjunction with popen to check (at intervals of 60 seconds) whether one or more people from a list of users has logged on. The list of names should be passed to arrived via command line arguments. When it detects a user from the list, arrived should display a message. Your program must be efficient. Make sure you use sleep to suspend execution between checks. The who command will be described in your system's user manual.

9.14 Miscellaneous calls

In this section we will describes the remaining, miscellaneous calls from the Standard I/O Library in brief. For more details consult your system's official documentation.

9.14.1 freopen and fdopen

Usage

```
#include <stdio.h>

FILE *oldstream, *newstream;
char *type, *filename;
int filedes;
  .
  .
  .

newstream = freopen(filename, type, oldstream);

oldstream = fdopen(filedes, type);
```

freopen closes the stream identified by oldstream, then reopens it for input from filename. type determines the mode of access for the new stream and takes the same value as its counterpart for fopen (r, w, etc.). It is usually used for reassigning stdin, stdout, or stderr. For example,

```
if(freopen("new.input", "r", stdin) == NULL)
        fatal("stdin could not be reassigned");
```

fdopen associates a new stream with an integer file descriptor filedes that has been obtained from a previous call to one of the system calls creat, open, pipe or dup.

Both routines return NULL on error.

9.14.2 Word I/O: getw and putw

Usage

```
#include <stdio.h>

int word, res;
FILE *inf, *outf;
  .
  .
  .
word = getw(inf);

res = putw(word, outf);
```

These two routines perform I/O in terms of words, which correspond to the integer type supported by the C compiler. The size of a word, and therefore use of these functions, is machine-dependent.

getw fetches the next word (that is, binary integer) from the stream identified by inf. putf places a word onto the stream identified by outf.

Both routines return EOF on error. Since this is a valid integer, ferror should be used to detect errors instead.

9.14.3 Buffer control: setbuf and setvbuf

Usage

```
#include <stdio.h>

FILE *stream;
char buf1[BUFSIZ], buf2[SOMEVALUE];
int type, size, res;
  .
  .
  .
setbuf(stream, buf);

res = setvbuf(stream, buf2, type, size);
```

Both these routines allow the programmer to control to some extent the buffering associated with a stream. They must be used after a stream has been opened, but before it is read or written.

setbuf is used to substitute buf1 in place of the buffer normally allocated by the Standard I/O Library. The size required of buf1 is determined by the constant BUFSIZ from stdio.h.

If setbuf is passed a NULL character pointer instead, then input or output will be unbuffered. This can be useful during debugging when the program is terminating abnormally, and data held in buffers is being lost.

setvbuf is a newcomer to the Standard I/O Library and allows finer control than setbuf. The buf2 parameter gives the address of an optional new buffer. size specifies the size of buf2. If NULL is passed, instead of an actual address, then default buffering will be used. The type parameter to setvbuf determines how stream is to be buffered. It can be used to tailor the stream for use with disk files or terminal devices. The three permitted values for type are taken from stdio.h. They are:

_IOFBF The stream will be fully buffered. This is the default for all streams not attached to a terminal. Data will therefore be written, or read, in chunks of BUFSIZ bytes to maximize efficiency.

_IOLBF Output will be line-buffered, and the buffer will be flushed whenever a newline is written. It will also be flushed when the buffer is full, or input is requested. This is the default for terminals, and is designed to aid interactive use.

_IOBNF This causes input and output to be unbuffered. In this case buf2 and size will be ignored. This is a mode suitable, among other things, for error logging.

Note that if an illegal value for either type or size is given, setvbuf returns a non-zero value. Conversely, zero denotes success.

Chapter 10 Screen Handling

10.1 Introduction

In Chapter 8 we studied the system calls UNIX provides for controlling the basic characteristics of terminal lines. In this chapter we will introduce some standard tools for controlling the CRT/VDU terminal screens commonly attached to these lines.

The screen-handling tools come in the form of two closely linked C libraries:

1. `curses` This is the highest level of screen control. The library allows the programmer to control screens via terminal-independent data structures called **windows**. It protects the programmer from the nitty-gritty of low-level terminal control, and for this reason its use is always preferred to low-level counterparts. When `curses` routines actually update the screen, they attempt to do this as efficiently as possible. Indeed, the library name `curses` is derived loosely from the expression *cursor motion optimization*.

   `curses` was first developed at the University of California, Berkeley, and has a long history. However, it has only recently been adopted as part of AT&T System V. The current version is a superset of the library that originated from Berkeley. It is defined in *Issue 2* (not *Issue 1*) of the AT&T *System V Interface Definition* as an optional extension to System V.

2. `terminfo`. This library provides a low-level counterpart to `curses`. It provides the programmer with detailed descriptions of the individual capabilities of different types of terminal. These include, for example, the output strings required to clear a terminal screen, or position the cursor at a given set of screen coordinates. Again, `terminfo` is defined in *Issue 2* of the *SVID* as an optional extension.

Both the current versions of `curses` and `terminfo` use a database of terminal descriptions also called `terminfo`. Within this database, each type of terminal has its individual capabilities defined in a file with a name of the form

```
/usr/lib/terminfo/<c>/<name>
```

Here, `<name>` stands for the actual terminal, for example `vt100`, and `<c>` will be replaced by the first character of `<name>`. Hence

```
/usr/lib/terminfo/v/vt100
```

is the name of the file containing a `vt100` description.

The `curses` and `terminfo` libraries usually find out the name of the relevant `terminfo` database by looking at the current value of the `TERM` environment variable. So the sequence of shell commands

```
$ TERM=vt100
$ export TERM
```

tells both libraries that the user is working on a *vt100* terminal. Notice that only the terminal name is usually given, not the pathname of the `terminfo` file.

Users can add new terminal descriptions by using a special language (which we won't describe). Each terminal description can be compiled into a form usable by programmers with the `tic` command. Existing definitions can be used at shell level with the `tputs` command. Both commands, and the specification language, are defined in the *SVID*.

The `termcap` library

`terminfo` is a relative newcomer to UNIX, developed by AT&T. In some variants of the UNIX System you may instead meet the now obsolete `termcap` or `termlib` library, which was originally developed as part of the Berkeley UNIX System and is not included in the *SVID*. Instead of the `terminfo` database, `termcap` uses terminal descriptions embedded in the text file `/etc/termcap`. To add a new terminal description, this file must be edited manually. Like the routines offered in `curses`, the `termcap` routines find out the terminal type by looking at the `TERM` shell environment variable. The `/etc/termcap` file was also used by the original version of `curses`.

Thankfully, to ensure compatibility for software developers, the `terminfo` library has been designed to be upwards compatible with `termcap`.

10.2 The `curses` library: an overview

`curses` allows the programmer to generate a data structure called a window, which corresponds to all or part of the physical screen. Characters can be 'written' into this window at any position. This is a logical operation; the physical screen is only updated when a program explicitly requests so. `curses` also provides routines for controlling the video attributes of a screen and accepting keyboard input.

Windows are represented with the data type `WINDOW`, which is itself defined in the standard include file: `curses.h`. A window is really nothing more than a two-dimensional array of characters which match all or part of the screen. (There are also more complex structures called `pads` which can be larger than the physical screen.) However, each character is stored as a short integer, rather than a single byte. This allows flags which represent video attributes to be bitwise ORed with each character.

As we shall see, the programmer can create new windows using the `newwin` routine. However, a standard, globally accessible window called `stdscr` (for standard screen) is provided. For simplicity, it is this object we shall concentrate on in this chapter.

Before looking at `curses` in some detail, we should make two important points. First, note that `curses` routines are not automatically linked into programs. The `curses` library must be explicitly named in the command line that creates a program. For example,

```
$ cc -o scrnprog scrnprog.c -lcurses
```

The same command is used to link `terminfo` routines into a program.

Second, many `curses` routines are actually macros defined using the C preprocessor. For this reason, the programmer should exercise some care while using them and should also be prepared for some unusual error messages during compilation.

10.3 General structure of a `curses` program

All `curses` programs have the same basic structure, as shown in the following skeleton program:

```
#include <curses.h>

main()
{
        initscr();

        /*main body*/

        endwin();
        exit(0);
}
```

We will consider this short program line by line. First, the header file `curses.h` must be included by all programs that use `curses` routines. Under System V, `curses.h` automatically includes the terminal header file `termio.h`. It also contains definitions of `curses` data structures, and some important macros.

The `initscr` routine must be called prior to any other `curses` function. It initializes certain `curses` data structures and also determines the type of terminal from the `TERM` variable in the environment. Similarly, `endwin` should always be called before the program exits. It will restore the original terminal state and move the terminal's cursor to the lower left-hand corner.

The simplest useful curses program has just one additional line, which calls the refresh routine:

```
#include <curses.h>

main()
{
        initscr();
        refresh();
        endwin();
}
```

refresh, or a more general version called wrefresh, must be called to get any output on the screen, and so make the physical screen look like the program's logical picture. refresh copies the contents of the default window stdscr to the screen. wrefresh does the same thing for a named window. In the case of the example program, since no data has been written to any window, the screen is simply cleared.

In the following discussion, we will study the different types of facility provided by curses. Be warned; curses is a rich library with many routines and we have not tried to be exhaustive. For a full description, refer to your system's own documentation.

10.4 Mode setting

After the call to initscr, a program that calls curses routines will usually set the terminal modes for input and output. The most important routines available to do this are described in the following list. You might like to work out how they are implemented.

```
echo();        /*enable echoing*/

noecho();      /*disable echoing*/
```

These enable a program to turn echoing by the terminal driver on or off. The default is to have echoing on, but many applications do their own echoing, and so suppress automatic echoing with noecho. Like all the mode setting routines, these routines do not take arguments.

```
nl();          /*enable CR-NL mappings*/

nonl();        /*disable mappings*/
```

If nl is called, newline is mapped to newline/carriage-return on output, and return is converted to newline on input. nonl turns these mappings off.

Initially, these mappings do occur, but again many applications switch them off. It is worth noting that, if `nonl` has been called, `curses` can better optimize cursor movement.

```
cbreak();     /*enable CBREAK mode*/

nocbreak();   /*disable CBREAK mode*/
```

The `cbreak` function places the terminal into `CBREAK` mode. In essence, this means that canonical processing is turned off within the terminal driver. Interrupt and flow control keys maintain their meanings however. `nocbreak` turns canonical processing back on. The term `CBREAK` comes from the terminal driver on Berkeley UNIX – the system on which the first version of curses was developed. (The Berkeley UNIX terminal driver is based upon the AT&T Version 7 release of UNIX, which predates System V by several years. The terms `CBREAK` and `RAW` therefore ultimately originate from Version 7.)

```
raw();        /*enable RAW mode*/

noraw();      /*disable RAW mode*/
```

`raw` places the terminal into `RAW` mode, which is the same as `CBREAK` mode, except that signal processing and flow control are also disabled. `noraw` reverses `RAW` mode. Again, the term `RAW` comes from the Berkeley terminal driver.

```
savetty();    /*save tty state*/

resetty();    /*reset tty state*/
```

These functions save and restore the terminal state. `savetty` places the current terminal state into a buffer internally held by `curses`. `resetty` restores the state to that stored by the last call to `savetty`.

The following sequence of calls is often encountered in `curses`-based applications. It puts the screen under the complete control of the program, and leaves signal handling and flow control switched on.

```
noecho();
nonl();
cbreak();
```

10.5 Writing characters and strings

`curses` provides four routines for writing single characters and simple strings to the standard window `stdscr`. These are `addch`, `mvaddch`, `addstr` and `mvaddstr`.

Usage

```
#include <curses.h>


int c, y, x;
char *string;
  .
  .
  .
addch(c);

mvaddch(y, x, c);

addstr(string);

mvaddstr(y, x, string);
```

The `addch` routine places character `c` into `stdscr` at the current cursor position. (The cursor position can be explicitly changed with the `move` routine, described in Section 10.7.) Again it is worth making the general point that this is a logical operation only. The physical screen will not be updated until `refresh` is called.

If the character is printable it will be placed in the window, and the cursor position incremented. If the character is a tab, a newline or a backspace, `curses` will move the cursor appropriately. If the character is not one of these, but still not printable, it will be displayed with the `^X` notation. For example, `CTRL-C` will be echoed as `^C`.

The routine `mvaddch` is identical to `addch`, except that the cursor is first moved to line `y`, column `x`. Here, coordinates begin at (0, 0) in the top left-hand corner of the screen. In fact, many curses routines have an equivalent which is prepended with `mv...` and takes `y` and `x` arguments. In all cases, the cursor is moved before any action is taken.

`addstr` and `mvaddstr` place all the characters within `string`, which must be null terminated, into the window `stdscr`. `addstr` starts at the current cursor position, while `mvaddstr` first moves the cursor to `(y,x)`. Both routines are identical to a sequence of calls to `addch`.

The next example `addex` uses `mvaddch` and `mvaddstr` to alter the standard screen. The integer variables `LINES` and `COLS` are internal to `curses`, and are defined as `extern` within `curses.h`. They give the current screen size.

```
/*addex -- mvaddch/mvaddstr demo*/

#include <curses.h>

main()
{

   int j, k;
```

```
    initscr(); /*initialization*/

    /*fill stdscr with asterisks*/
    for(j = 0;j < LINES; j++)
        for(k = 0;k < COLS; k++)
            mvaddch(j, k, '*');

    /*write some text*/
    for(j = 10;j < LINES && j < 20; j++)
        mvaddstr(j, 20, "This is a string added with mvaddstr");

    /*nothing will appear until refresh() is called*/
    refresh();

    sleep(5);

    /*finish up*/
    endwin();
}
```

If you run this example you will find that the lower right-hand character position is left blank. `curses` prevents programs from writing to this position to stop the terminal scrolling automatically.

10.6 Formatted output

`curses` offers a number of facilities that parallel `printf` from the Standard I/O Library (discussed in full in the previous chapter). For `stdscr` these routines are `printw` and `mvprintw`:

Usage

```
#include <curses.h>

char *fmt;
int y, x;

/*NB arg0, arg1 ... argn have arbitrary type*/
  .
  .
  .
printw(fmt, arg0, arg1, ... argn);

mvprintw(y, x, fmt, arg0, arg1, ... argn);
```

If you know how to use `printf` (see Section 9.11), you know how to use `printw` and `mvprintw`. The following simple example uses `mvprintw` to write a short message in the centre of the screen:

```
/*d2 -- mvprintw example*/

#include <curses.h>

char fmt[] = "LINES = %2d, COLS = %2d";

main()
{
   initscr();

   mvprintw(LINES/2, COLS/2 - 10, fmt, LINES, COLS);

   refresh();
   sleep(5);
   endwin();
}
```

10.7 Cursor movement

The cursor can be moved relative to `stdscr` using the `move` command.

Usage

```
#include <curses.h>

int y, x;
  .
  .
  .
move(y, x);
```

The parameters `y` and `x` give the new coordinates relative to the top left-hand corner: `y` is the line coordinate, and `x` the column number. As you might by now expect, the physical cursor is not actually moved unless `refresh` is called.

The routine `getyx` can be used to get the current coordinates of the cursor.

Usage

```
#include <curses.h>

int y,x;
WINDOW *w;
  .
  .
  .
```

```
/*general use*/
getyx(w, y, x);

/*standard screen*/
getyx(stdscr, y, x);
```

`getyx` is a general routine and so requires a pointer to a `WINDOW` as its first argument. For our current purposes, we can substitute `stdscr` which is defined in `curses.h` and denotes the 'standard screen'. In this latter case, the cursor coordinates relative to the top left-hand corner of the physical screen are placed into `y` and `x`. Experienced C programmers might begin to feel uncomfortable at this point, since no ampersand (`&`) is placed before either of these parameters in the usage description, indicating that values are passed, not pointers as this sort of routine would normally require. The reason is that `getyx` is actually a macro, not a true C function. As we said back in the introduction to this chapter, many **curses** routines are implemented in this way, and care should be taken when using them.

Using `move`, `getyx` and `addch`, the following routine prints a message on the last line on the screen, then restores the cursor to its original coordinates. It uses two new `curses` routines, `beep` which rings the terminal bell, and `clrtoeol` which erases the line to the right of the cursor.

```
/*scrn_warn -- print error on last line*/

#include <curses.h>

scrn_warn(string)
char string[];
{
        int j, y, x;

        /*save original coords*/
        getyx(stdscr, y, x);

        /*clear message line*/
        move(LINES-1, 0);
        clrtoeol();

        /*print error message*/
        mvaddstr(LINES-1, 0, string);

        /*ring bell*/
        beep();

        /*restore orig. position*/
        move(y, x);
        refresh();
}
```

10.8 Input from the keyboard: getch

curses provides several routines for accepting input from the user. The most basic of these is getch, which reads a single character from the keyboard. getch returns an integer, rather like the getc routine in the Standard I/O Library.

Usage

```
#include <curses.h>

int in_ch;
  .
  .
  .
in_ch = getch();
```

If the terminal driver is not in canonical processing mode, i.e. if either cbreak or raw has been called, a call to getch will return immediately. Otherwise, a character will be returned after the first newline. (Why?)

The next example is a screen-oriented version of the yesno function we introduced in Section 9.8. Like the scrn_warn function we met above, this version of yesno displays a message on the bottom line of the screen. It next uses getch to receive input characters until either 'y' or 'n' is pressed, and then returns 1 or 0, respectively. It also echoes the strings [Yes] or [No] to provide some positive feedback.

```
/*yesno -- get yes or no response from user*/

#include <curses.h>

yesno(prompt)
char *prompt;
{
        int reply;

        /*save current terminal state*/
        savetty();

        /*set appropriate terminal mode*/
        noecho();
        raw();

        /*clear message line*/
        move(LINES-1, 0);
        clrtoeol();

        /*print prompt*/
        mvaddstr(LINES-1, 0, prompt);
```

```
        move(LINES-1, strlen(prompt)+1 );
        refresh();

        /*get response from user*/
        for(reply = -1; reply == -1;){
                switch(getch()){        /*call to getch*/
                  case 'y':
                  case 'Y':
                        reply = 1;
                        break;
                  case 'n':
                  case 'N':
                        reply = 0;
                        break;
                  default:
                        beep();
                        break;
                }
        }

        /*display feedback string*/
        addstr(reply == 1? "[Yes]" : "[No]");
        refresh();

        /*restore terminal state and return*/
        resetty();
        return (reply);
}
```

Reading function keys

Many terminals have special keys, such as function keys, arrows keys, editing keys and so on. Pressing one of these usually results in a special sequence of characters being sent to the UNIX system. Fortunately, the current version of `curses` enables the programmer to deal with these in a general way. (This is one of several facilities not provided in the original Berkeley implementation of `curses`.) The first step is to initialize the terminal's keypad by calling the `curses` `keypad` routine as follows:

```
keypad(stdscr, TRUE);
```

Special keys will then be returned via codes defined in `curses.h`. The values of these codes start at 401 (octal) to prevent confusion with normal ASCII characters. They have names like `KEY_DOWN` for the down arrow key, `KEY_UP` for the up arrow key, `KEY_F(5)` for function key F5 and so on. They are often used in code fragments such as:

```
int in_ch;
  .
  .
```

```
  .
in_ch = getch();

switch(in_ch){
   case KEY_DOWN:
        /*down arrow key processing*/
        .
        .
        .
   case KEY_UP:
        /*up arrow key processing*/
        .
        .
        .
}
```

We will use this technique in the `domenu` example in Section 10.13.

Exercise 10.1 Write a routine modelled on `yesno` that presents a short, one-line menu such as:

Press 1) to exit, 2) to save, 3) to run.

Your routine should return the number of the selected option.

10.9 Input from the screen: `inch`

`getch` is, as we have seen, concerned with input from the keyboard. A different problem is finding out what character is located at a particular point on the screen, or, to put it more precisely, what character occupies a given position on `stdscr`. Two routines are provided for this purpose, `inch` which returns the character from the current cursor position, and `mvinch` which allows the programmer to give coordinates.

Usage

```
#include <curses.h>

int in_ch;
  .
  .
  .
in_ch = inch();

in_ch = mvinch(y, x);
```

As usual, `y` and `x` denote the screen coordinates desired. Also notice how both functions return integers. As we shall see later, the integer that represents a character on a screen can also contain attribute information concerned with highlight types and the like. To get just the actual character part, the integer should be bitwise ANDed with the `A_CHARTEXT` constant from `curses.h`. For example,

```
cvalue = ivalue & A_CHARTEXT;
```

10.10 Editing an existing screen

Once a screen has been drawn, it may need to altered. For example, new characters may need to be inserted into a string, or part of a line may need to be erased. This sort of thing will often occur in applications such as word processors or screen editors.

`curses` provides a number of useful functions for this purpose (including one we have already met: `clrtoeol`). It is also worth noting that `curses` may use hardware features built into a terminal to perform this kind of operation. This ensures efficiency and a quick response for the end user. (However, specific use of any such hardware feature is not guaranteed.)

These routines can be divided into three classes: those that clear whole areas of the screen, those that delete text and also rearrange the screen, and those that non-destructively insert text in the screen. The routines provided for clearing parts of `stdscr` are listed in the following usage description.

Usage

```
#include <curses.h>
  .
  .
  .
erase();

clear();

clrtobot();

clrtoeol();
```

The `erase` and `clear` functions both copy spaces to every position in the standard screen `stdscr`. The difference is that `clear` will also arrange that the screen is automatically cleared when `refresh` is next called.

`clrtobot` will erase all characters from the cursor to the end of the screen. In other words, the current line to the right of the cursor is erased, as well as all lines below the current.

`clrtoeol` will erase all characters on the current line to the right of the cursor.

The next group of routines will also delete characters from the screen, but in addition they will move up the rest of the screen to fill the gap.

Usage

```
#include <curses.h>

int y, x;
  .
  .
  .
delch();
mvdelch(y, x);

deleteln();
```

In the case of `delch`, the character under the cursor is deleted. All characters to the right of the cursor are moved one space to the left to fill the gap. `mvdelch` is exactly the same except that the cursor is first moved to the given coordinates.

The `deleteln` routine deletes the current line, as indicated by the current `y` coordinate. To fill the gap, all lines below the current line are moved up by one.

The final group of routines are concerned with character insertion.

Usage

```
#include <curses.h>

int c, y, x;
  .
  .
  .
insch(c);
mvinsch(y, x, c);

insertln();
```

`insch` inserts the character `c` at the current position. All characters to the right of the cursor are moved along by one. If there is a non-space character at the rightmost position on that line, it will be lost. `mvinsch` performs the same function, but, as you might expect, first moves the cursor to the specified position.

The routine `insertln` inserts a blank line above the current line. All lines below this are moved down by one. As a consequence, the bottom line will disappear off the end of the screen.

The following example demonstrates the action of some of these functions more explicitly:

```
/*text.c -- simple curses example*/

#include <curses.h>

main()
{
        char *p;

        initscr();

        move(10, 0);
        addstr("hello, world");

        refresh(); sleep(2);   /*A*/

        move(10, 6);
        clrtoeol();
        addstr(" unix user");

        refresh(); sleep(2);   /*B*/

        mvdelch(10, 6);
        delch(); delch(); delch(); delch();

        refresh(); sleep(2);   /*C*/

        for(p = "sesruc "; *p != '\0'; p++)
                insch(*p);

        refresh(); sleep(2);  /*D*/

        endwin();
        exit(0);
}
```

After the initial `refresh` statement – labelled with the comment string `/*A*/` – the screen will contain the string `hello, world` on line 11 (remember, counting starts at zero). The program then calls `move`, `clrtoeol` and `addstr`. The result of this group of statements is that line 11 contains the string `hello, unix user` when the program reaches `/*B*/`. The next sequence of calls to `mvdelch` and `delch` has the effect of removing the word *unix* from the screen by the the time the program reaches `/*C*/`. Finally, the `for` loop at the end of the program uses `insch` to insert the word `curses` between `hello` and `user`. So, the final string displayed on the screen is `hello, curses user`. Notice the way the characters within `curses` are inserted in reverse order. This is because `insch` inserts text *before* the current cursor position.

10.11 Video attributes

Most modern terminals can display text in a variety of different ways. For example, many terminals allow characters to be displayed in normal video mode (light on a dark background), or reverse video (dark against a light background). `curses` provides constants which can be bitwise ORed with a character to place it into a given mode. For example

```
addch(ch|A_BOLD);
```

will place `ch` in bold, i.e. brighter than the surrounding text, at the current screen position. Some other constants you might encounter are:

`A_STANDOUT`	This mode is intended to make text stand out. It is normally implemented as reverse video or bold, depending on what the terminal can do and what looks most attractive.
`A_REVERSE`	Reverse video mode.
`A_BOLD`	Text will be displayed bold.
`A_DIM`	Text will be displayed at less intensity than normal.
`A_UNDERLINE`	Text will be underlined.
`A_BLINK`	Text will be displayed 'blinking' on and off.

A number of routines are provided specifically for dealing with attributes.

Usage

```
#include <curses.h>

int  atts;
  .
  .
  .
attrset(atts);

attron(atts);

attroff(atts);


standout();

standend();
```

`attrset` is used to turn on attributes for the standard screen. All text written to the standard screen `stdscr` after the call will be automatically given the attributes in `attrset` (text already on the screen is unaffected).

Several different attributes can be combined using the C bitwise OR operator. For example,

```
attrset(A_BLINK|A_BOLD);
```

will cause text to be displayed both bold and flashing. Note that calling `attrset` with an argument of zero turns off all current attributes.

`attron` turns on the named attributes in `atts` for all text written after the call. It does not affect any currently set attributes. Similarly `attroff` can be used to turn off selected attributes. The two routines `standout` and `standend` are equivalent to `attron(A_STANDOUT)` and `attroff(A_STANDOUT)`, respectively. In the original Berkeley version of `curses`, only these last two routines are available.

10.12 Creating and manipulating new windows

Thus far we have considered only routines that affect the standard window `stdscr`. For a great number of applications this is all that is required. However, the structure of some problems can be best expressed via the concept of multiple windows, several of which may occupy the screen simultaneously, perhaps overlapping. Here we give a flavour of the facilities provided for the management of new windows. For more details you will have to consult your system's documentation.

The most fundamental window management routine is `newwin`.

Usage

```
#include <curses.h>

WINDOW *win;
int lines, cols, startline, startcol;
  .
  .
  .
win = newwin(lines, cols, startline, startcol);
```

This creates a window of size `lines` by `cols` which has its upper left-hand corner at position (`startline`, `startcol`) on the standard screen. The window is identified through the window pointer `win`. A new full-size window can be created with the call

```
w = newwin(0, 0, 0, 0);
```

Text can be manipulated by using generalized versions of the routines we have met before. For example,

```
wmove(win, y, x);
```

This moves the cursor associated with the window win (which in general will not be associated with the physical cursor) to the coordinates (x, y). These coordinates are relative to the top left-hand corner of win, not the standard screen stdscr.

The sequence:

```
mvwaddstr(win, y, x, "hello, ");
waddstr(win, y, x, "world");
```

adds two strings to the named window. Notice the routine names. They are prepended either with a w or an mvw. The same formulations can be used to derive other routine names for handling windows other than stdscr. The call

```
wrefresh(win);
```

copies the contents of the window win to the physical screen. Other routines provide for moving and deleting windows and so on.

10.13 A curses example: domenu

In this section we will discuss a simple, menu routine called domenu. This uses a number of curses functions to display and manipulate a menu (that is a list of options from which the user makes a single selection) on the standard screen stdscr.

Each menu is defined by a data structure with tag menu. We will assume the template for this structure is contained in the header file menu.h as follows:

```
/*menu.h -- contains definition of menu structure*/

struct menu {
        int m_height;           /*menu height    */
        int m_width;            /*menu width     */
        char *m_title;          /*menu title     */
        char **m_data;          /*pointer to data*/
};
```

The purpose of most of the members of this structure should be clear. m_height and m_width describe the size of the menu area. domenu will calculate the screen coordinates of the menu from these. The member m_title will point to a title which will be displayed centred on the first line of the screen. Finally, m_data will point to the base of an array of character pointers, each of which will in turn point to a line of the menu. This will become clearer later.

The domenu routine accepts a pointer to a menu structure as its only argument. At the heart of the routine is a loop where a character is accepted via getch. Depending on what the user types, the program then changes the 'current' line of the menu, which is highlighted via use of the standout function. (In the actual body of domenu the code that alters the current line occurs before the call to getch. This enables the first line of the menu to be initialized as the current line at startup.)

The user can alter the current line of the menu, either by typing a character which matches the first on another line (as a corollary, all lines should begin with a unique character), or by pressing one of the cursor control keys; for example, pressing KEY_UP will move the current line up by one. The user 'selects' an option by pressing the RETURN or ENTER key. domenu then returns the number of the current line to the calling routine. Many other types of menu are possible of course – at the time of writing, horizontal 'ring' menus are particularly fashionable. domenu should provide you with a framework for your own preference:

```
/*domenu -- handle a simple menu on stdscr*/

#include <curses.h>
#include "menu.h"

domenu(m)
struct menu *m;
{

   int option, lastoption, j, c, y, x;
   char *p;

   /*save current terminal state, then set required modes*/
   savetty();

   cbreak(); nonl(); noecho(); standend();

   /*empty screen*/
   clear();

   /*initialize keypad, TRUE is defined in curses.h*/
   keypad(stdscr, TRUE);

   /*print centred title on line one*/
   move(0, (COLS - strlen(m->m_title))/2);
   addstr(m->m_title);

   /*work out position for top left corner of menu*/
   y = (LINES - m->m_height)/2 + 1;
   x = (COLS  - m->m_width)/2;

   /*display menu*/
   for(j = 0;j < m->m_height;j++)
      mvaddstr( y+j, x, m->m_data[j]);
```

```
/*initial values for cursor pos. and option setting*/
move( y, x);

/*this assumes first line in menu isn't blank*/
lastoption = option = 0;

for(;;){

   /*remove highlight bar from last option*/
   if(lastoption != option)
      mvaddstr( lastoption+y, x, m->m_data[lastoption]);

   /*put highlight bar on current option*/
   standout();
   mvaddstr( option+y, x, m->m_data[option]);
   standend();
   move(option+y, x);

   /*save current option*/
   lastoption = option;

   refresh();

   /*process input*/
   switch( (c = getch()) ){

    case '\r':     /*option selected, so return*/
    case '\n':
     if(option < 0){
        beep();
        break;
      }

      /*restore initial state and return*/
      resetty();
      return option;

    case KEY_DOWN:  /*move current down if possible*/
    case KEY_RIGHT: /*or wrap around                */

      do{
         option = (++option < m->m_height) ? option: 0;
      }while( isblank(m->m_data[option]));
      break;

    case KEY_UP:   /*move current line up or wrap*/
    case KEY_LEFT: /*around                      */
      do{
         option = (--option >= 0) ? option : m->m_height -1;
```

```
          }while( isblank(m->m_data[option]));
          break;

        default:        /*try to match character*/
          for(j = 0; j < m->m_height; j++){

             for(p = m->m_data[j]; *p == ' '; p++)
                ;


             if( *p == '\0') /*blank line*/
                continue;

             if( *p == c){
                option = j;
                break;
             }
          }
          if(j >= m->m_height) /*no match*/
             beep();
          break;
      }
   }
}
```

The isblank routine is used to check if a string is all spaces:

```
isblank(s) /*is string all spaces*/
char *s;
{
   while(*s == ' ')
        s++;

   return *s == '\0' ? 1: 0;
}
```

To put all this together we have constructed a small example, which allows a user to select a fruit or vegetable of his or her choice! Note how the menu data structure is initialized, and the fact that a menu can contain blank lines:

```
/*example use of domenu*/

#include "menu.h"

char *mtab[8] = {
"apples",
"bananas",
"carrots",
"",
```

```
"melons",
"",
"peaches",
"zucchini",
};

struct menu m1 = {
        8, 8,
       "Select a Fruit or Vegetable",
        &mtab[0]
};

main()
{

       initscr();
       domenu(&m1);
       endwin();
}
```

Exercise 10.2 Add a 'help' facility to the domenu routine. Do this by adding a character pointer to the menu structure which points to the name of a help text file. Then adapt domenu so that it displays the help text when a special key is pressed (? is one option here). The routine should restore the menu display when the user has finished reading the help text.

Exercise 10.3 This is a rather more ambitious exercise: Extend domenu so that different menus can be 'chained' together, the domenu routine allowing the user to descend a menu hierarchy automatically. One way of doing this would be to optionally associate a pointer to another menu structure with each non-empty menu line. Allow the user to go back up to the previous menu level. Extend the structure further, so that menu items can also be associated with actions, represented either as pointers to functions or, if you prefer, program names. Finally, devise a way of generating the definitions for a chained list of menu structures from a simple, more understandable form of specification (imagine you are developing a tool for non-C programmers).

10.14 Low-level terminal control: terminfo

curses centres on high-level structures, not the physical characteristics of the terminal. This is a great strength, and ensures maximum portability between systems for an application. Whenever possible, curses should be used for screen handling.

However, there may be circumstances when a programmer needs to gain access to the low-level aspects of a terminal; for example, in programming a 'soft' function key or controlling a terminal status line. The `terminfo` library serves this purpose in UNIX System V.2. The programmer can use it to obtain descriptions of the individual capabilities provided by a given terminal as described in the `terminfo` database. Be warned, by going down to this level the programmer must get involved with hardware-specific features. The most obvious such problem area is **padding**. This term describes the insertion of deliberate, short delays into output which enable the terminal to keep up with the program.

Lack of space prevents us from discussing the `terminfo` library. However, the shortest useful `terminfo` program is probably

```
#include <curses.h>
#include <term.h>

main()
{

        setupterm(0, 1, 0);
        putp(clear_screen);
        reset_shell_mode();
        exit(0);
}
```

which clears the screen. The file `term.h` contains macro names for **capabilities** of which `clear_screen` is one. The call to `setupterm` initializes the `terminfo` package (the parameters passed to `setupterm` in this example cause it to use 'reasonable defaults'). The call to `putp` causes the clear screen sequence to be written out to the terminal screen. It is a specialized version of a more general routine called `tputs`. The final `terminfo` routine `reset_shell_mode` returns the terminal to its initial state.

Chapter 11 Miscellaneous System Calls and Library Routines

11.1 Introduction

In this final chapter we examine a handful of system calls and some useful library routines that didn't logically fit into previous chapters. The topics we will cover include memory management, time functions, character validation and string manipulation.

11.2 Dynamic memory management

Each of the programs we have examined so far has used data objects which were totally determined by standard C declarations, such as

```
struct something x, y, *z, a[20];
```

In other words, the layout of the data used by our examples has been determined at compile time. Many computing problems however are best approached by creating and destroying data objects dynamically, which means the data layout used by the program is only finally determined during execution. Pascal, for instance, supports the `new` primitive which can be used to create objects dynamically on the program 'heap'. Under UNIX, the `malloc` family of library functions (the name `malloc` stands for *memory allocation*) allow the C programmer to take this kind of approach. `malloc` itself is defined as follows.

Usage

```
char *malloc(), *p;
unsigned nbytes;
  .
  .
  .
p = malloc(nbytes);
```

This call normally causes `malloc` to return a pointer to `nbytes` worth of contiguous new storage. In effect, the program has gained an extra array of characters which it can use as it sees fit. If there is insufficient memory available, and `malloc` cannot allocate the requested amount, it returns instead a null, i.e. zero, pointer.

Perhaps more typically, `malloc` can also be used to create storage to hold one or more data structures. For example,

```
struct item  *p;
char *malloc();
 .
 .
 .

p = (struct item *) malloc( sizeof(struct item) );
```

If successful, this `malloc` call creates a new `item` structure, which can be referenced via the pointer `p`. Notice how the return value from `malloc` is cast into the appropriate pointer type. This will avoid complaints from the compiler. The cast is meaningful because `malloc` is implemented so that the storage it returns can hold any type of object, providing the amount of space requested is big enough. Problems such as word alignment are taken care of internally by the `malloc` algorithm. Note how the size of the `item` structure is obtained with the C operator `sizeof`, which returns a value measured in bytes. We were also careful to declare `malloc` as returning a pointer to `char`. If we hadn't, `malloc` would be assumed to return an `int`, but the cast would hide the error in the short term. On some computer architectures (such as the Intel 8086 family) this would produce a memory fault, and the cause can be very hard to track down – we speak from bitter experience!

The inverse of `malloc` is `free`, which releases storage previously allocated by the `malloc` algorithm, making it available for re-use. `free` is passed a pointer that was previously obtained from a call to `malloc`:

```
 .
 .
 .
ptr = (struct item *) malloc( sizeof(item) );

/*do the work...*/

free((char *)ptr);
```

After `free` has been called in this way, the space pointed to by `ptr` must not be used, since `malloc` may later reallocate all or part of it. It is very important that `free` is passed a pointer that really was originally generated by `malloc`, or one of its two sister functions `calloc` or `realloc` (described shortly). If the pointer doesn't fit this criterion, serious memory errors will almost certainly result, leading to erroneous program behaviour or even a catastrophic core dump.

Two more functions in the `malloc` family are directly concerned with memory allocation. The first of these is `calloc`.

Usage

```
char *ptr, *calloc();
unsigned nbytes, nelem;
 .
 .
 .
ptr = calloc(nelem, nbytes);
```

`calloc` allocates space for an array of `nelem` elements each of which is `nbytes` in size. It is typically used along the following lines:

```
/*allocate array of structures*/
aptr = (struct item *)calloc(nelem, sizeof(struct item));
```

Unlike `malloc`, the storage allocated by `calloc` is set to zeros, which obviously has an execution time overhead, but can be useful when such initialization is required.

The final allocation function in the `malloc` family is `realloc`.

Usage

```
char *oldptr, *newptr, *realloc();
unsigned newsize;
 .
 .
 .
newptr = realloc(oldptr, newsize);
```

`realloc` is used to change the size of the memory block pointed to by `oldptr`, which must have been obtained previously from either `malloc`, `calloc` or `realloc`. `realloc` may have to move the block within memory, so the pointer `newptr` is returned to mark its new starting position. The contents of the block are preserved up to the smaller of the new and old sizes.

UNIX System V.2 introduced two new routines for giving the programmer finer control over the `malloc` algorithm, both of which have been incorporated in the *SVID*. They are `mallopt`, which allows internal parameters associated with `malloc` to be fine tuned, and `mallinfo` which provides information about total space usage. See your system's manual for full details.

A `malloc` example: linked lists

There are many types of dynamic data structure encountered in computer science. One classical example is the linked list, where a group of identical objects are chained into a single logical entity. In this section we will develop a simple linked list example to demonstrate use of the malloc family. We will start by looking at the header file list.h:

```
/*list.h -- header for linked list example*/
#include <stdio.h>

/*fundamental structure definition*/

typedef struct list_member{
    char *m_data;
    struct list_member *m_next;
}MEMBER;

/*function definition*/
extern MEMBER *new_member();
```

The typdef statement introduces a type called MEMBER, which has two fields. The first m_data will, in an actual occurrence of a MEMBER, point to some arbitrary string. The second component m_next points to another MEMBER. In defining m_next we have to use struct list_member *m_next rather than MEMBER *m_next for syntactical reasons.

In a linked list of MEMBER-type structures, each m_next will point to the next MEMBER in the list, i.e. given one element of the list, we can find the next simply by using its m_next pointer. Because there is only one pointer for each MEMBER in the list, it can only be scanned in one direction. Such lists are described as being **singly linked**. If we had defined an m_prev pointer, the list could also be joined in the reverse direction, and would in this case be **doubly linked**.

The address of the start or head MEMBER of a list is usually recorded in a special pointer declared in a manner similar to

```
MEMBER *head = (MEMBER *)0;
```

The end of a list is marked by a null value in the m_next field of the last actual MEMBER in the list.

For clarity, a simple three-element list is shown in Figure 11.1. Its start is indicated by a pointer called headptr.

We will now introduce a small set of routines for manipulating these structures. The first function we shall look at is called new_member. It uses malloc to create enough store for a MEMBER structure. Notice the way we set the m_next pointer to a null pointer, here represented as (MEMBER *)0. This is because malloc doesn't zero the memory it allocates. So, when a MEMBER is created, m_next could well contain a spurious but seemingly plausible address.

```
/*new_member -- allocate memory for new member*/

#include "list.h"
MEMBER *new_member(data)
```

```
char *data;
{
    extern char *malloc();
    MEMBER *new;

    if( (new = (MEMBER *) malloc(sizeof(MEMBER) )) == (MEMBER *)0){
        fprintf(stderr, "out of memory in new_member\n");
    }else{
        new->m_data = data;
        new->m_next = (MEMBER *)0;
    }
    return(new);
}
```

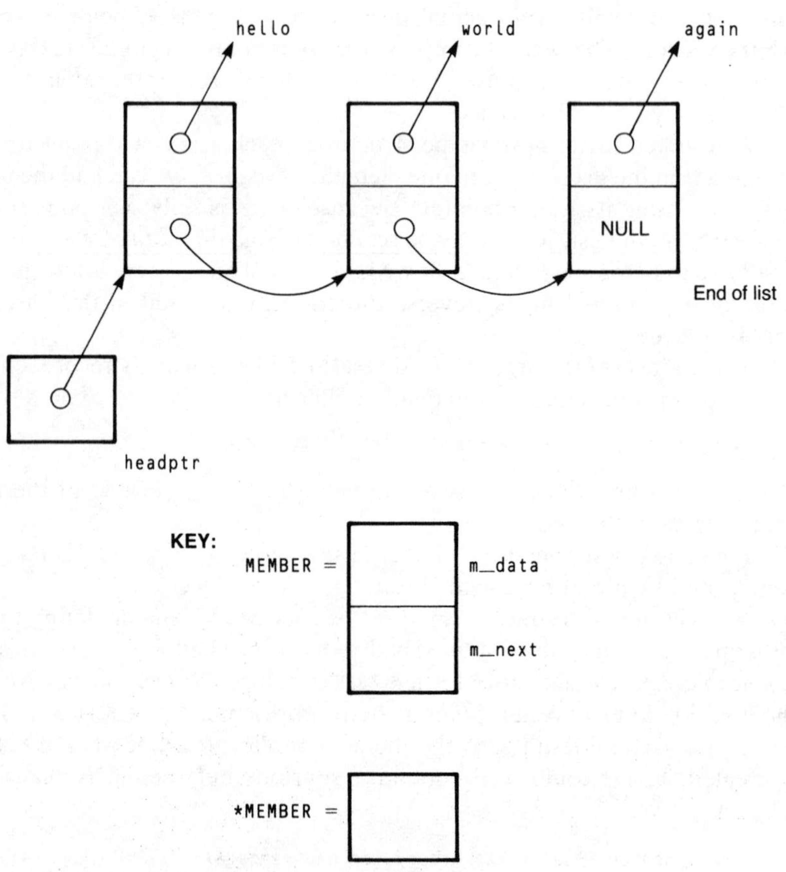

Figure 11.1 A linked list of MEMBERs.

The next routine `add_member` adds a `MEMBER` to the list rooted in `*head`. You should be able to see that the routine always adds the new `MEMBER` to the very start of the list.

```
/*add_member -- add MEMBER to list*/

#include "list.h"

add_member(head, newmem)
MEMBER **head;          /*start of list*/
MEMBER *newmem;         /*new MEMBER to add*/
{

    /*This simple routine pushes new member
     *onto the start of the list
     */

     newmem->m_next = *head;
     *head          = newmem;
}
```

The final utility routine we shall examine is `free_list`. It takes a pointer rooted in `*head` and frees the memory used by all its constituent `MEMBER` structures. It also sets `*head` to the null pointer, making sure that `*head` doesn't contain a now meaningless value (if we didn't, `*head` might be misused elsewhere).

```
/*free_list -- free entire list*/

#include "list.h"

free_list(head)
MEMBER **head;
{

    MEMBER *curr, *next;

    for(curr = *head; curr != (MEMBER *)0; curr = next){
        next = curr->m_next;
        free((char *)curr);
    }

    /*reset start of list pointer*/
    *head = (MEMBER *)0;
}
```

The simple example program that follows puts everything together. It creates the same linked list we saw in Figure 11.1, then frees it. Notice the way the routine `printlist` scans through the list. Its `for` loop is very typical of programs that use linked lists.

```
/*test program for list routines*/

#include "list.h"

char *strings[] = {
    "again",
    "world",
    "Hello"
};

main()
{
    MEMBER *head, *newm;
    int j;

    /*initialize list*/
    head = (MEMBER *)0;

    /*add members to list*/
    for(j = 0; j < 3; j++){
            newm = new_member(strings[j]);
            add_member(&head, newm);
    }

    /*display members of list*/
    printlist(head);

    /*free list*/
    free_list(&head);

    /*display members of list*/
    printlist(head);
}

/*scan list and print*/
printlist(listhead)
MEMBER *listhead;
{
    MEMBER *m;

    printf("\nList Contents:\n");

    if(listhead == (MEMBER *)0)
            printf("\t(empty)\n");
    else
            for(m = listhead; m != (MEMBER *)0; m = m->m_next)
                    printf("\t%s\n", m->m_data);
}
```

Notice the way we initialize the list at the beginning of the program by setting `head` to `(MEMBER *)0`. This is important, otherwise garbage may creep into the list, and again memory errors might result.

The program produces the following output:

```
List Contents:
        Hello
        world
        again


List Contents:
        (empty)
```

The `brk` and `sbrk` calls

For completeness, we should also mention the `brk` and `sbrk` calls. These aren't part of the *SVID*, but they are the primitive calls for dynamic memory allocation provided by actual implementations of UNIX. They work by adjusting the size of the process's data segment, or, to be more precise, the position of the first byte above the process's data segment. `brk` moves this position to an absolute address, while `sbrk` makes a relative adjustment. For most situations, you are very strongly advised to use `malloc` and its relations, not these two primitive calls.

Exercise 11.1 Our example linked list can be used to implement a stack where the member last added is the first used. `add_member` gives us the **push** operation; write the **pop** operation that removes the first element from the list.

Exercise 11.2 Write a program that uses members of the `malloc` family to create storage for a single integer, an array of `float` variables and an array of pointers to `char`.

11.3 Time

UNIX provides a handful of routines for finding out and setting the system's idea of the time. Time is measured in terms of the number of seconds elapsed since 00:00:00 GMT, 1st January, 1970, and this sort of figure must be held in a `long` integer. (Internally, the system itself uses a type `time_t` which is defined in `/usr/include/sys/types.h`. This will normally reduce to `long`.)

The most basic call is `time`, a true system call which returns the current time in the standard UNIX form.

Usage

```
long now1, now2, time();

now1 = time(&now2);
```

After this call, both `now1` and `now2` will contain the system's idea of the time. To save declaration of a dummy parameter, `time` can also be passed a null pointer value, which is then ignored:

```
now1 = time((long *)0);
```

Alternatively, just use

```
time(&now1);
```

Superuser (and *only* superuser) can reset the system's idea of the time using `stime`. Its single argument must be in the same form as the return value from `time`.

Usage

```
long newtime;
int ret;
  .
  .
  .
ret = stime(&newtime);
```

If this call is invoked by superuser, `ret` will be zero. Otherwise, it will be set to −1 and `errno` will contain the error `EPERM` from `errno.h`.

It is pretty hard for human beings to think in terms of large numbers of seconds, so UNIX provides a series of library routines for producing time information in a more understandable form. The most basic of these is `ctime`, which generates a 26-character string from the output of the `time` call. For example,

```
main()
{
    long timeval;
    extern char *ctime();

    time( &timeval );
    printf("GMT time is %s\n", ctime( &timeval ));
    exit(0);
}
```

produces output like

```
GMT time is Tue Mar 18 00:17:06 1986
```

and so proves how late some of us work.

Associated with `ctime` (and included under the same heading in the *SVID* and standard manuals) are a series of routines that use `struct tm` structures. The `tm` template is defined in the header file `time.h` as follows:

```
struct  tm {
        int     tm_sec;     /*seconds           */
        int     tm_min;     /*minutes           */
        int     tm_hour;    /*hours 0 to 24     */
        int     tm_mday;    /*day of month 1 to 31*/
        int     tm_mon;     /*month 0 to 11     */
        int     tm_year;    /*year minus 1900   */
        int     tm_wday;    /*weekday Sunday = 0  */
        int     tm_yday;    /*day of year 0 - 365 */
        int     tm_isdst;   /*Daylight saving flag*/
                            /*for USA only      */
};
```

The purpose of each member should be self-explanatory. The routines that use this structure are `localtime`, `gmttime`, and `asctime`.

Usage

```
#include <time.h>
#include <sys/types.h>

long timeval;
struct tm *tptr, *localtime(),
   gmttime();
char *timestring, *asctime();
  .
  .
  .

tptr = localtime(&timeval);

tptr = gmttime(&timeval);

timestring = asctime(tptr);
```

Both `localtime` and `gmttime` take a value previously obtained from `time` and convert it into a `tm` structure, returning local and GMT versions, respectively. For example,

```
/*tm -- tm struct demo*/

#include <time.h>

main()
{
        long t;
        struct tm *tp, *localtime();
```

```
        /*get time from system*/
        time(&t);

        /*get tm structure*/
        tp = localtime(&t);

        printf("Time %d:%d:%d\n", tp->tm_hour, tp->tm_min,
        tp->tm_sec);

        exit(0);
}
```

produces a message like

```
Time 1:13:23
```

`asctime` converts a `tm` structure into a `ctime`-like string.

Exercise 11.3 Write your own version of `asctime`.

Exercise 11.4 Write a function `weekday` that returns 1 if it is a weekday, zero otherwise. Write its inverse `weekend`.

Exercise 11.5 Write routines that return the difference in days, months, years and seconds between two dates obtained from `time`. Remember leap years!

Exercise 11.6 Write routines that convert `ctime` style strings and `tm` structures into a form suitable for `stime`.

11.4 String and character manipulation

The UNIX libraries are rich in functions that manipulate string or character data. These are useful enough to warrant a brief examination.

The `string` family

We have already used some of these well known routines in the text, for example, `strcat` and `strcpy`. The complete list follows.

Usage

```
/*NB: optional header file "string.h"
 *includes declarations for functions
 */

#include <string.h>

char *s1, *s2, *s3;
int cmp, length, c;
```

```
.
.
.

s3 = strcat(s1, s2);
s3 = strncat(s1, s2, length);

cmp = strcmp(s1, s2);
cmp = strncmp(s1, s2, length);

s3 = strcpy(s1, s2);
s3 = strncpy(s1, s2, length);

length = strlen(s1);

s3 = strchr(s1, c);
s3 = strrchr(s1, c);

s3 = strpbrk(s1, s2);

length = strspn(s1, s2);
length = strcspn(s1, s2);

s3 = strtok(s1, s2);        /*first call*/
s3 = strtok((char *)0, s2); /*later calls*/
```

`strcat` concatenates `s2` onto the end of `s1`. `strncat` does the same, but concatenates only `length` characters at the most. Both return a pointer to `s1`. An example usage of `strcat` is

```
strcat(fileprefix, ".dat");
```

If `fileprefix` initially contains `"file"`, it will end up containing `"file.dat"`. An important point to note is that `strcat` alters the string pointed to by its first argument. This characteristic is shared by `strncat`, `strcpy`, `strncpy` and `strtok`. Since a C routine cannot find out the size of an array passed to it, a programmer must make sure that the first argument for these routines is large enough to hold the result of the requested operation.

`strcmp` compares the two strings `s1` and `s2`, returning an indicator variable `cmp`. If `cmp` is positive, it means `s1` is *lexicographically greater than* `s2` according to the ordering of the ASCII character set. A negative value means that `s1` is *lexicographically less than* `s2`. If `cmp` is zero, the strings are identical. `strncmp` is similar, but compares only `length` characters at most. An example use of `strcmp` is

```
if(strcmp(token, "print") == 0){

      /*process print keyword*/
}
```

strcpy is a close relation to strcat. It copies the contents of s2 into s1, overwriting the original contents of s1. strncpy copies exactly length characters, truncating or adding nulls as necessary (which can mean that s1 is not null-terminated).

strlen simply returns the length of s1. In other words, it returns the number of characters in s1, not including the terminating null.

strchr returns a pointer to the first occurrence of character c (actually declared as int) in string s1, or a null pointer if no match is found. strrchr does the same for the *last* occurrence of c. We used strrchr in Chapter 4 to strip off the pathname part of a file name:

```
/*strip off pathname part*/
filename = strrchr(pathname, '/');
```

strpbrk returns a pointer to the first occurrence in s1 of any character in the string s2. A null pointer is returned if there is no match.

strspn returns the length of that part of the string s1, starting from the first character in s1, which consists entirely of characters from s2. strcspn returns the length of the initial segment of s1 which does *not* include any character from s2.

Finally, strtok allows a program to split a string s1 into individual lexical tokens. Here the string s2 contains the characters that can separate the tokens (for example: spaces, tabs and/or newlines). The first call, with the first argument set to s1, causes strtok to remember the string. A pointer to the first token will be returned. Subsequent calls, with the first argument set to the null pointer, will produce further tokens from s1. A null pointer is returned when no tokens remain.

The memory family

Less well known than the string family functions are the memory routines which act on arbitrary sequences of bytes, rather than well formed strings. One of the more useful members is memcpy, which is called as follows.

Usage

```
#include <memory.h>

char  *buf1, *buf2;
int size;
  .
  .
  .

memcpy(buf1, buf2, size);
```

This moves size bytes of storage from the region starting at buf2 to that starting at buf1. One application of memcpy gives a portable way of allowing structures to be assigned directly, even with compilers that do not specifically support this feature. For example,

```
#ifdef NO_ASSIGN /*ie no structure assignment supported*/
#define ASGN(x, y)  memcpy( (char *)&x, (char *)&y, sizeof(x))
#else
#define ASGN(x, y)  ((x) = (y))
#endif
```

Since character movement may be performed differently on different machines, the effect of copying overlapping regions is not defined in the *SVID*. This differs from the ANSI C Standard, so might well change.

Characters: validation and conversion

UNIX provides two useful sets of macros and functions for manipulating characters, both of which are defined in the header file `ctype.h`. The first set, which is grouped under the heading `ctype`, is intended for validation of single characters. They are all Boolean macros which return 1 (*true*) if a condition is true, 0 (*false*) if it is not. For example, `isalpha` tests whether a character is a letter, i.e. in the range a–z or A–Z, or not:

```
#include <ctype.h>
int c;
 .
 .
 .
/*"isalpha" is a ctype macro*/

if( isalpha(c) ){
      /*process alphabetic character, ie a letter*/
}else
     warn("Character is not a letter");
```

Notice the way `c` is declared as an `int`. The full list of `ctype` macros is:

`isalpha(c)`	Is `c` a letter?
`isupper(c)`	Is `c` an upper-case letter?
`islower(c)`	Is `c` a lower-case letter?
`isdigit(c)`	Is `c` a digit (0 to 9)?
`isxdigit(c)`	Is `c` a hexadecimal digit?
`isalnum(c)`	Is `c` a letter or digit?
`isspace(c)`	Is `c` a white-space character, i.e. one of `space`, `tab`, `carriage-return`, `newline`, `form-feed` or `vertical-tab`?
`ispunct(c)`	Is `c` a punctuation character?
`isprint(c)`	Is `c` a printable character? In the ASCII character set, this means any character in the range `space` (040) to `tilde` (~ or 0176).
`isgraph(c)`	Is `c` a printable character, and not a `space`?

`iscntrl(c)` Is `c` a control character? ASCII `delete` is counted as a control character, as well as anything with a numeric value of less than 040.

`isascii(c)` Is `c` in the ASCII character set at all? Note that an integer value passed to any of the other `ctype` routines must satisfy this test, with the one exception of `eof` from `stdio.h` (this exception allows `ctype` macros to be used with `getc`, etc.).

The other set of character-based utilities is intended for simple character translation, and is grouped under the heading `conv`. For example, `tolower` is a function that translates an upper-case character to its lower-case equivalent:

```
#include <ctype.h>
int newc, c;
  .
  .
  .

/*translate uppercase to lowercase*/
/*eg: map 'A' to 'a'              */

newc = tolower(c);
```

If `c` is an upper-case letter, it is converted to lower-case. Otherwise, it is left alone. The other routines and macros are:

`toupper(c)` A function that converts `c` to upper case, if it is a lower-case character. Otherwise it leaves `c` alone.

`toascii(c)` A macro that converts a non-ASCII integer value to ASCII by stripping off non-ASCII bits.

`_toupper(c)` A faster macro version of `toupper` that does no checking, and so *must* be passed a lower-case character.

`_tolower(c)` A fast macro version of `tolower`, with similar limitations to `_toupper`.

11.5 A selection of other useful functions

In this last section we will briefly list other functions that you may find useful. Our aim is no more than to bring their existence to your attention.

11.5.1 Interrogating the local environment

There are a variety of system calls and library routines concerned with interrogating the local peculiarities of a system. These include:

`uname` — `uname` returns a pointer to a `utsname` structure (the template for which comes from `/usr/include/sys/utsname.h`). The structure contains a system name, a node name that might be used by the system on a communications network, and release and version data for UNIX itself.

`getpwent` — This family of routines allows access to data from the password file. It is also worth mentioning the routine `getpw` which returns a user name given a numeric user-id.

`getgrent` — This family of routines is concerned with accessing the group file.

11.5.2 Mathematical routines

UNIX provides a largish library of mathematical routines for the scientific or technical programmer. Some of these routines should be used in conjunction with the header file `math.h`, which includes `extern` function definitions, definitions for some important constants (such as e and π), and structure definitions to do with error handling. To use the majority of the routines we will touch on below, you will also need to link your programs against the maths library with a command like

```
cc -o mathprog mathprog.c -lm
```

The routines appear in UNIX manuals and the *SVID* under the following headings:

`abs` — Returns the absolute value of an integer. Part of the standard C library, so you don't need to link against the maths library.

`bessel` — A group of routines that implement the various Bessel functions.

`drand48` — A set of functions to generate pseudo-random numbers. (See also `rand`.)

`erf` — The mathematical error function (which is not to be confused with error handling in the programming sense).

`exp` — A set of exponential and logarithmic functions.

`floor` — Routines for truncating or obtaining the absolute value of floating-point expressions.

`frexp` — Routines for manipulating parts of floating-part numbers.

`gamma` — A version of the log gamma function.

`hypot` — The Euclidean distance function. Useful for proving to your children that computers are really quite useful.

`matherr` — Used when the mathematical functions generate an error such as overflow or loss of significance.

`rand` The heading covers `rand`, a simple pseudo-random number generator, and `srand` a seed function for the generator. (See also `drand48`.)

`sinh` This heading covers `sinh`, `cosh` and `tanh` functions.

`trig` Denotes a group of trigonometric functions: `sin`, `cos`, `tan`, `asin`, `acos`, `atan` and `atan2`.

It is also worth investigating the headings `strtod` and `strtol` which, although outside the maths library proper, cover routines for translating strings to floating-point numbers and integers, respectively.

11.5.3 Sorting, searching and structure management

The *SVID* defines a number of useful routines for sorting and manipulating objects which are held in memory in various ways. They are grouped under the following names:

`qsort` The `qsort` routine is an implementation of the 'quicker sort' algorithim of C.A.R. Hoare. `qsort` can be used on a collection of arbitrary data items, the programmer passing it a function to perform comparisons between items, a technique also used by the following 'search' functions.

`bsearch` This function implements a binary search algorithm.

`hsearch` `hsearch` provides a hash table search mechanism. It has two companion routines: `hcreate` which creates a hash table and `hdestroy` which destroys a hash table.

`lsearch` A linear search routine.

`tsearch` `tsearch`, and the associated functions `tfind`, `tdelete` and `twalk`, aid the manipulation of binary search trees. They can be used to dynamically build, contract or search tree structures.

Appendix errno Error Codes and Associated Messages

Introduction

As we saw first in Chapter 2, UNIX provides a set of standard error codes and messages that describe the errors that can be produced by system calls. More specifically, each system call error has an error number, a mnemonic code and (usually) a message string. These can be used by including the following set of lines within a program:

```
#include <errno.h>    /*contains mnemonic codes*/

extern int   errno;
extern char *sys_errlist[];
extern int   sys_nerr;
```

`errno` is set by a system call whenever an error occurs. In almost all cases, the system call will also return −1 to the calling process to tell it an error has arisen. `errno` can then be tested against the mnemonic codes defined in `errno.h`. For example,

```
#include <stdio.h>
#include <errno.h>

extern int errno;
int pid;
  .
  .
  .

if((pid = fork()) == -1){
  if(errno == EAGAIN)
        fprintf(stderr, "process limit reached, try again\n");
  else
        fprintf(stderr, "not enough memory\n");
}
```

The external array `sys_errlist` is a table of the error messages printed by the `perror` routine. `errno` can be used as an index into the array when the message appropriate to an error situation is required. The external integer `sys_nerr` gives the current size of the `sys_errlist` table. `errno` should always be checked against `sys_nerr` if you want to index into `sys_errlist`, since new error numbers may be added before the string table is extended.

A list of error codes and messages

A complete list of the system call error messages which are possible under System V follows. It is based on information from *Issue 2* of the AT&T *System V Interface Definition*. Each entry gives the mnemonic code from `errno.h`, the system error message contained in `sys_errlist` and a short description. Note that the text of the error messages may vary in the future, as AT&T intend to adopt a more formal structure for system messages.

`E2BIG` *Arg list too long*. This simply means that an over-long argument list (in terms of total number of bytes) has been passed to an `exec` call.

`EACCES` *Permission denied*. A file permission error occurred. Can occur with `open`, `link`, `creat` and similar system calls. It can also be generated with `exec` if execution permission isn't set.

`EAGAIN` *Resource temporarily unavailable, try again later*. This usually means a particular system table is full. It can be generated by `fork` (too many processes) and the IPC calls (too many of a particular IPC object type).

`EBADF` *Bad file number*. This means that either a file descriptor does not represent an opened file, or that the access mode, i.e. read-only, write-only, does not allow the requested operation. Generated by a great many calls, including `read` and `write`.

`EBUSY` *Device or resource busy*. Can be generated when a process tries to mount an already mounted file system, or unmount a file system which is being used.

`ECHILD` *No child processes*. `wait` was called, but no suitable child processes existed.

`EDEADLK` *Deadlock avoided*. This means that, if successful, the call would have produced a deadlock (in other words, a situation where two processes were sleeping, each awaiting an action from the other). This error can be set by `fcntl` and `lockf`. It is also used by `lockf` to indicate a full lock table within the kernel.

`EDOM` *Math argument*. A mathematics package error, it means that the argument of a function is outside the domain of that function. It can be set by the `trig`, `exp` and `gamma` functions among others.

EEXIST *File exists.* This indicates that a file exists which prevents an operation from being carried out. Can be set by `link`, `mknod` and `open`.

EFAULT *Bad address.* Generated by the system after a memory protection hardware fault. Usually means an absurd address has been specified. The ability of systems to generate this error will vary considerably.

EFBIG *File too large.* An attempt was made to extend a file beyond the process's file size limit (as set by `ulimit`) or the system's maximum file size.

EINTR *Interrupted system service.* Returned when a signal is caught while a program is executing a system call. (Only certain calls are affected – see Chapter 6.)

EINVAL *Invalid argument.* Simply means an invalid parameter or set of parameters was passed to a system call. Can be generated by `fcntl`, `signal`, and some of the IPC routines. Can also be set by mathematical routines.

EIO *I/O error.* A physical error has occurred during I/O.

EISDIR *Is a directory.* An attempt was made to open a directory file for writing. This error is generated by `open` and `creat`.

EMFILE *Too many open files in a process.* Occurs when a file is being opened; it means that the per-process limit on open file descriptors has been reached. Typically this limit is 20.

EMLINK *Too many links.* Generated by `link` when the maximum number of links associated with a single physical file has already been reached.

ENFILE *File table overflow.* Generated by calls which return an open file descriptor (such as `creat`, `open` and `pipe`). It means that the internal file table within the kernel is full, and no more file descriptors can be opened.

ENODEV *No such device.* An attempt was made to perform an invalid system call on a device.

ENOENT *No such file or directory.* This occurs when no actual file corresponds to a pathname (for example, with `open`), or one of the directories in a pathname does not exist (for example, with `creat`).

ENOEXEC *Exec format error.* The program file to be executed is not recognized as being in a valid executable format. Produced by `exec`.

ENOLCK *No locks available.* There are no more record locks available for an `fcntl` lock.

`ENOMEM` *Not enough space*. A general memory error, occurring when a process asks for more space than the system can supply. Can be generated by `exec`, `fork` and the non-*SVID* routines `brk` and `sbrk`, which are concerned with memory allocation.

`ENOSPC` *No space left on device*. The device in question is full, and a file cannot be extended or a directory entry created. Can be generated by `write`, `creat`, `open`, `mknod` and `link`.

`ENOTBLK` *Block device required*. Means a non-block file was given when a block-device special file was wanted. Can be generated by `mount` and `umount`.

`ENOTDIR` *Not a directory*. This occurs when a pathname does not represent a directory when the context demands it. Can be set by `chdir`, `chroot`, and `mount`.

`ENOTTY` *Not a character device*. A call was made to `ioctl` on an open file that is not a special character device.

`ENXIO` *No such device or address*. Occurs when an attempt is made to access a device, or device address, which does not exist. Off-line devices can cause this error.

`EPERM` *Not owner* or *No permission match*. This indicates that a process tried to manipulate a file in a manner allowed only to the file owner or superuser (`root`). It can also mean that an attempt was made to perform an operation allowed only to superuser. Calls that can generate this error include `chmod` and `link`.

`EPIPE` *Broken pipe*. Set by `write`, to signify that an attempt was made to write on a pipe which is not open for reading by any process; in fact, this condition would normally cause the writing process to be interrupted by the signal `SIGPIPE`. `EPIPE` is only set if `SIGPIPE` is caught and the process does not terminate.

`ERANGE` *Result too large*. A maths error, it means that the return value of a function cannot be represented on the host processor.

`EROFS` *Read-only file system*. An attempt to write to, or modify, a directory entry, was made on a file system that has been mounted (with `mount`) read-only for protection purposes.

`ESPIPE` *Illegal seek*. A meaningless call to `lseek` was made on a pipe.

`ESRCH` *No such process*. Non-existent process specified. Generated by `kill`.

`ETXTBSY` *Text file busy*. When generated by `exec` calls, it means that an attempt was made to run a shared-text program which is currently open for writing. When generated by calls which return a file descriptor, it means that an attempt was made to open for writing a shared-text program that is being executed.

`EXDEV` *Cross-device link.* Occurs when `link` is called to link files across file systems.

Selected Bibliography

Note: the following list of books is necessarily partial since so many UNIX and C books are now available. Our apologies to any authors we have omitted.

Standards documents

ANSI Technical Committee X3J11. (1985). *C Information Bulletin (Preliminary Draft ANSI Standard).* X3 Secretariat.

AT&T. (1985). *System V Interface Definition, Issue 2, Volumes 1 and 2.* AT&T.

Technical Committee on Operating Systems of the IEEE Computer Society. (1986). *IEEE Trial-Use Standard Portable Operating System for Computer Environments (POSIX).* IEEE.

The X/OPEN Group. (1985). *X/OPEN Portability Guide.* Elsevier Science Publishers BV.

The C language

AT&T. (1985). *The C Programmer's Handbook.* Prentice-Hall.

Harbison, S. P., and Stevens, G. L. (1984). *C: A Reference Manual.* Prentice-Hall.

Kernighan, B. W., and Ritchie, D. (1978). *The C Programming Language.* Prentice-Hall.

Plum, T. (1983). *Learning to Program In C.* Plum-Hall.

Plum, T. (1985). *Reliable Data Structures in C.* Plum-Hall.

Plum, T., and Brodie, J. (1985). *Efficient C.* Plum-Hall.

UNIX environment

AT&T. (1985). *The UNIX System User's Handbook.* Prentice-Hall

Bach, M. J. (1986). *The Design of the UNIX Operating System.* Prentice-Hall.

Banahan, M., and Rutter, A. (1982). *UNIX – The Book.* Sigma Technical Press.

Bourne, S. R. (1983). *The UNIX System.* Wokingham, England: Addison-Wesley.

Brown, P. (1983). *Starting with UNIX.* Wokingham, England: Addison-Wesley.

Foxley, E. (1985). *UNIX for Superusers.* Wokingham, England: Addison-Wesley.

Kernighan, B. W., and Pike, R. (1984). *The UNIX Programming Environment.* Prentice-Hall.

Various. (1978). *The Bell System Technical Journal (Computer Science and Systems).* AT&T Bell Laboratories. July–August.

Various. (1984). *AT&T Bell Laboratories Technical Journal (Computer Science and Systems), The UNIX System.* AT&T Bell Laboratories. October.

Index